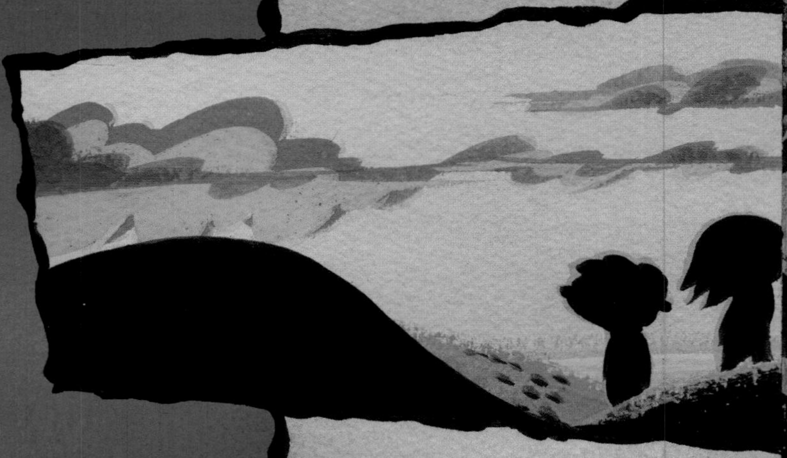

The
Barefoot Serpent

ISBN 1-891830-37-6
1. Film / Directors (Kurosawa, Akira)
2. Graphic Novels

Top Shelf Productions, PO Box 1282
Marietta, GA 30061-1282, USA
www.topshelfcomix.com

Published in 2003 by Top Shelf Productions,
Inc.
Printed in Canada.

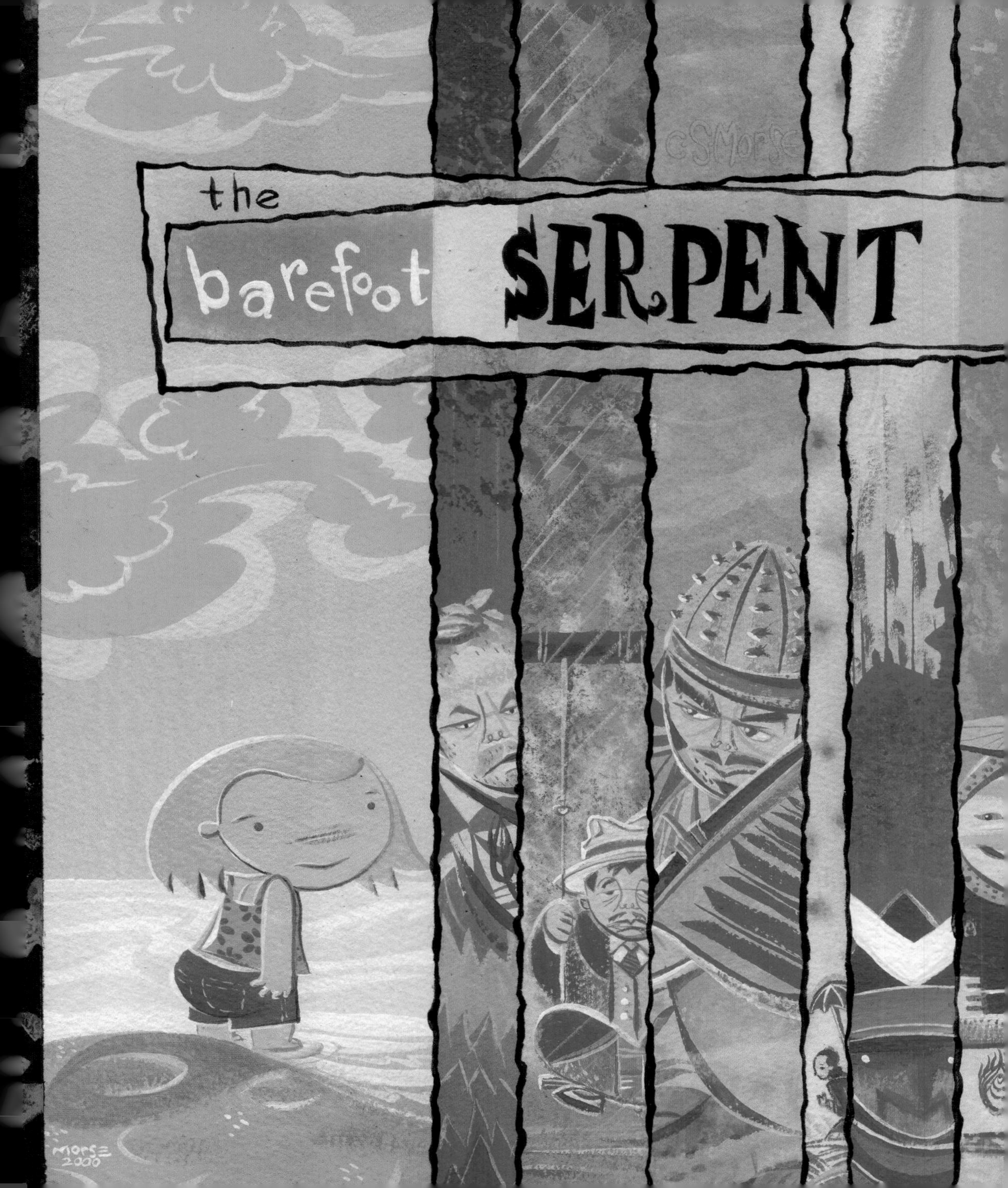
the barefoot SERPENT
CSMorse
Morse 2000

introduction

by
Stan
Sakai

If you have never before experienced C. Scott Morse's work, you are about to be awed and excited. Then you are going to run out and ferret everything else by this wonderful storyteller. And you are in luck, because from where I'm sitting I can see at least ten of his books up on my bookshelf (I haven't gotten around to shelving his more recent works). I discovered Scott's work pretty early in his comic book career when I bought *LittleGreyMan* (Image Comics, 1997). I was impressed by this new creator, whose work I had never seen before. Since then, Scott has honed his abilities to become one of the most distinctive and respected storytellers working in comics.

I am especially delighted to have been asked to write this introduction because *The Barefoot Serpent* details two passions in my life—Akira Kurosawa and Hawaii. As the creator of Usagi Yojimbo, the samurai rabbit, I am more than a little influenced by Kurosawa. The series title, itself, is an homage to the great director, and one of my characters is a direct steal from Toshiro Mifune's performances in *Yojimbo* and *Sanjuro*. Also, I was raised in Hawaii, though not the Hawaii that Scott depicts. I grew up in the Hawaii of high rises, traffic jams, and blazing humidity. I much prefer Scott's version.

Some may find the transition from the biography of Kurosawa to the story of the little *haole* girl a bit jarring. I did, at first. However, look into the story and you'll see a lot of Kurosawa in Scott's work. They are both visionaries, unique in their mediums, working with a cinematic beauty all their own. They both work with an economy of dialogue, letting the visuals carry the story. Kurosawa was enamored with silent films, and always imagined what a scene would be like without words. Both Kurosawa and Scott are storytellers who can work on an intimate scale or on grand epics, but the focus is always on the individual, on characters, and that is what makes them succeed.

Kurosawa once said, "There is nothing that says more about the creator than the work." So even if you have never met C. S. Morse, enjoy this book. You're about to meet one heck of a nice guy.

Stan Sakai

(Stan Sakai is the creator of USAGI YOJIMBO and the recipient of numerous awards, including an American Library Association Award and a National Cartoonists Society Reuben.)

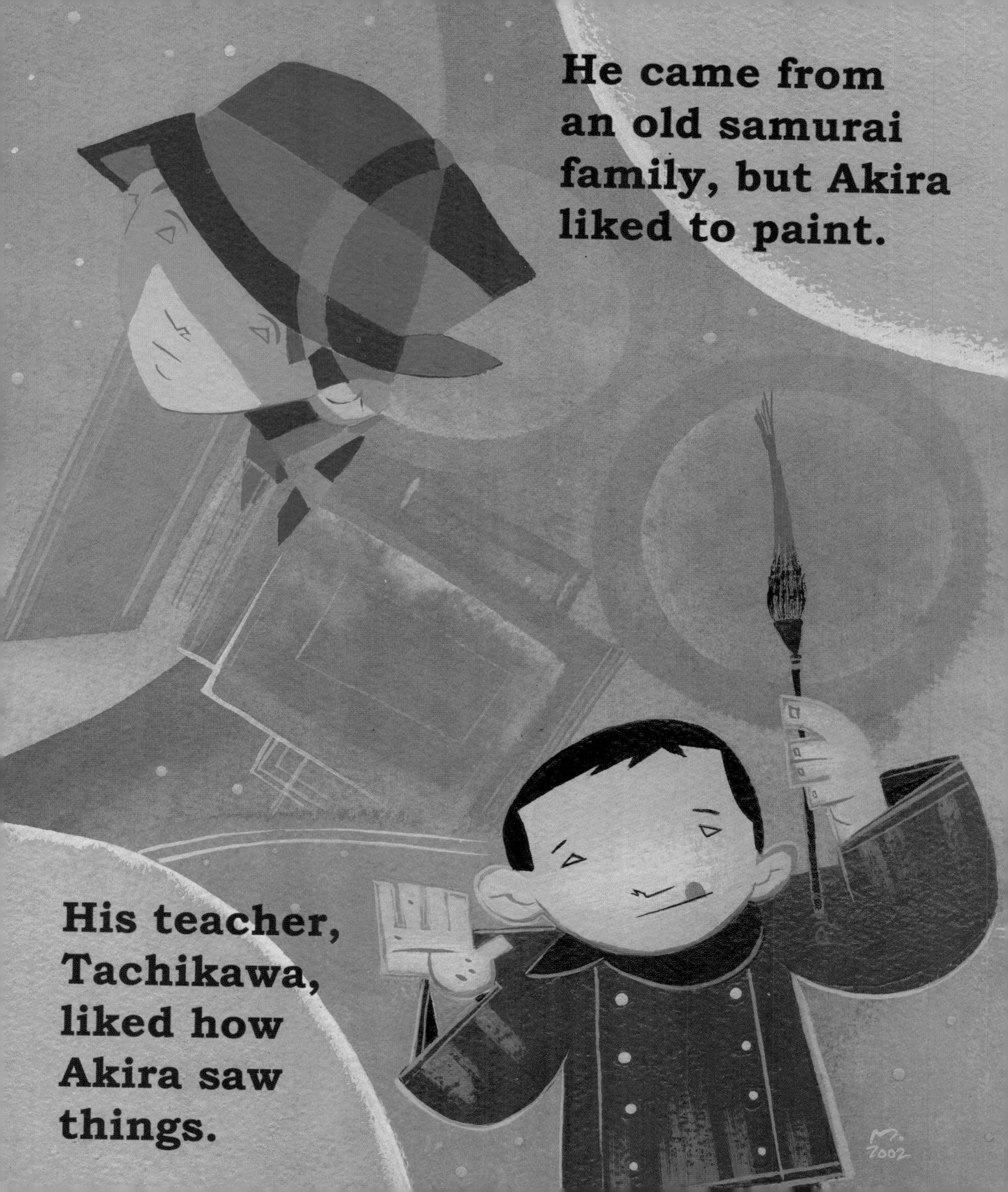

He came from an old samurai family, but Akira liked to paint.

His teacher, Tachikawa, liked how Akira saw things.

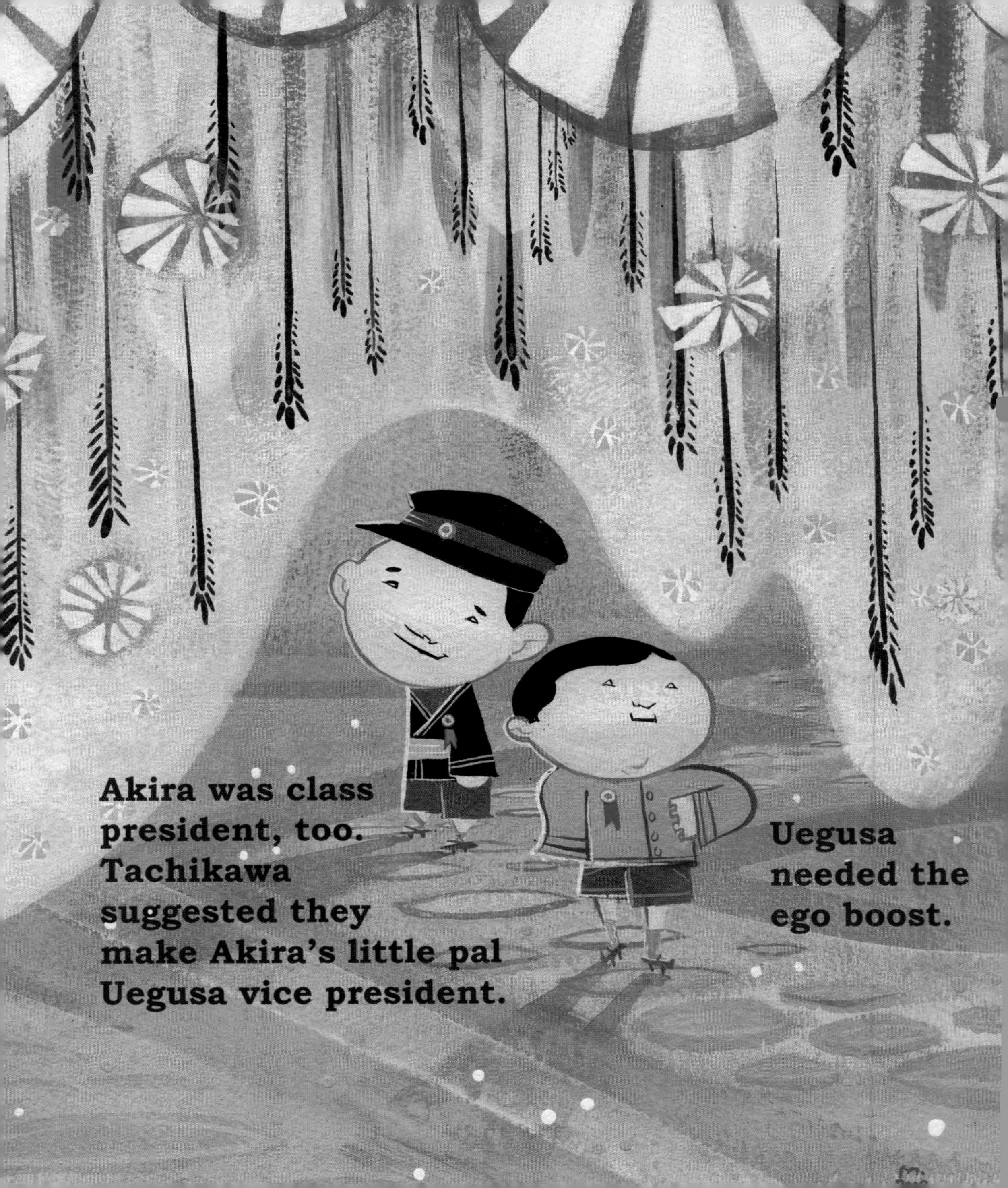

Akira was class president, too. Tachikawa suggested they make Akira's little pal Uegusa vice president.

Uegusa needed the ego boost.

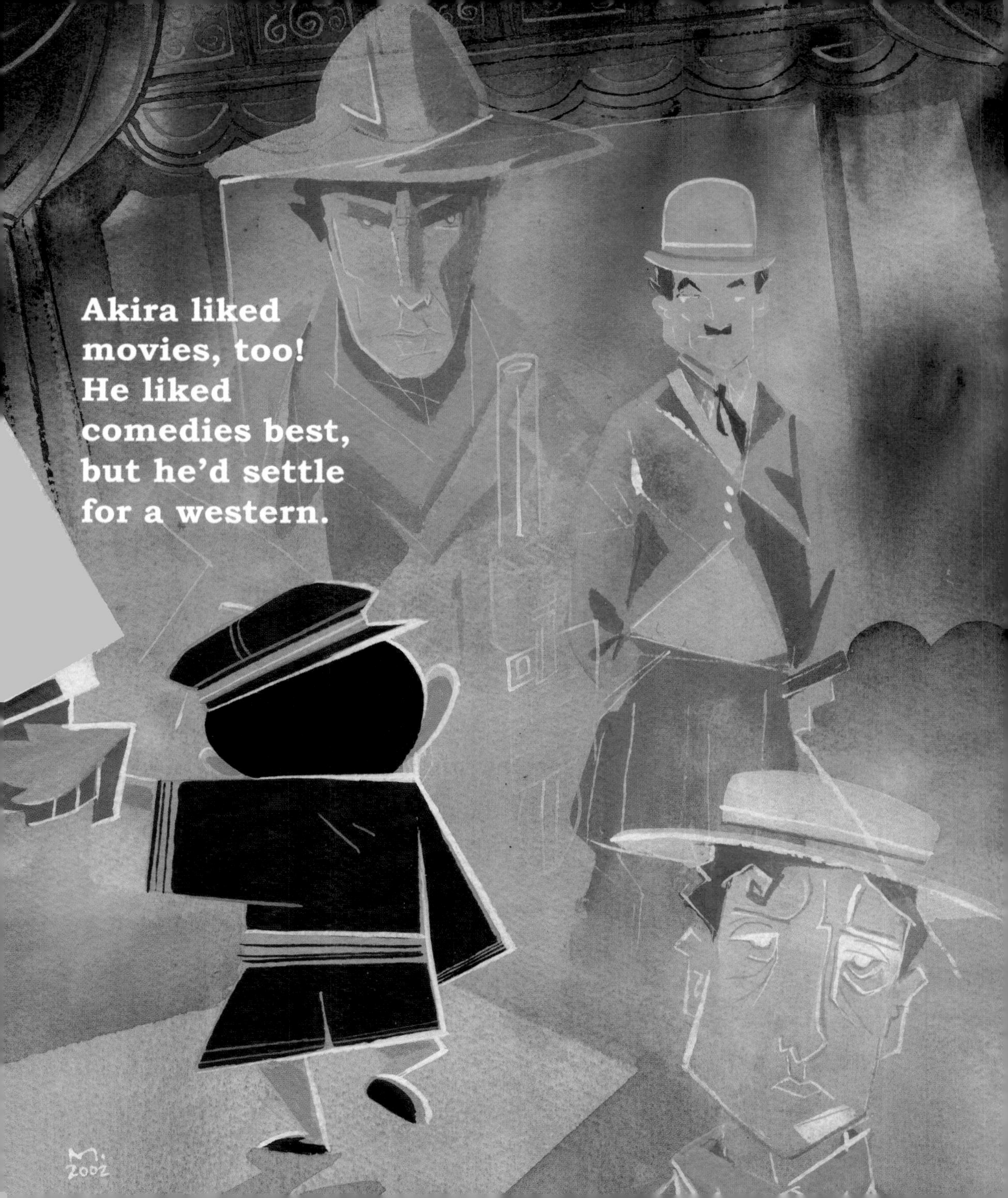
M.
2002

Akira liked movies, too! He liked comedies best, but he'd settle for a western.

Akira liked fencing, too. This made his father proud as punch...and left his brother, Heigo, in the shadows.

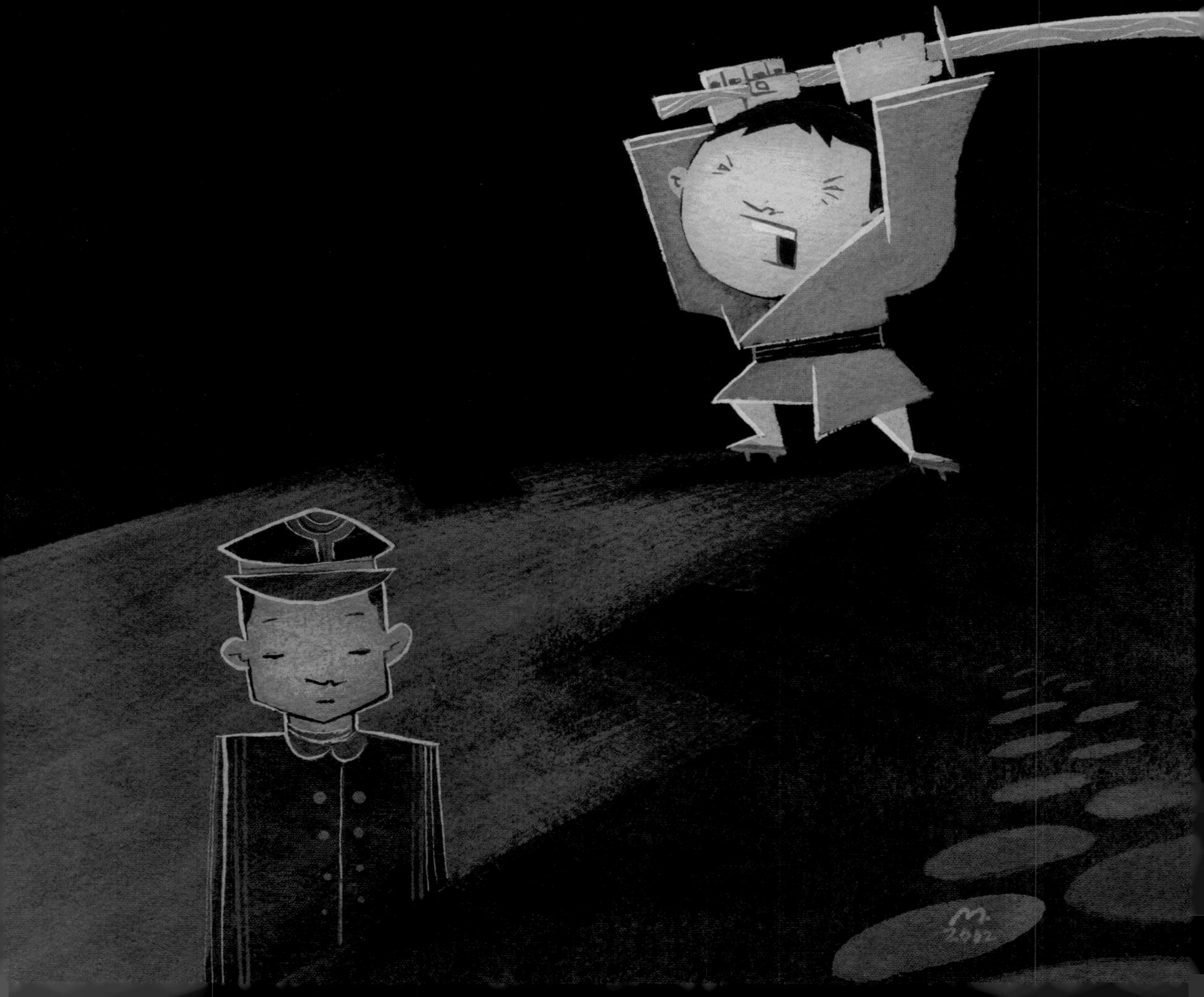

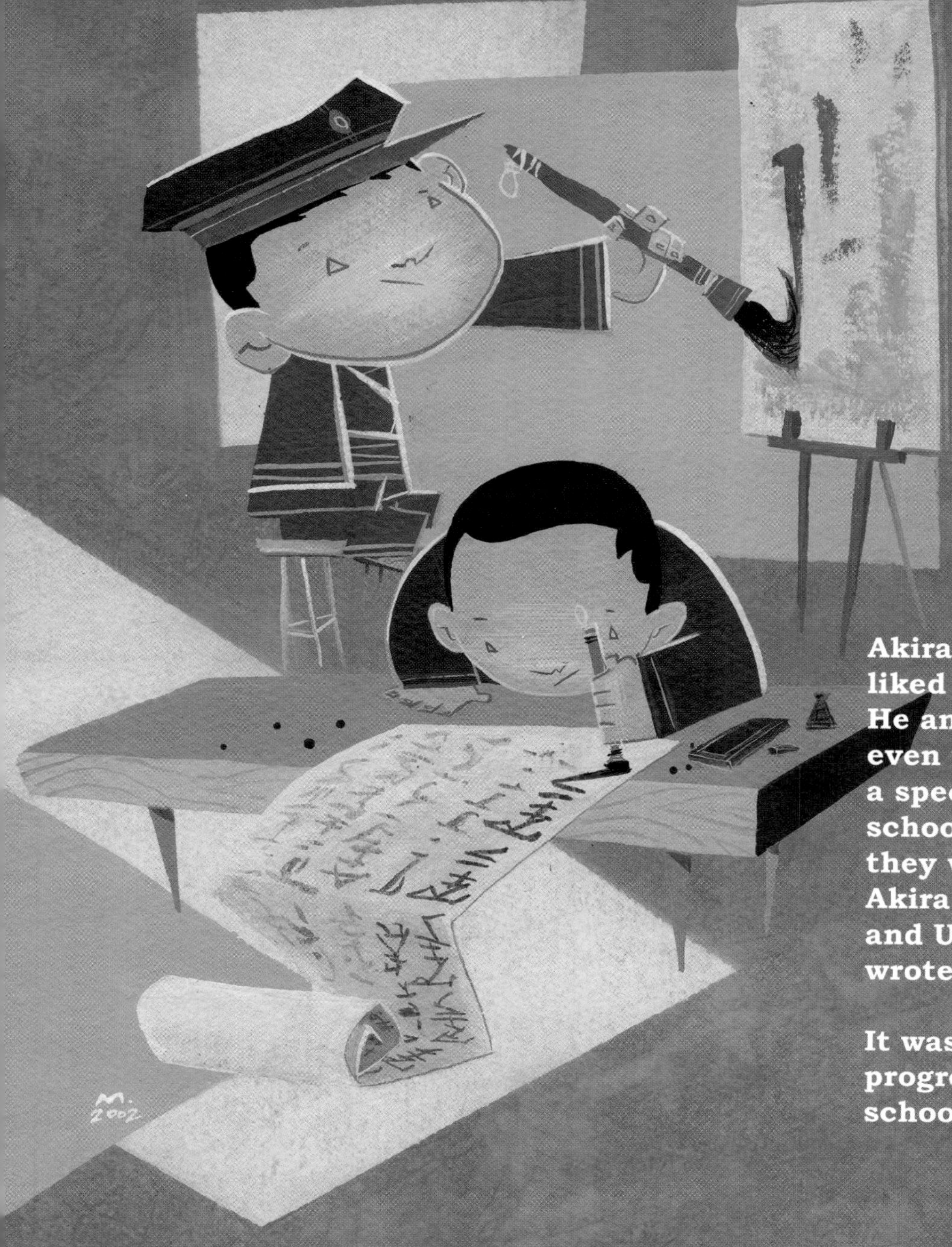

Akira really liked to paint. He and Uegusa even went to a special art school when they were bigger. Akira painted, and Uegusa wrote stories.

It was a very progressive school.

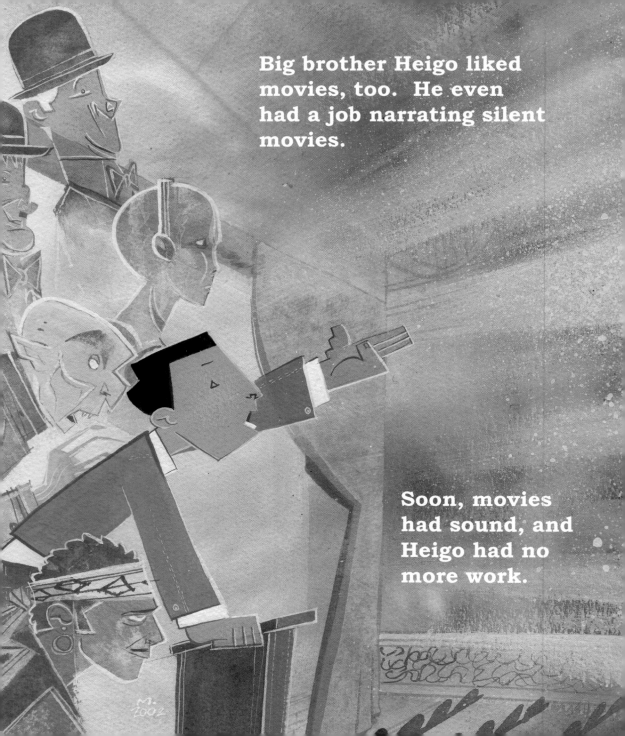

Big brother Heigo liked movies, too. He even had a job narrating silent movies.

Soon, movies had sound, and Heigo had no more work.

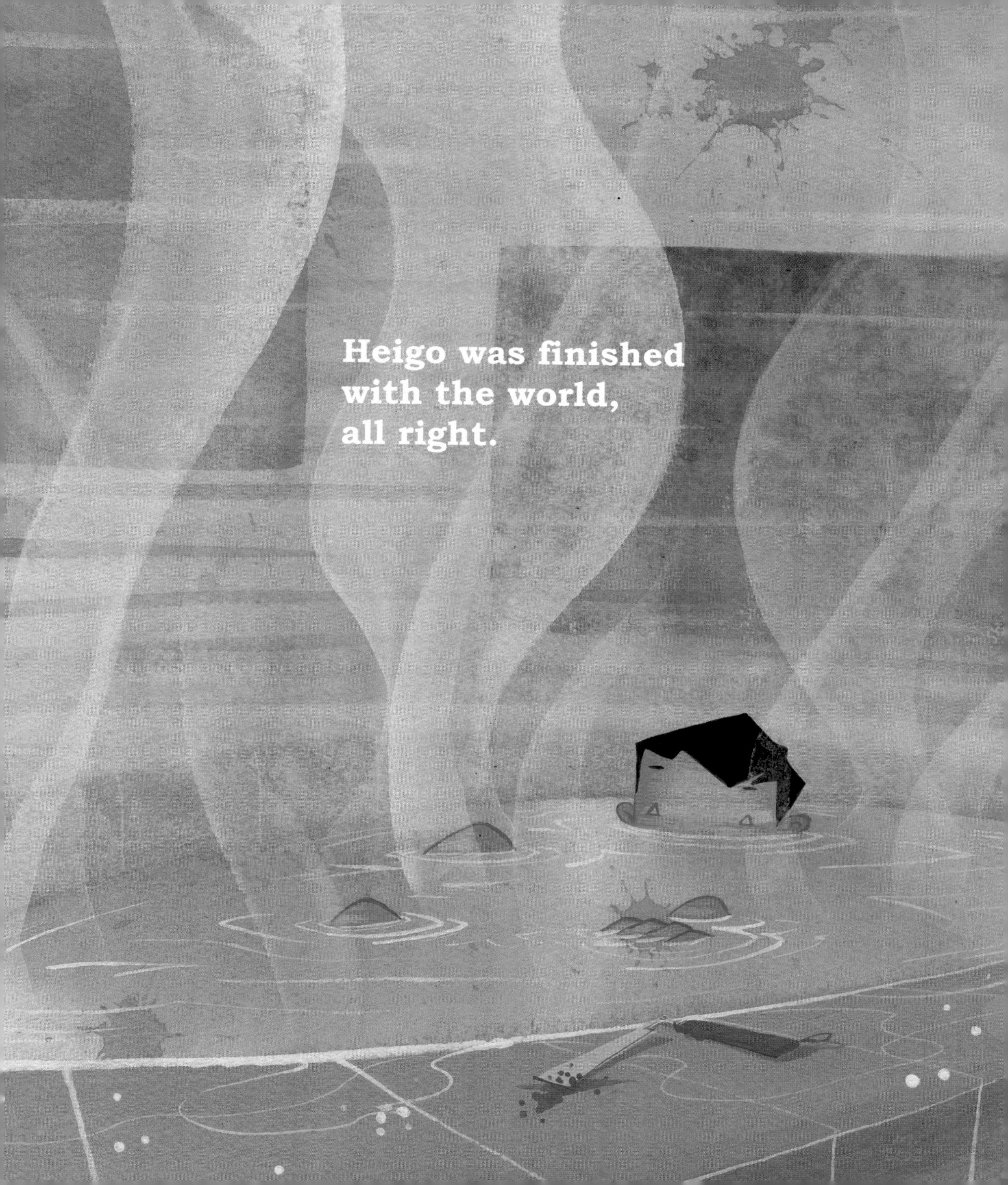

Heigo was finished
with the world,
all right.

Akira kept painting, but the bills kept coming, too. He didn't want to suck his folks dry! It was time to get a real gig.

In 1936, a movie studio hired Akira.

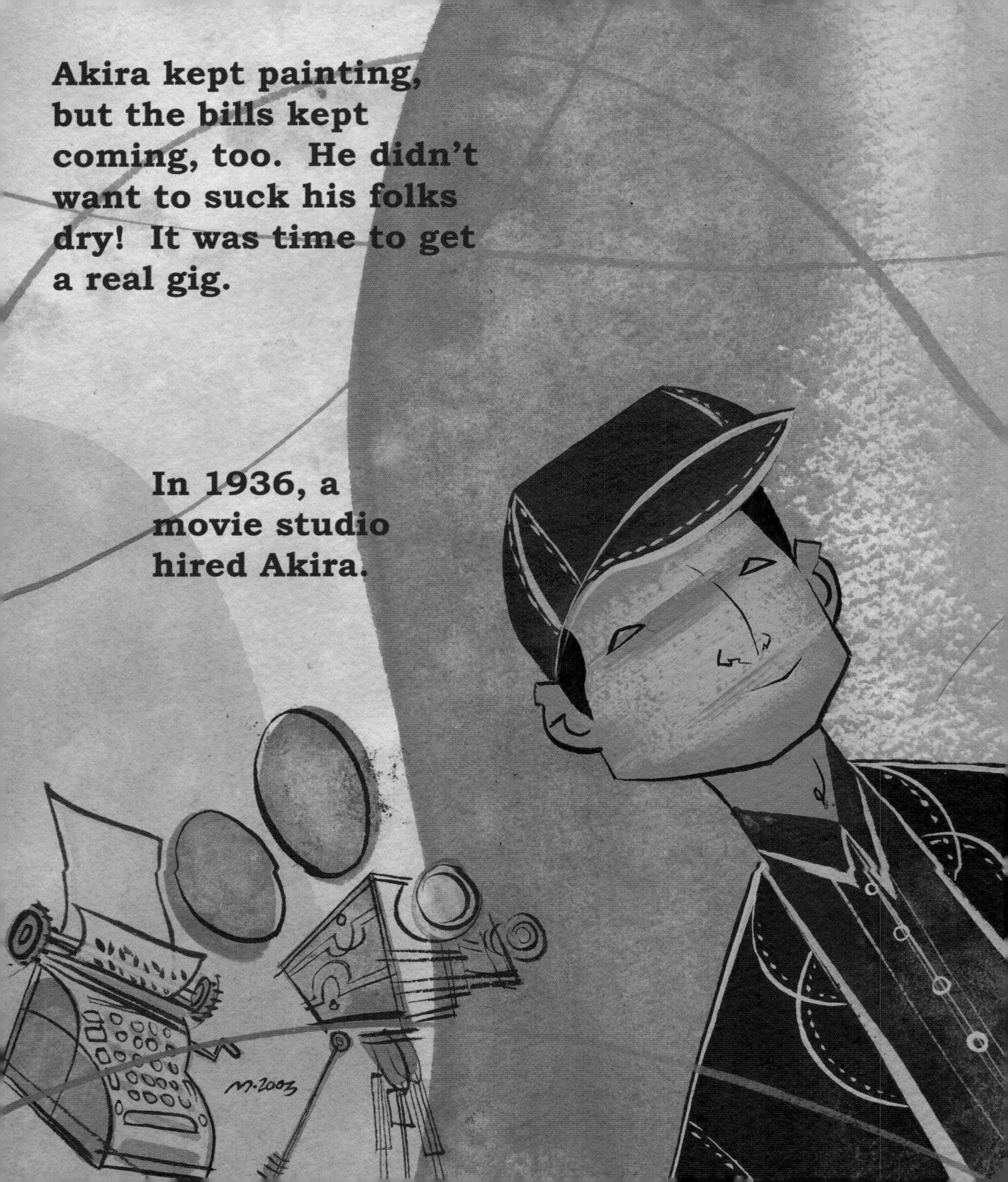
M·2003

Kajiro Yamamoto, a big director at the studio, showed Akira what to do. "He's a perfectionist... a real artist," thought Yamamoto.

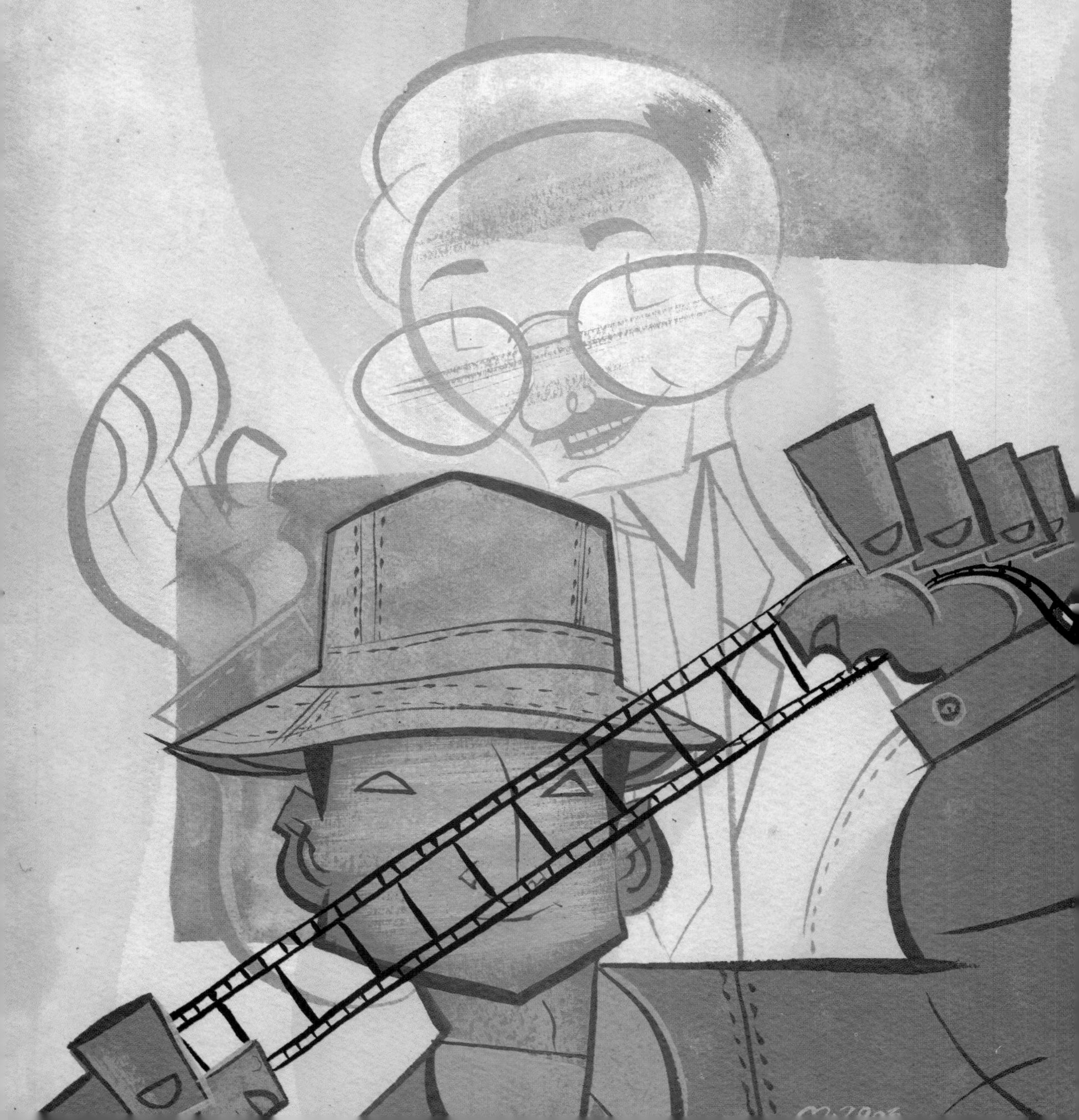

Uegusa worked there too. He and Akira made pictures to support the war effort... and that meant restrictions on how to best tell stories.

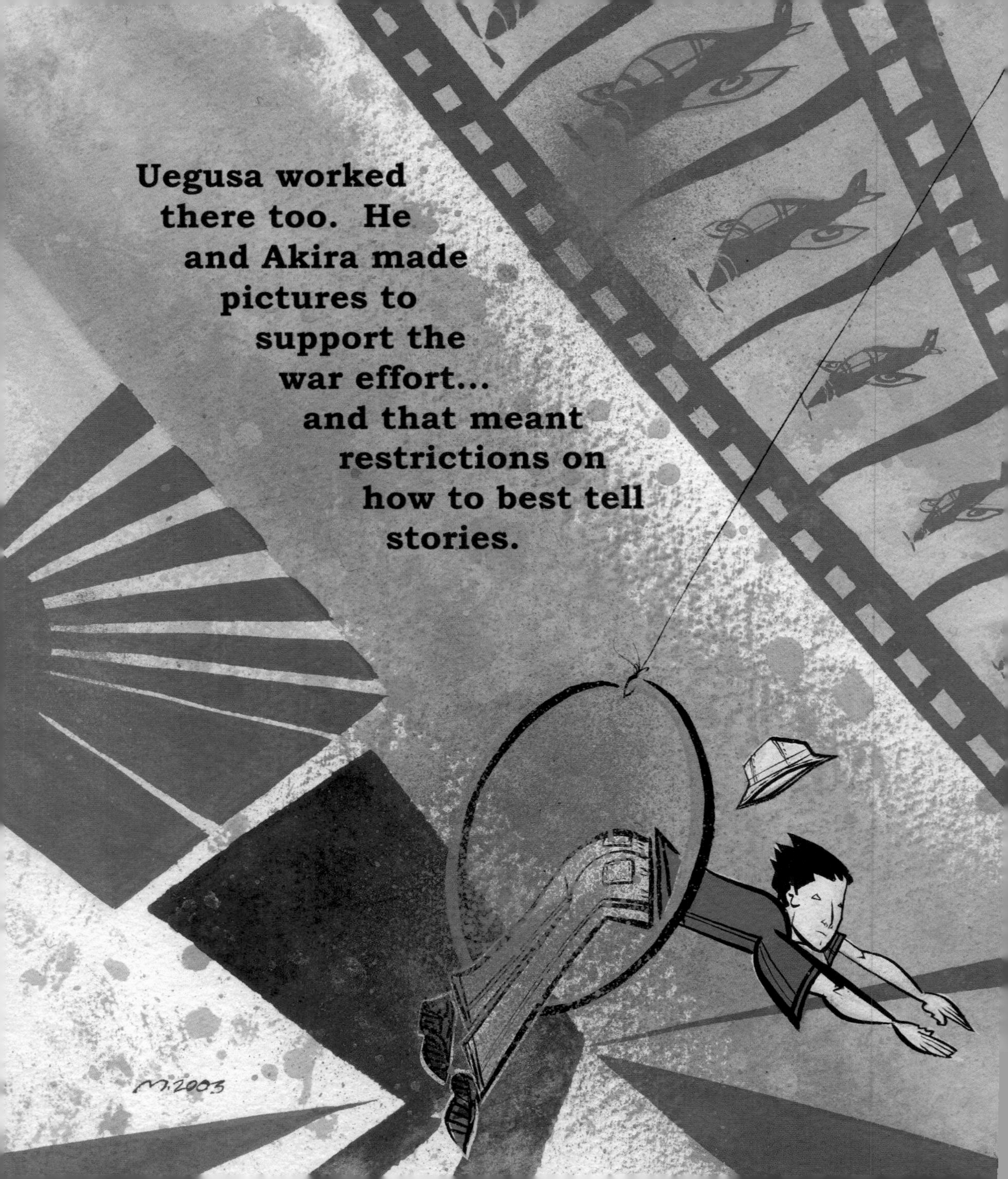
Mi 2003

Soon, the allied forces occupied Japan...and Akira had no more limits! He could breath an air of youth and freedom into his stories.

Akira could be an individual!

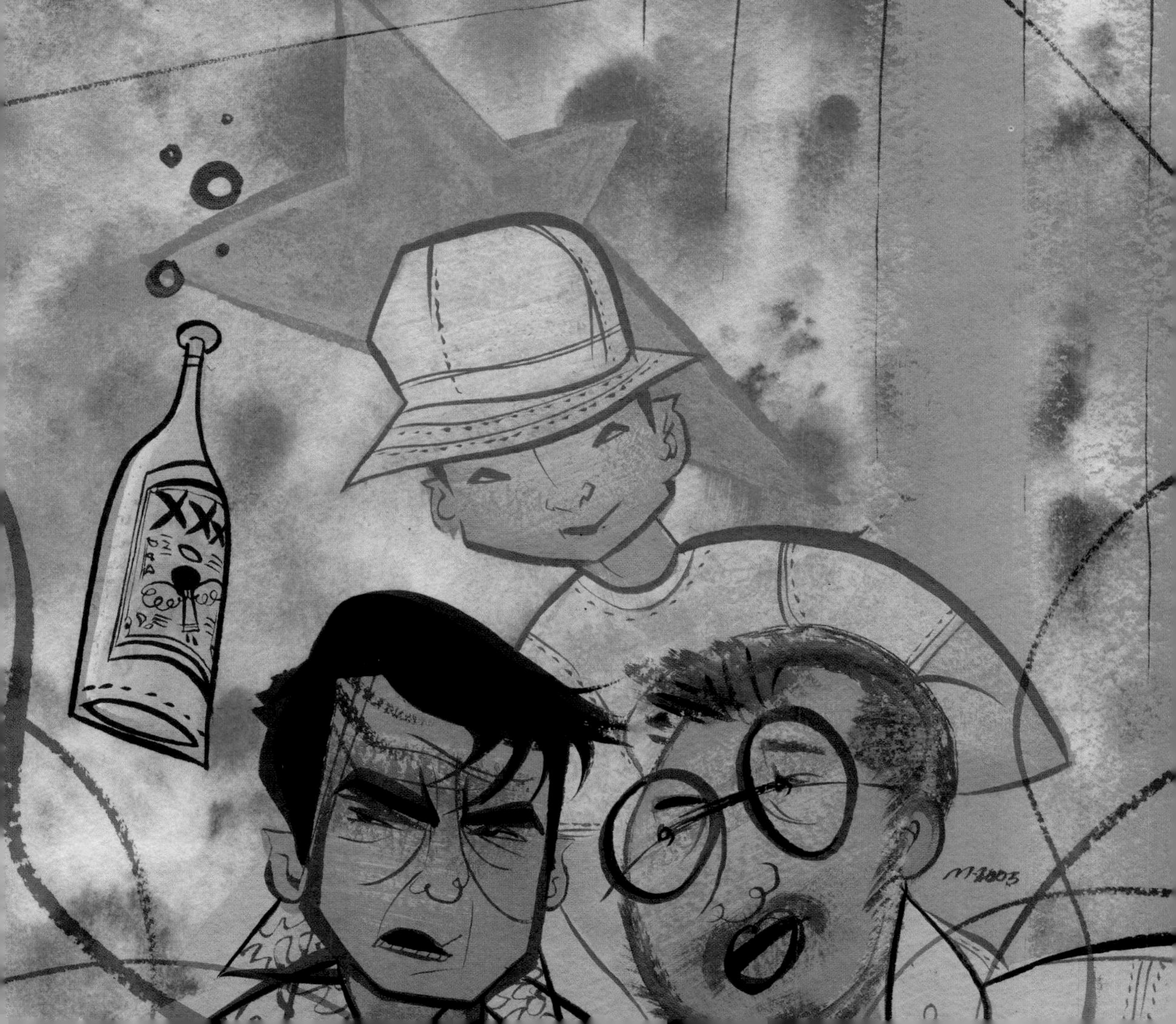

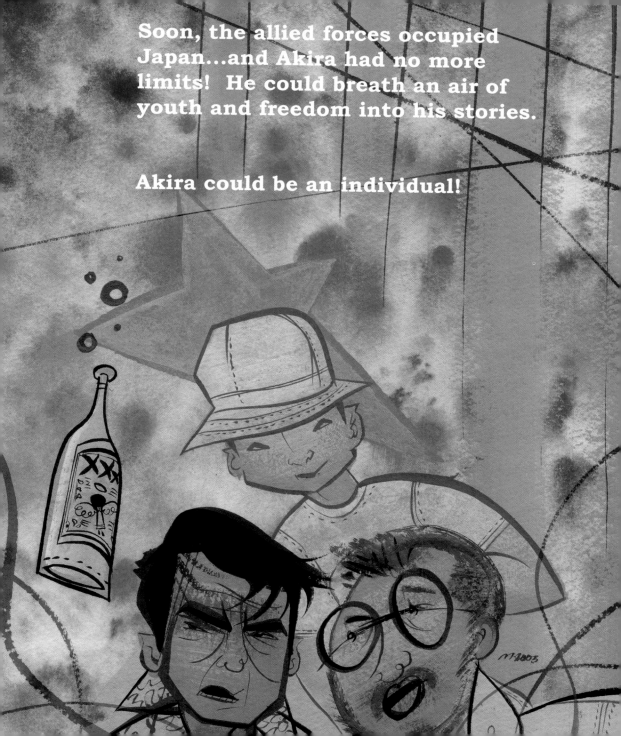

Akira showed the world what youth and freedom could do...

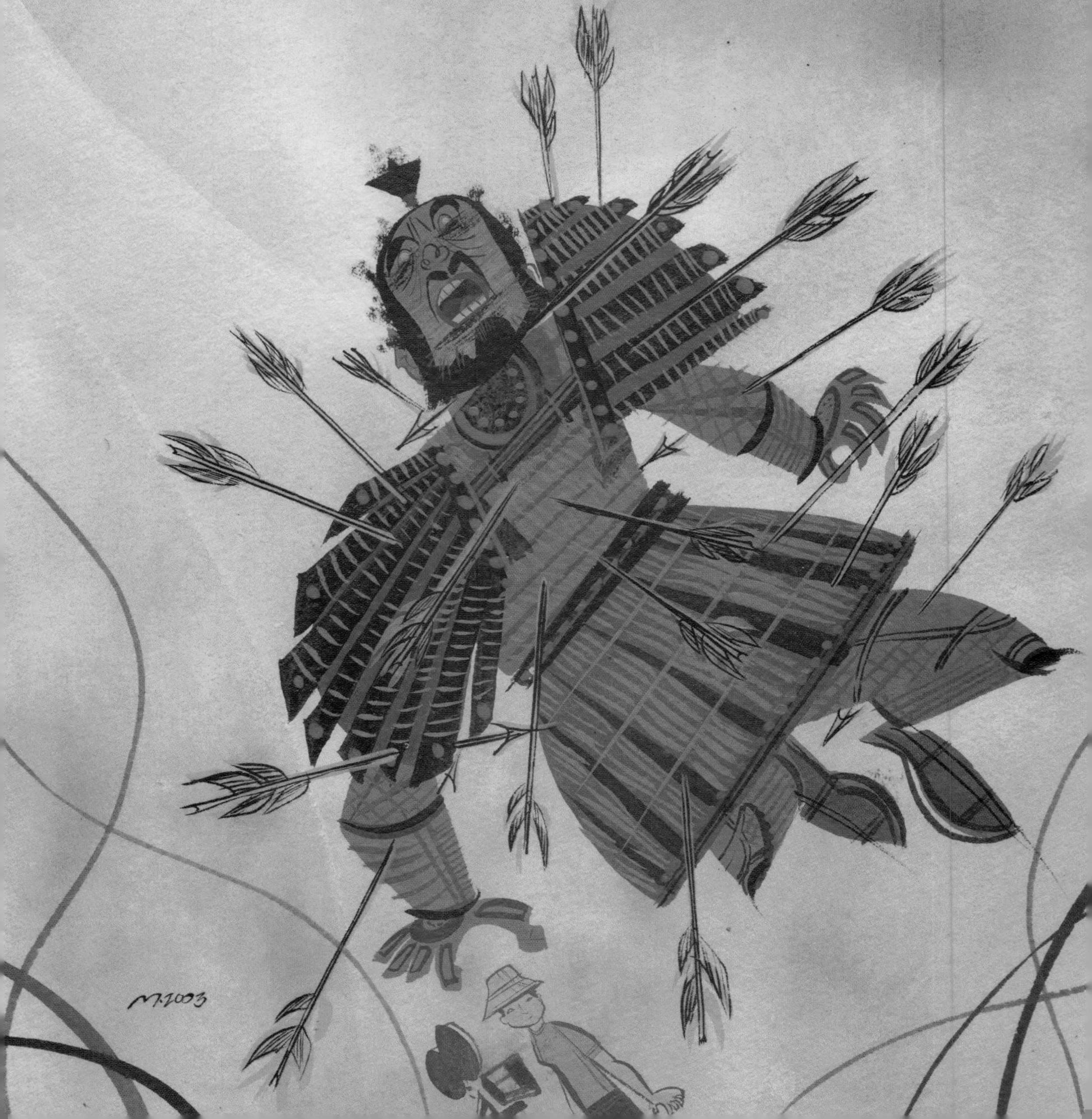

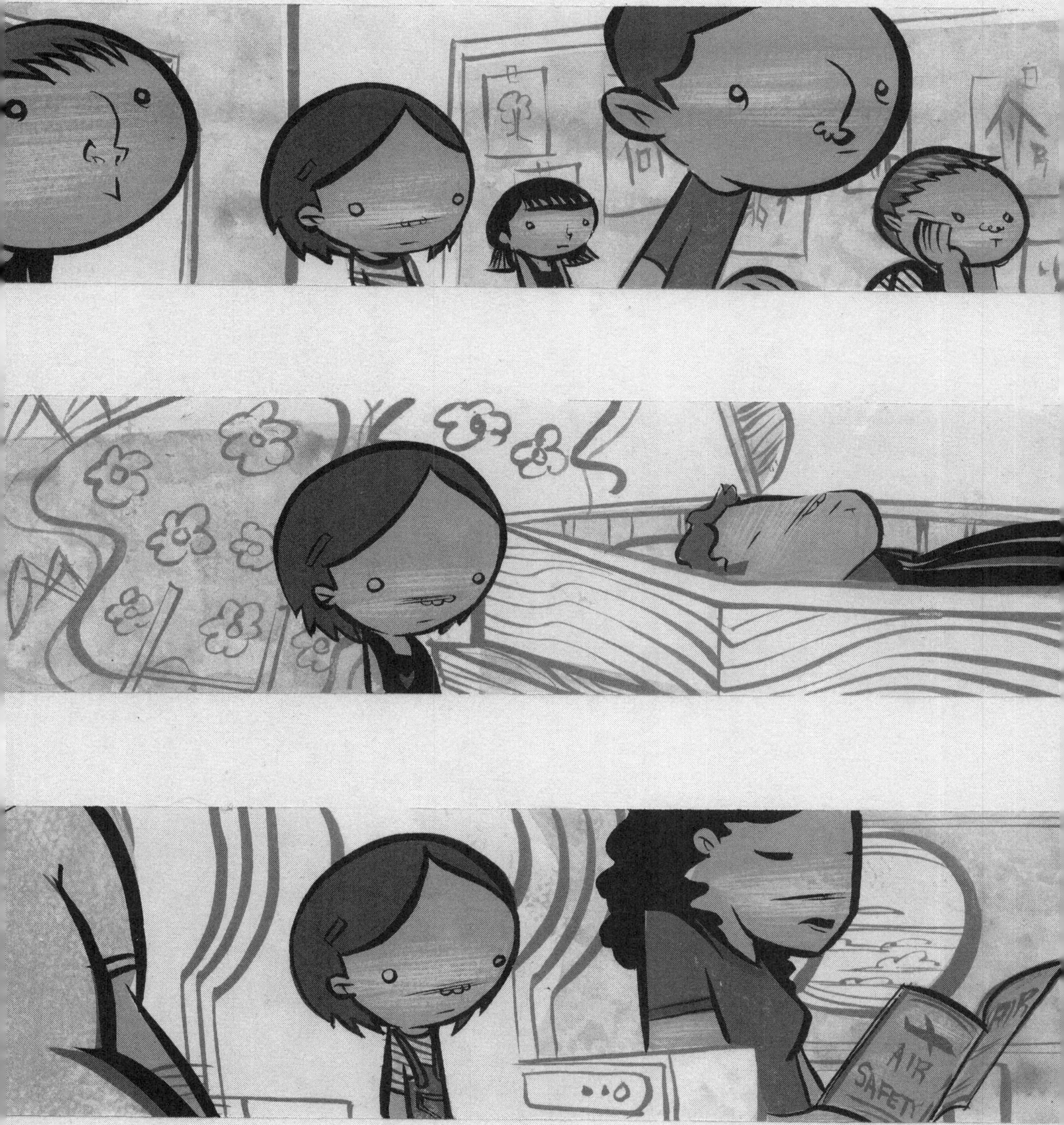
AIR SAFETY

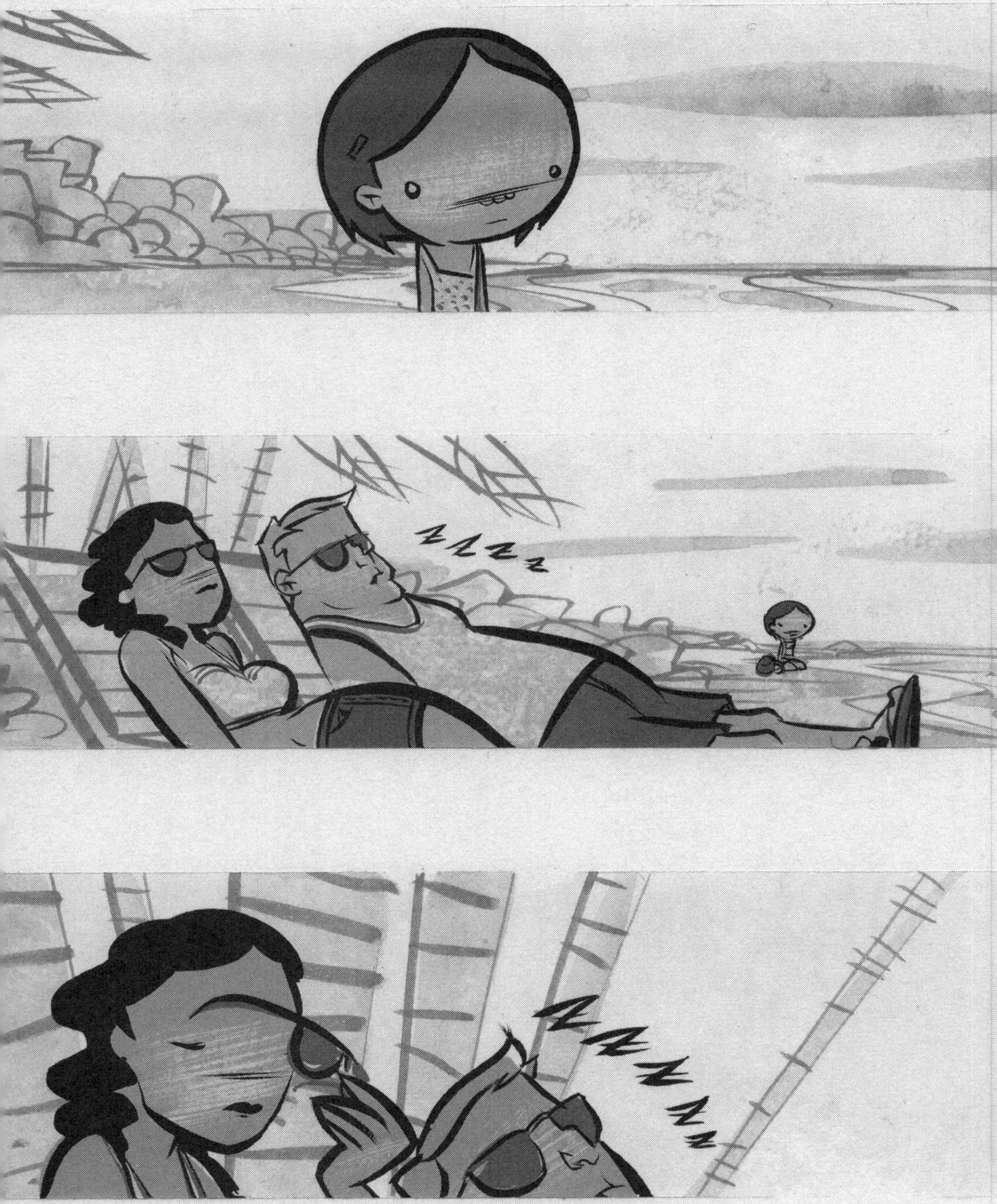

ZZZZZZ
ZZZZZZ

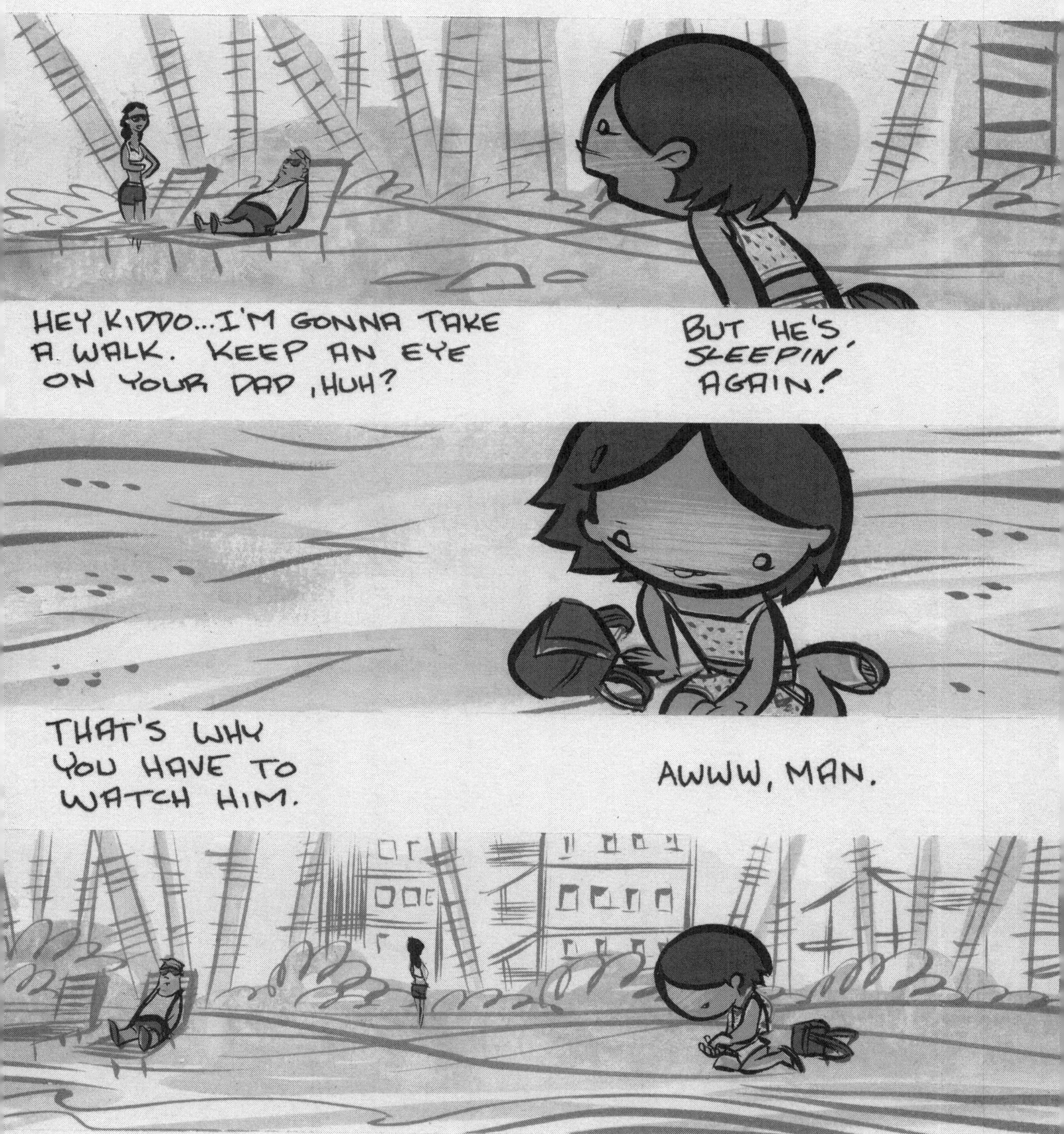
HEY, KIDDO... I'M GONNA TAKE A WALK. KEEP AN EYE ON YOUR DAD, HUH?
BUT HE'S SLEEPIN' AGAIN!
THAT'S WHY YOU HAVE TO WATCH HIM.
AWWW, MAN.

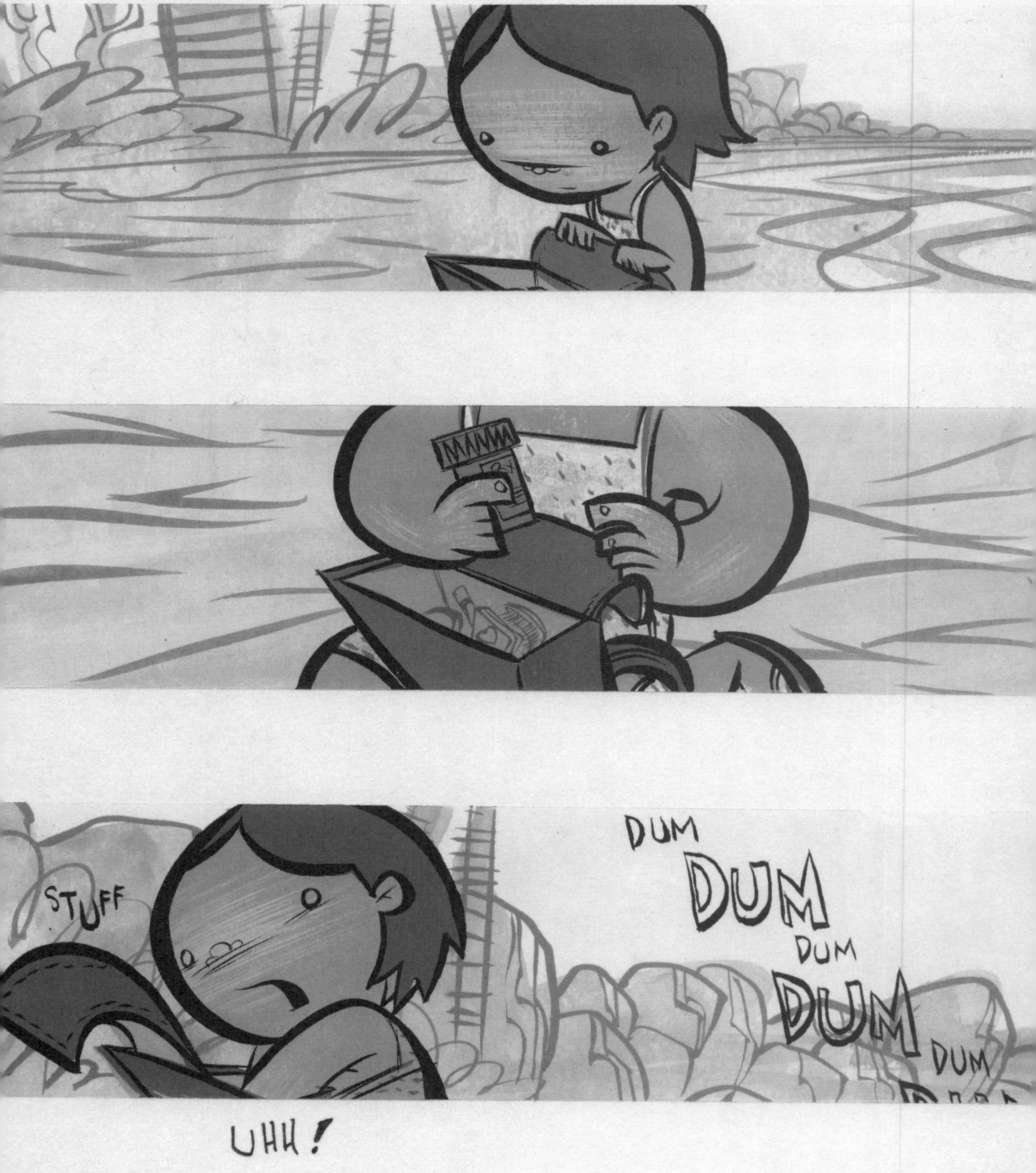
STUFF
DUM
DUM
DUM
DUM
DUM
UHH!

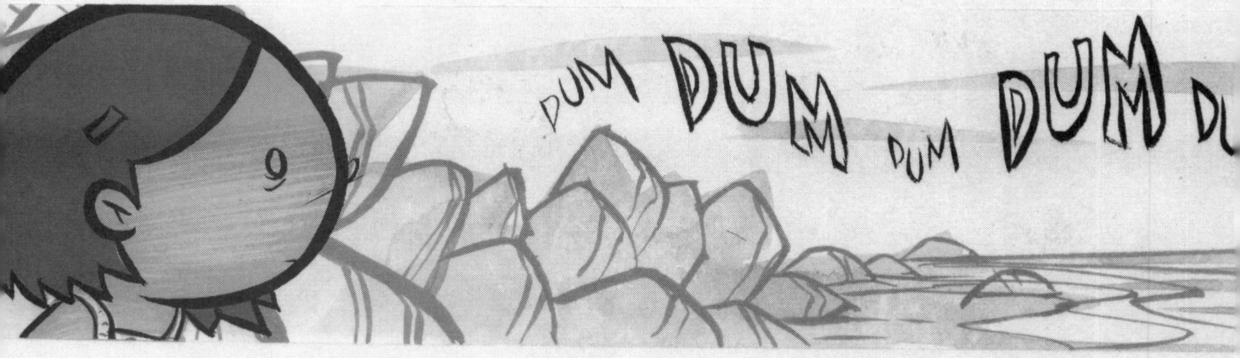
DUM DUM DUM DUM DU

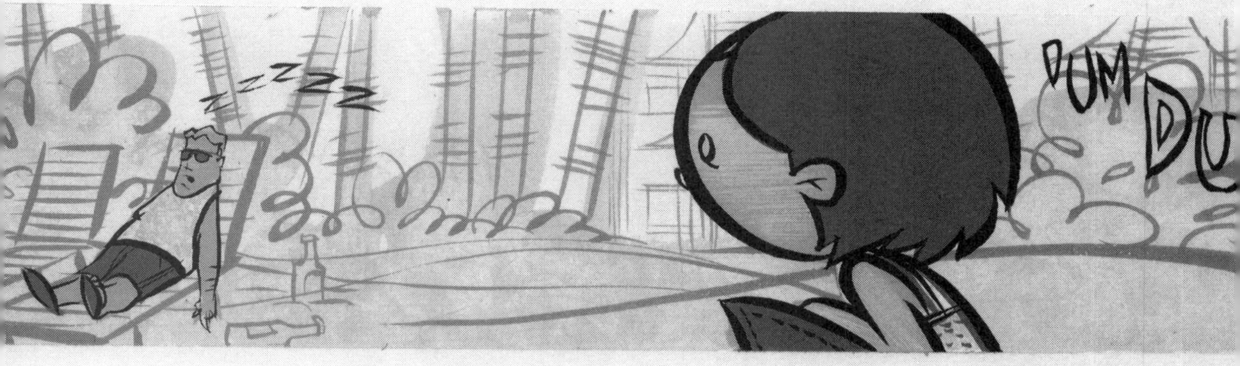
ZZZZZZ
DUM DU

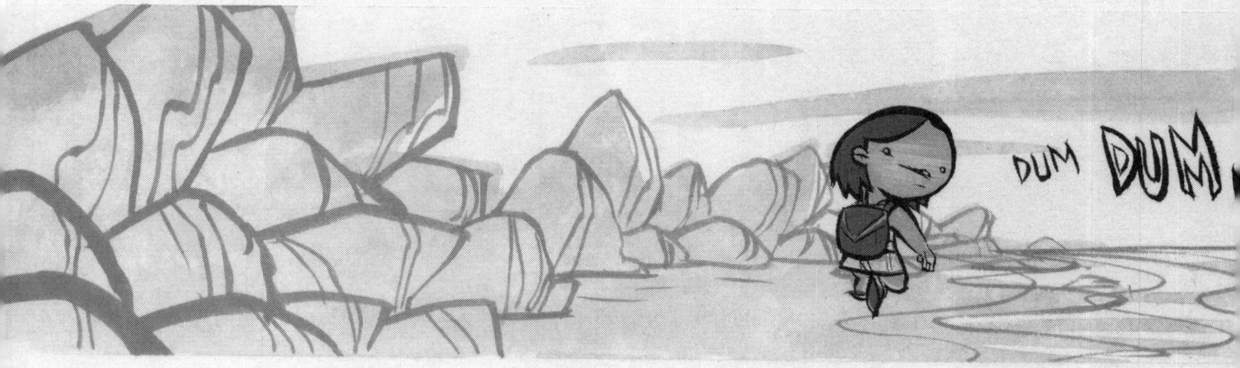
DUM DUM

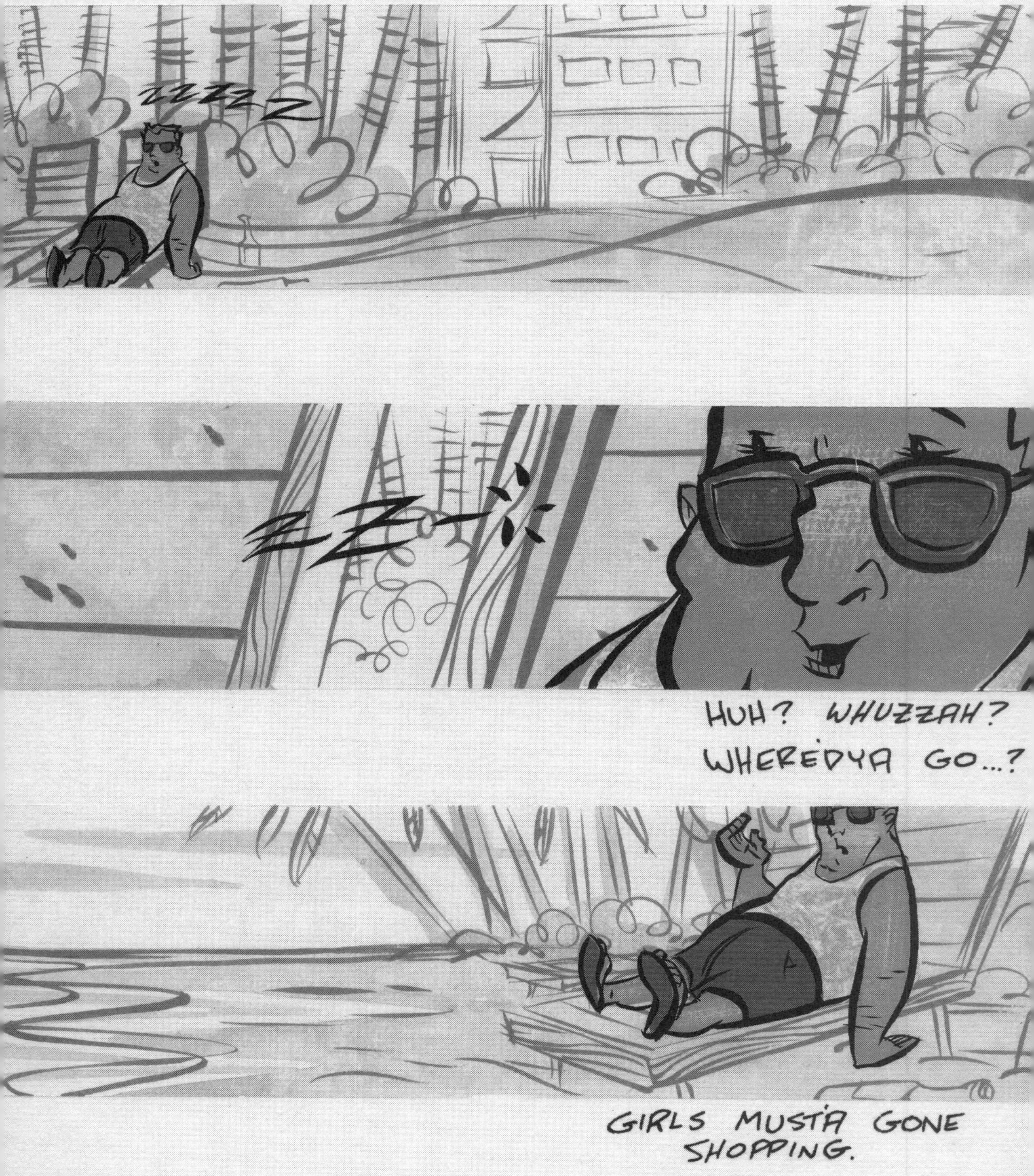
HUH? WHUZZAH? WHEREDYA GO...?
GIRLS MUSTA GONE SHOPPING.

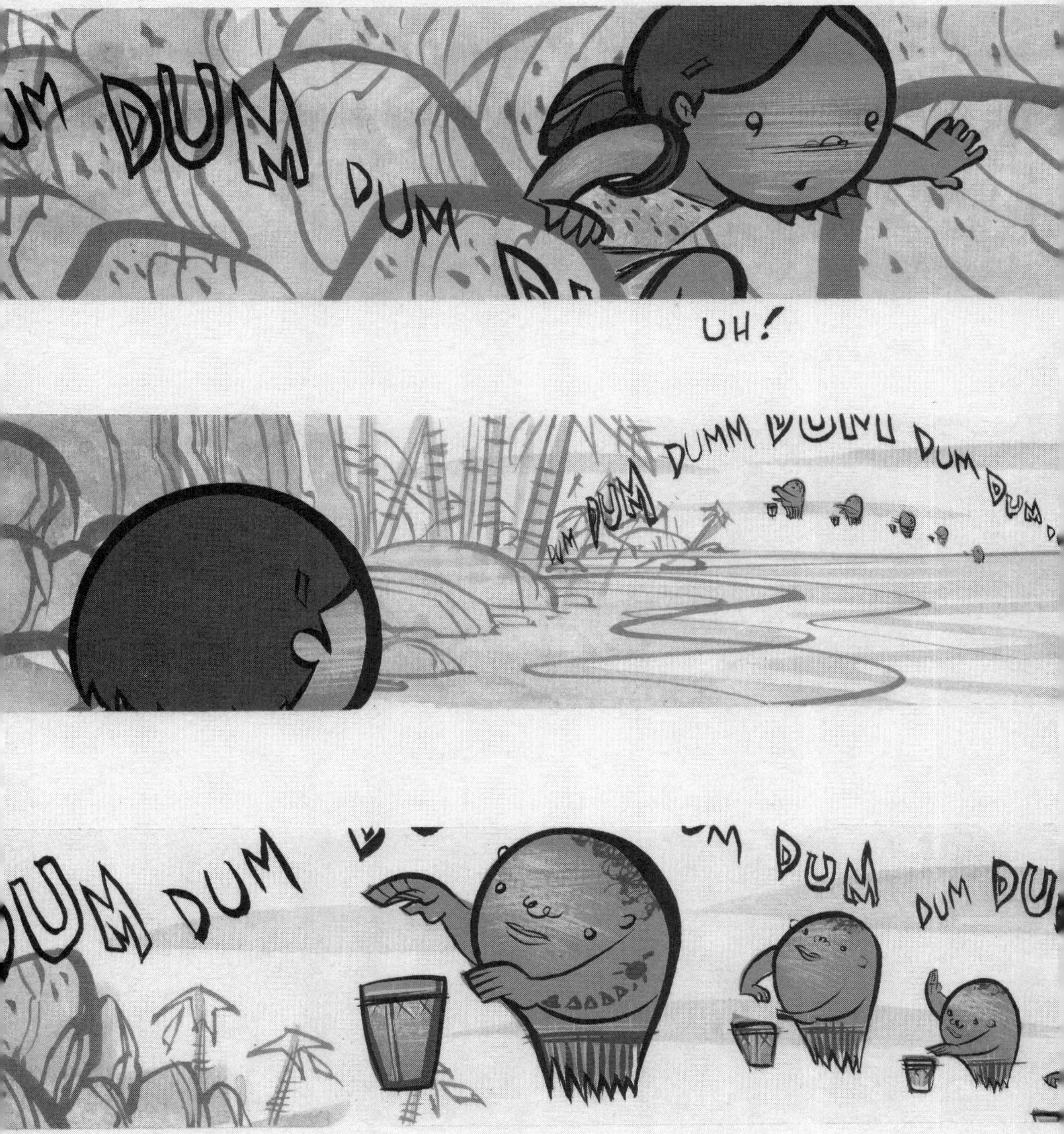
UM DUM DUM
UH!
DUM DUM DUMM DUM DUM DUM
UM DUM DUM DUM DU

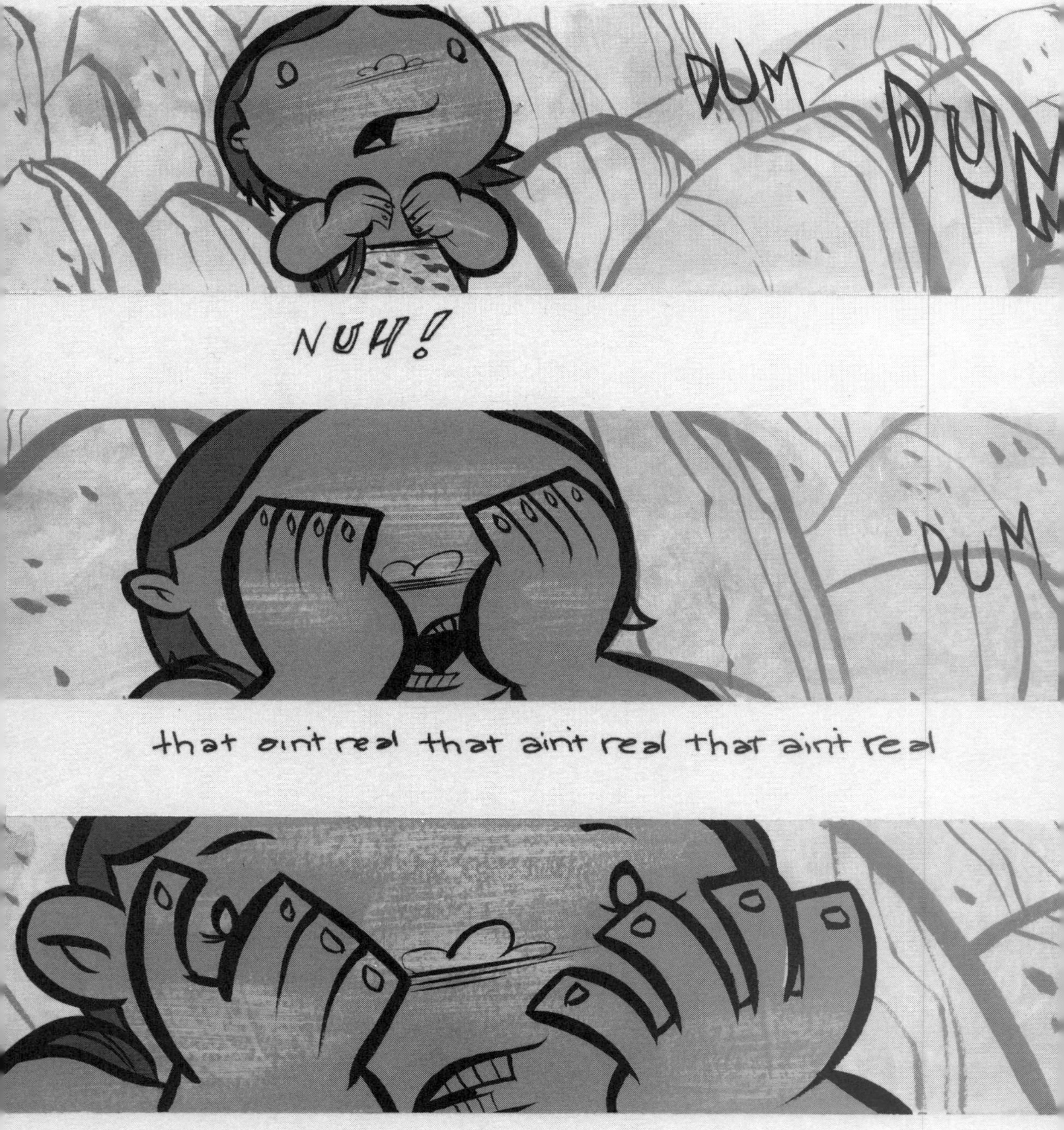
DUM
DUM
NUH!
DUM
that aint real that aint real that aint real

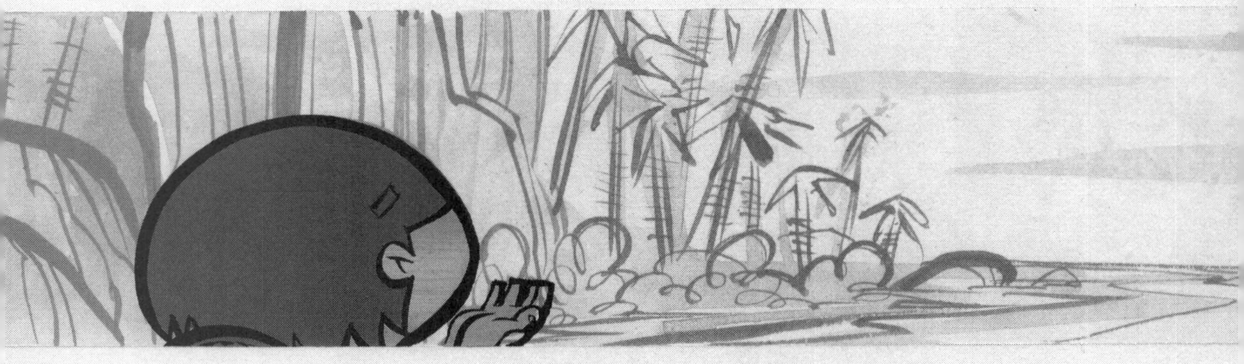
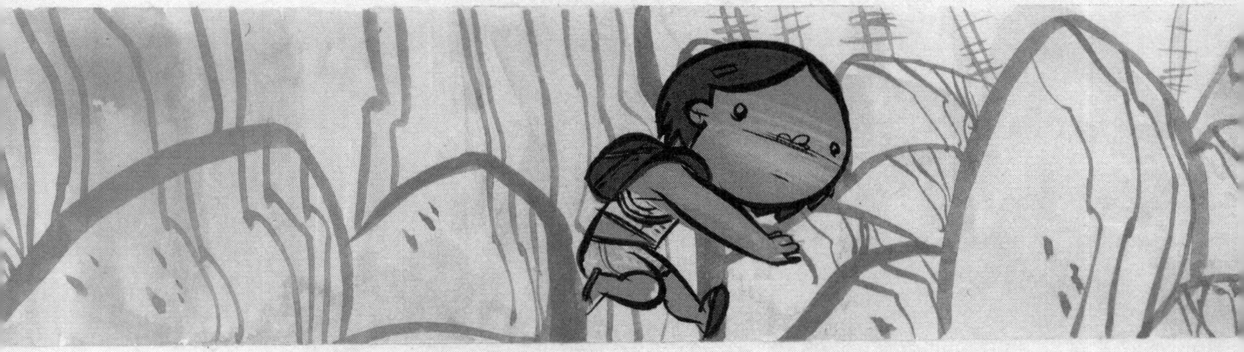
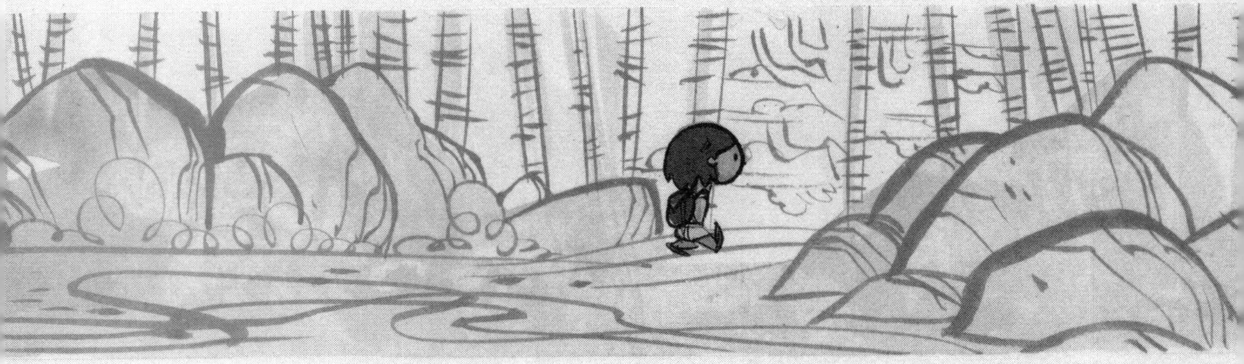

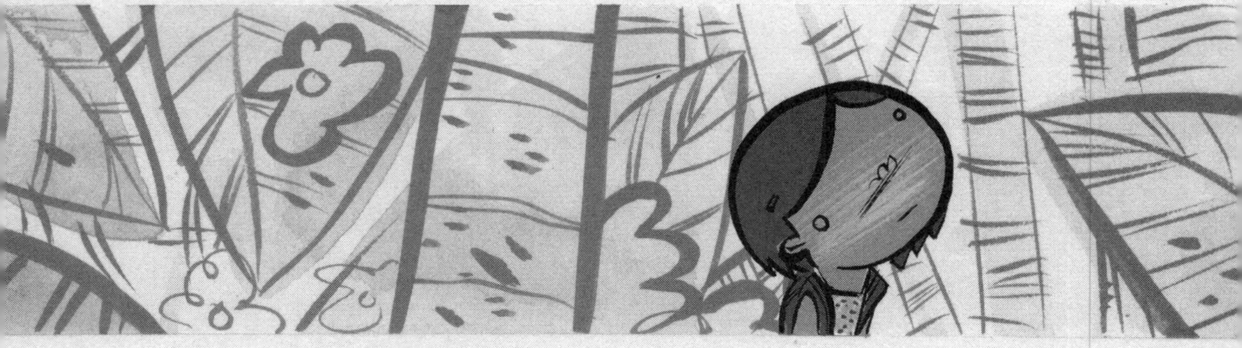

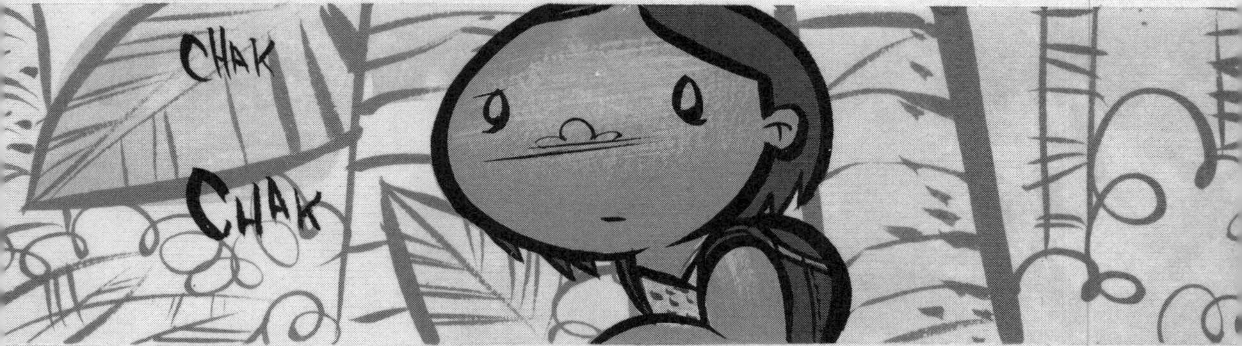
CHAK
CHAK

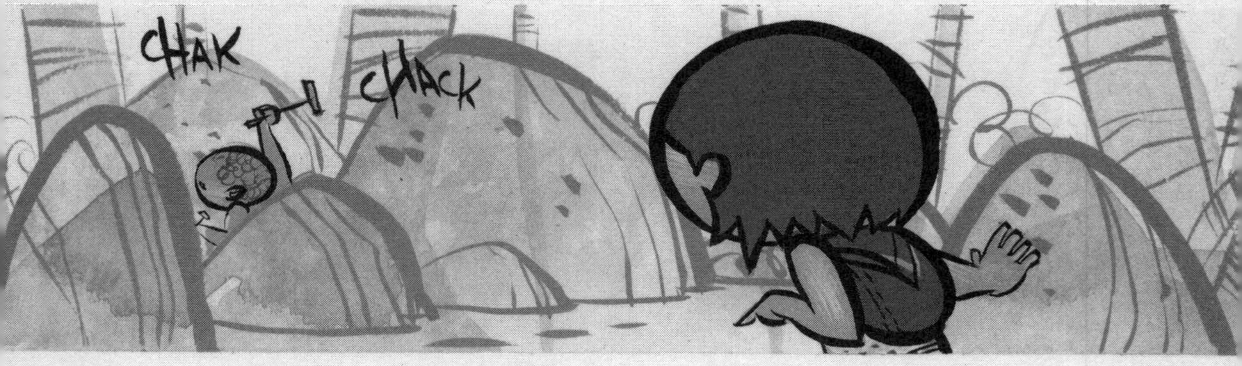
CHAK
CHACK

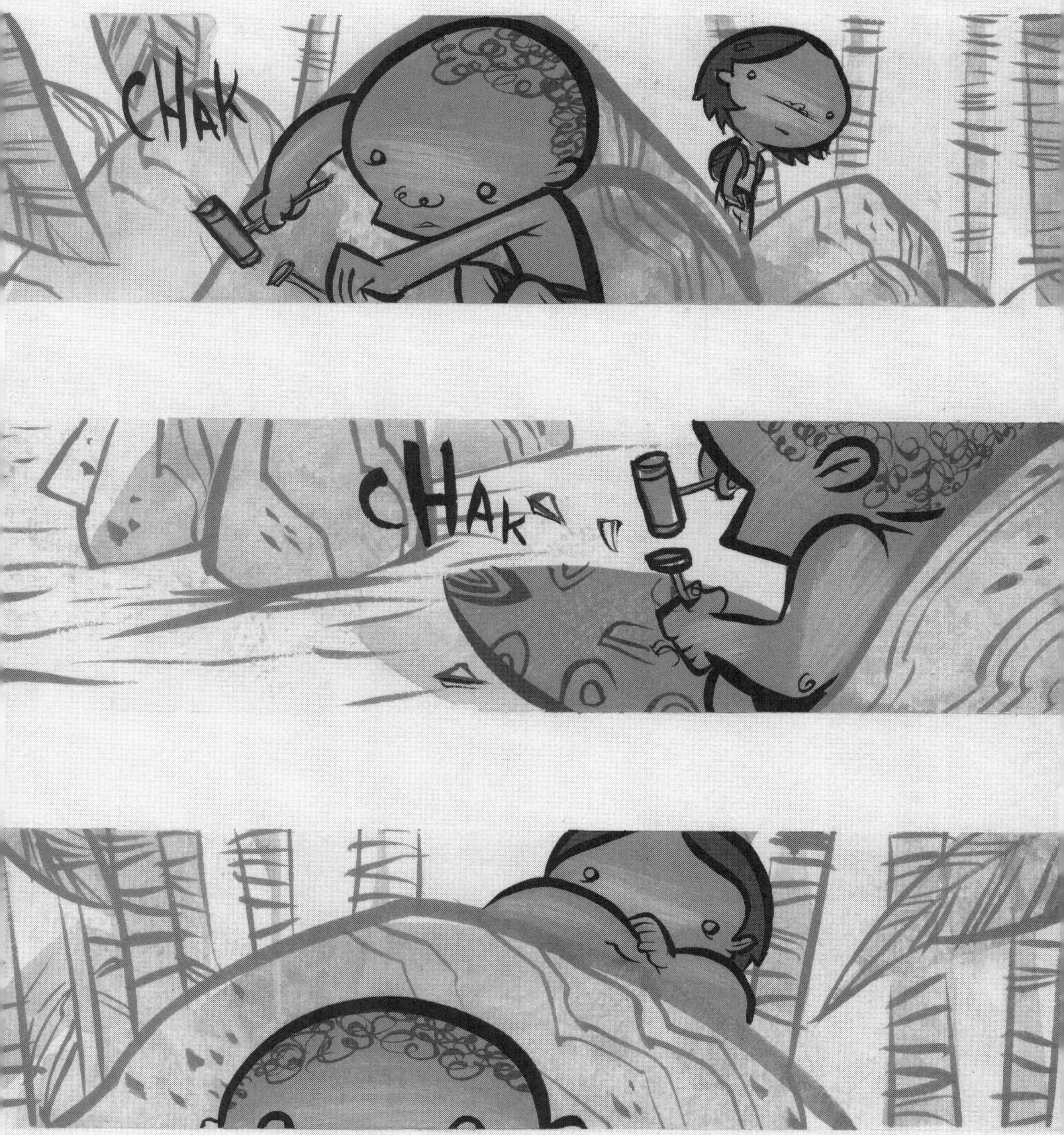
CHAK
CHAK

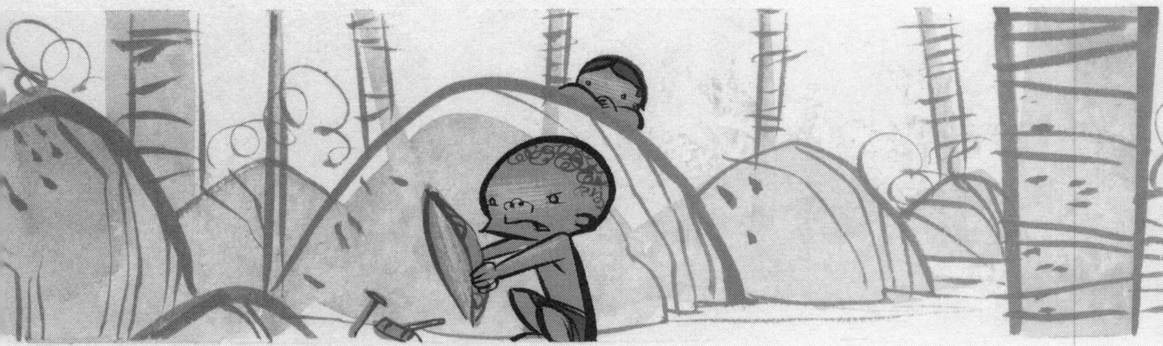

WAIT... WHAT?

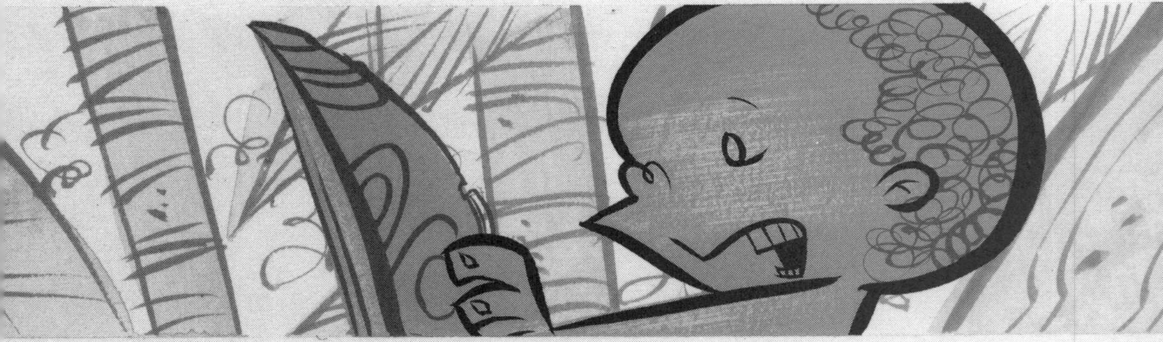

BEHIND ME?

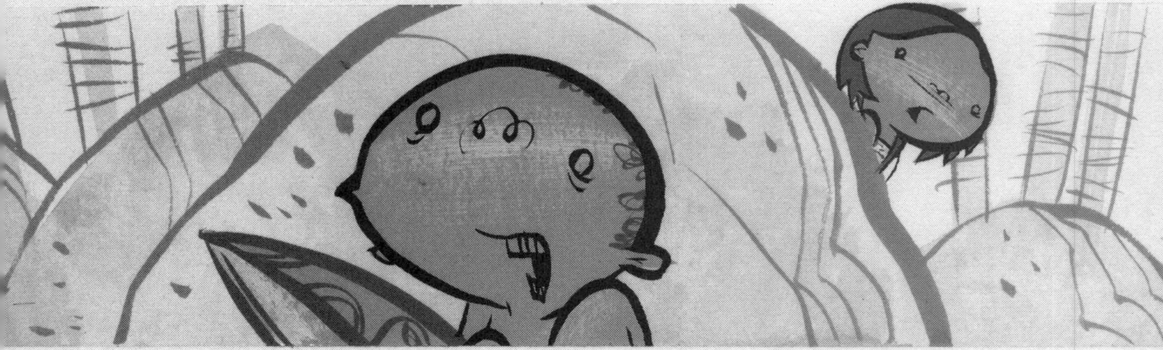

UT!

WHO ARE YOU TALKING TO?

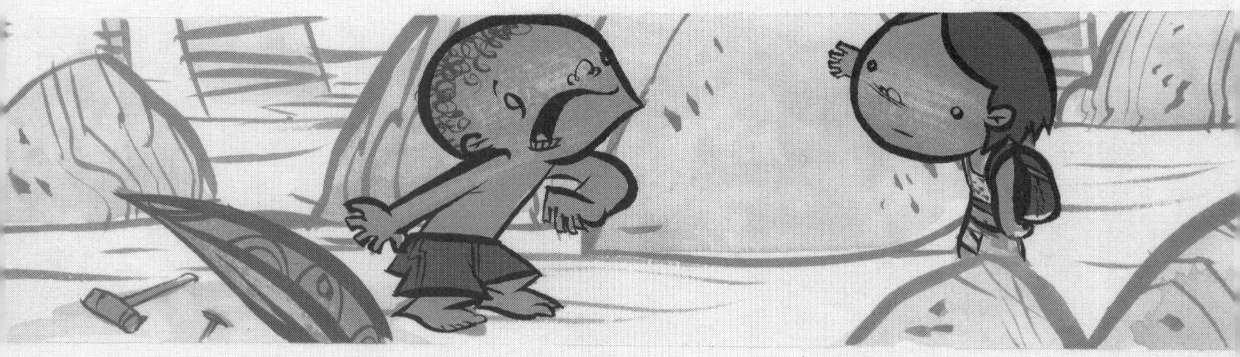
NOBODY!
WHADDA YA WANT?

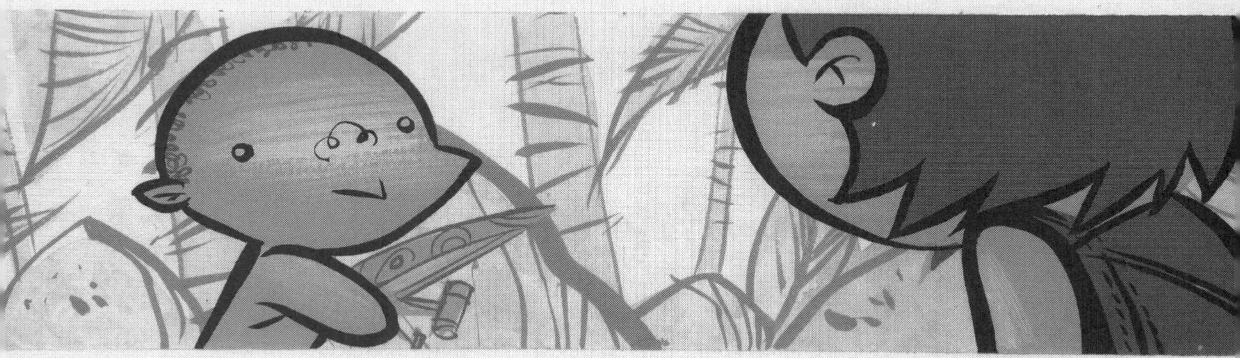
NOTHING..
ARE YOU ANOTHER GHOST?

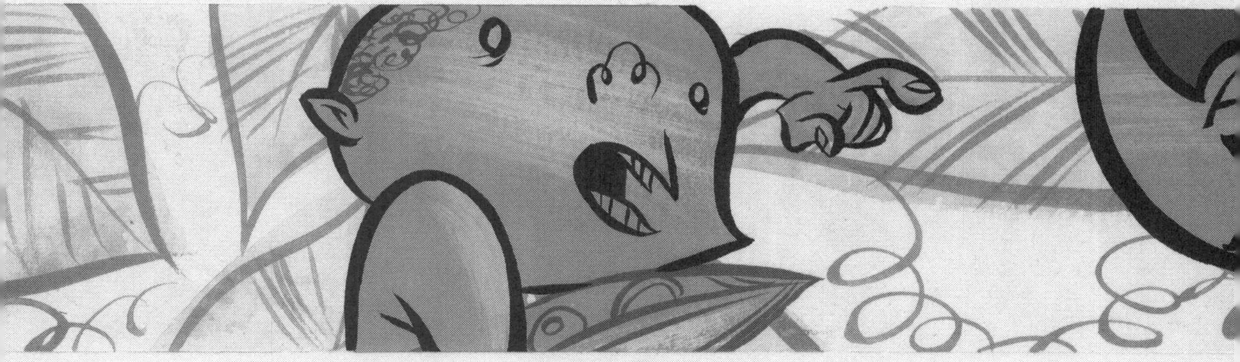
YOU SAW A GHOST? STAY AWAY FRM'E!

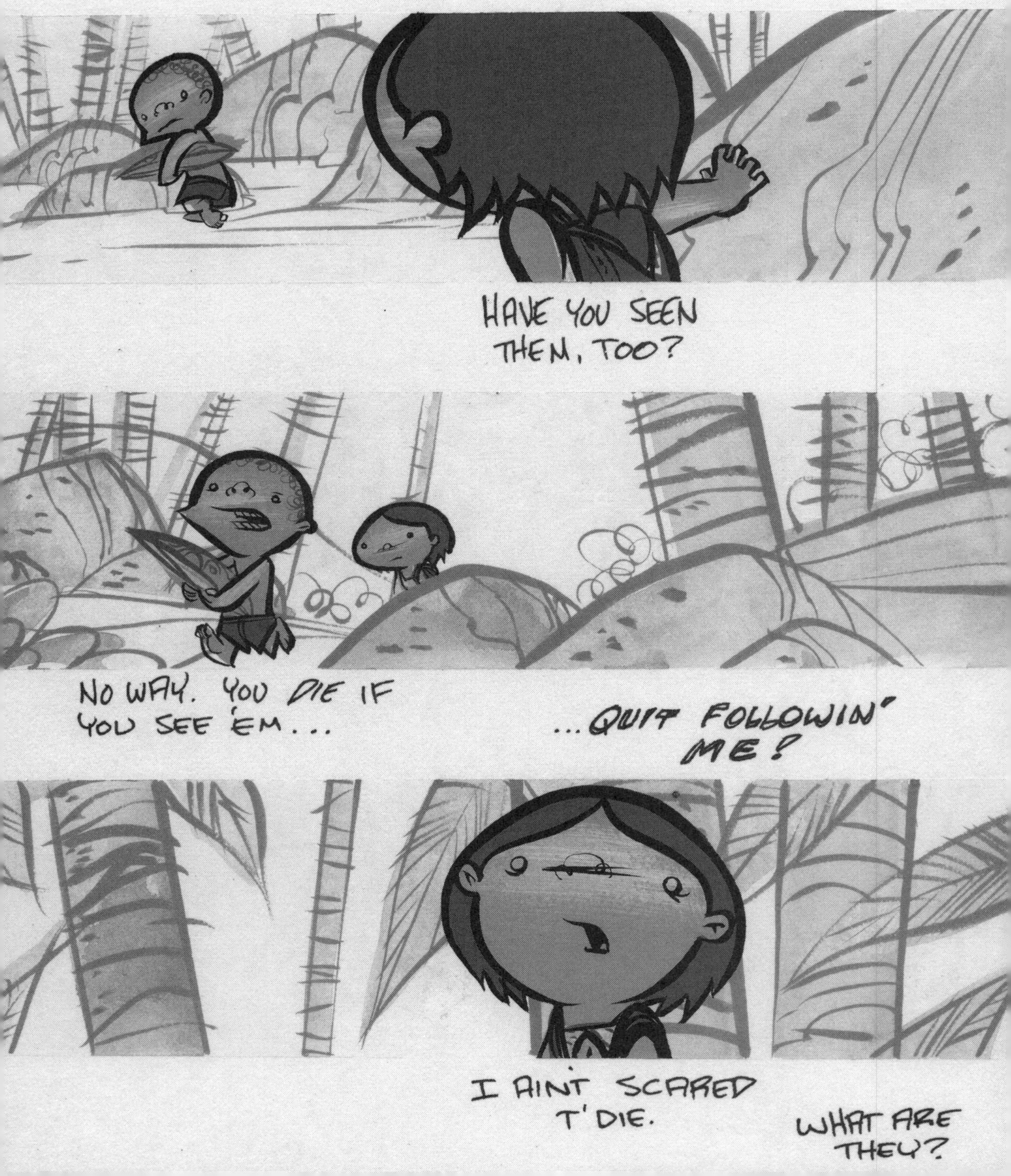
HAVE YOU SEEN THEM, TOO?
NO WAY. YOU DIE IF YOU SEE 'EM...
...QUIT FOLLOWIN' ME!
I AINT SCARED T'DIE.
WHAT ARE THEY?

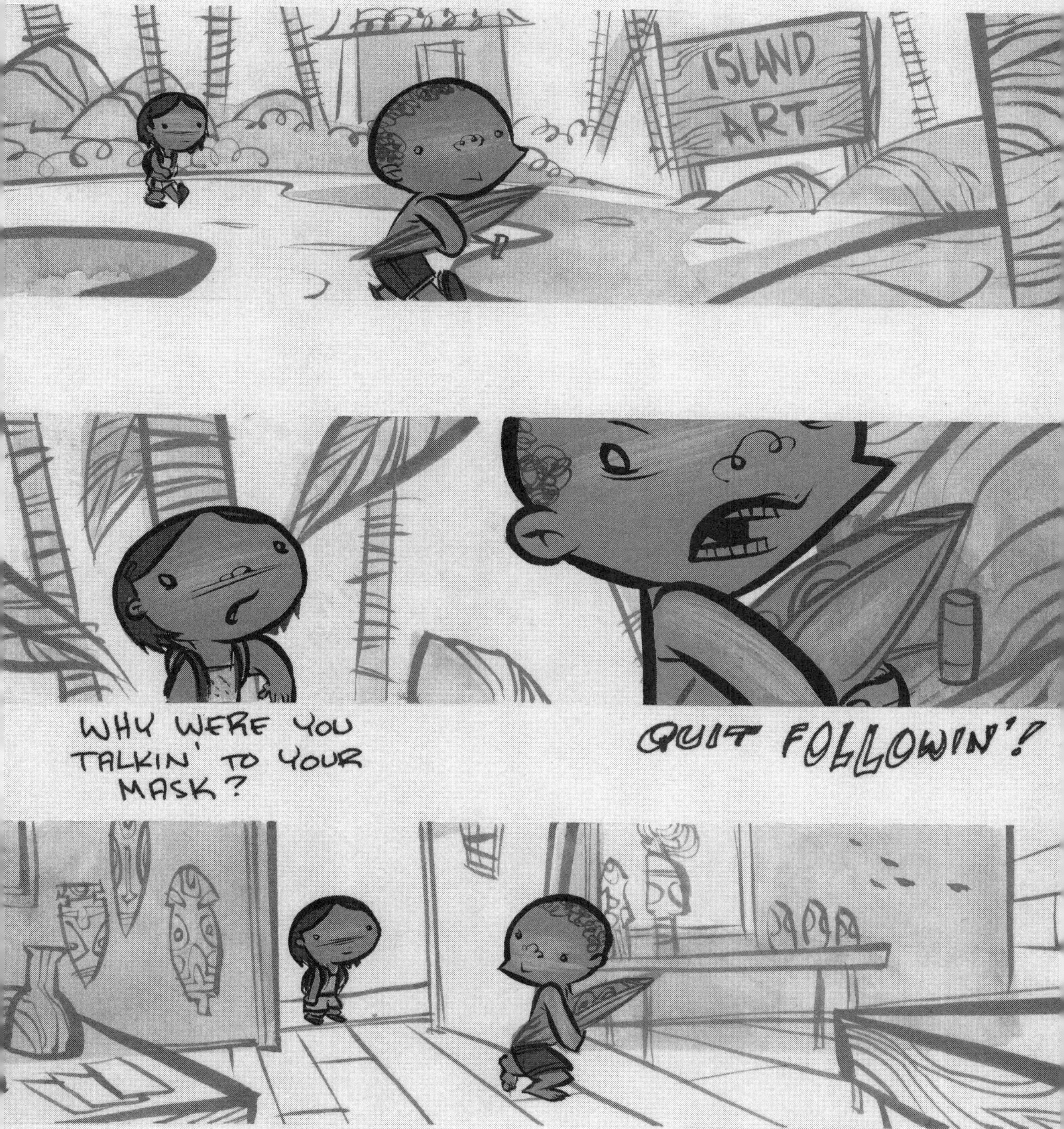
ISLAND ART
WHY WERE YOU TALKIN' TO YOUR MASK?
QUIT FOLLOWIN'!

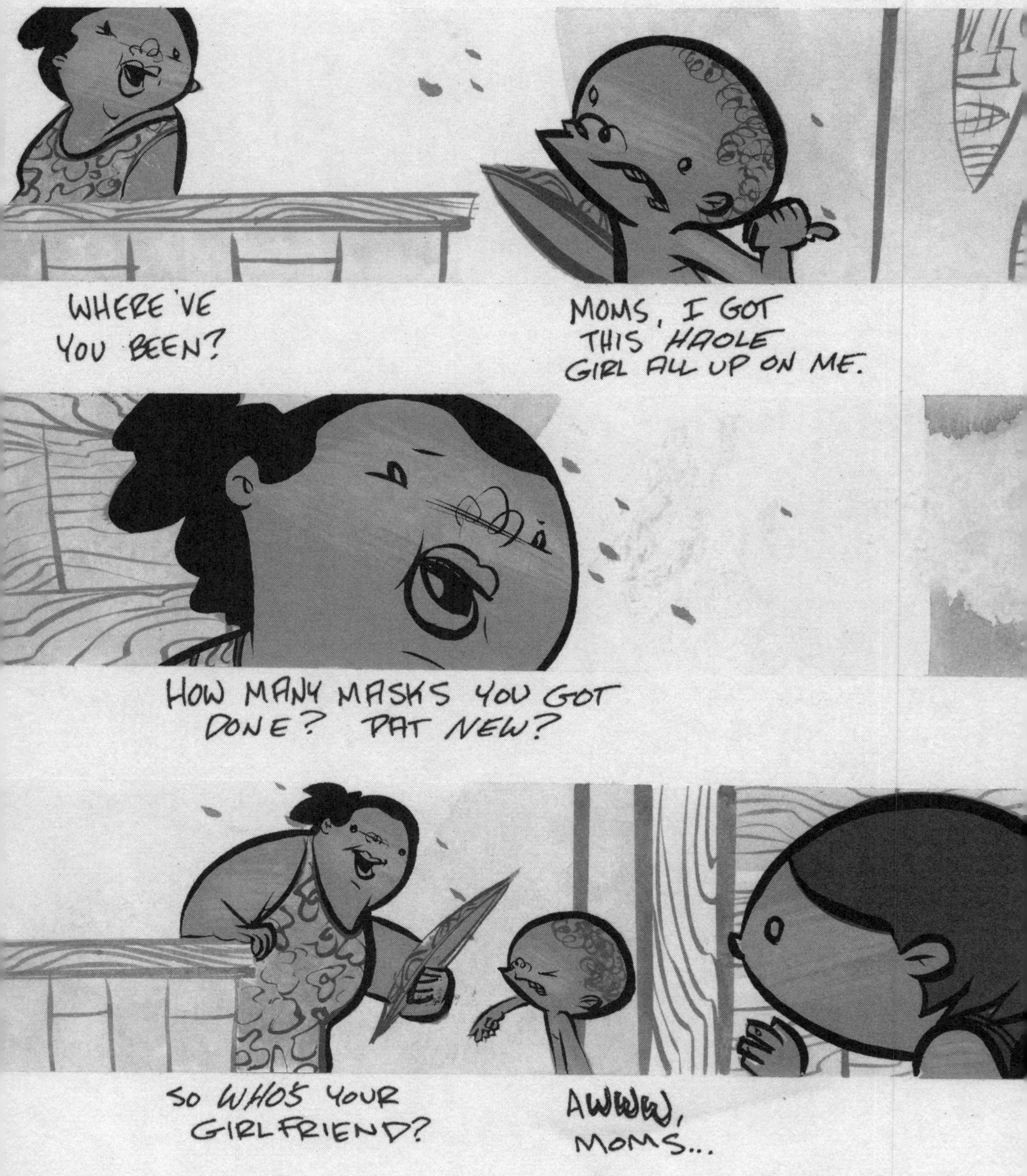
WHERE'VE YOU BEEN?
MOMS, I GOT THIS HAOLE GIRL ALL UP ON ME.
HOW MANY MASKS YOU GOT DONE? DAT NEW?
SO WHO'S YOUR GIRLFRIEND?
AWWW, MOMS...

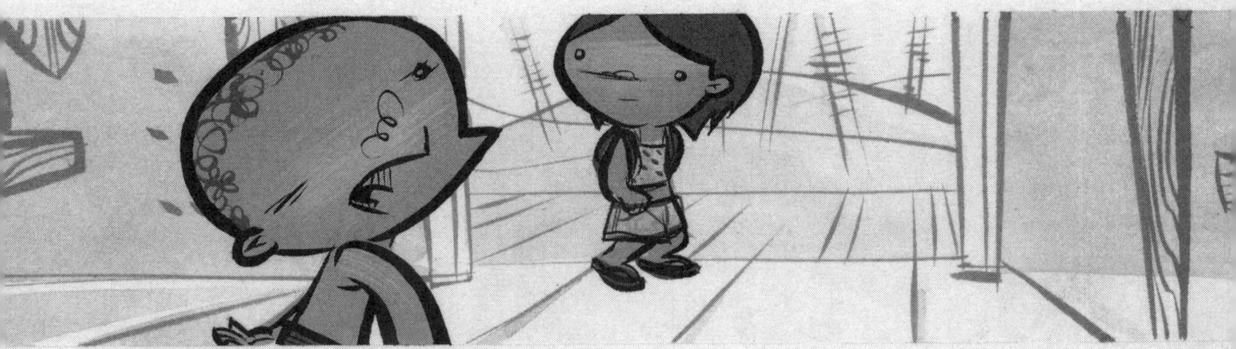

DANG! SHE AIN'T
MY GIRLFRIEND... SHE
SAW TH' *NIGHT MARCHERS.*

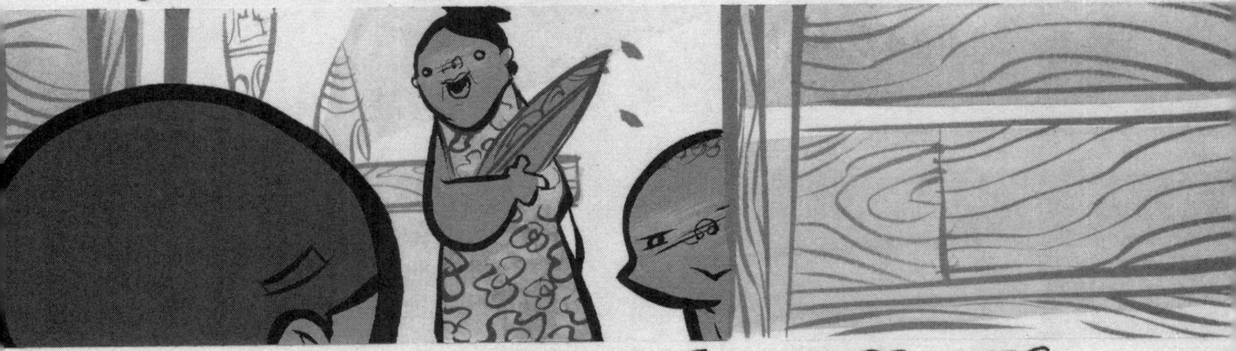

OH, SHE DID, HUH? IN THE *DAYTIME?*
INVITE HER IN. SHE'S CUTE.

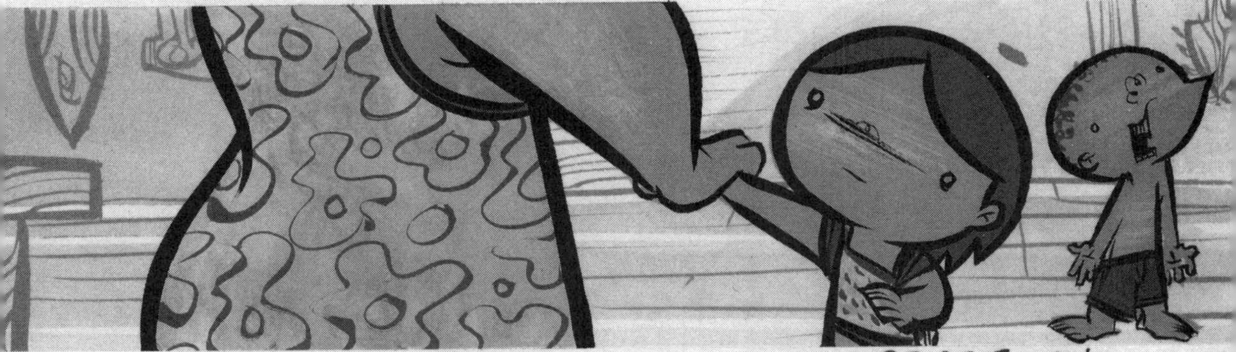

NICE TO MEET YOU. ARE
YOU VISITING THE ISLANDS?

DANG! WHY'S
MY LIFE GOTTA
BE SO *HARD*
FOR?

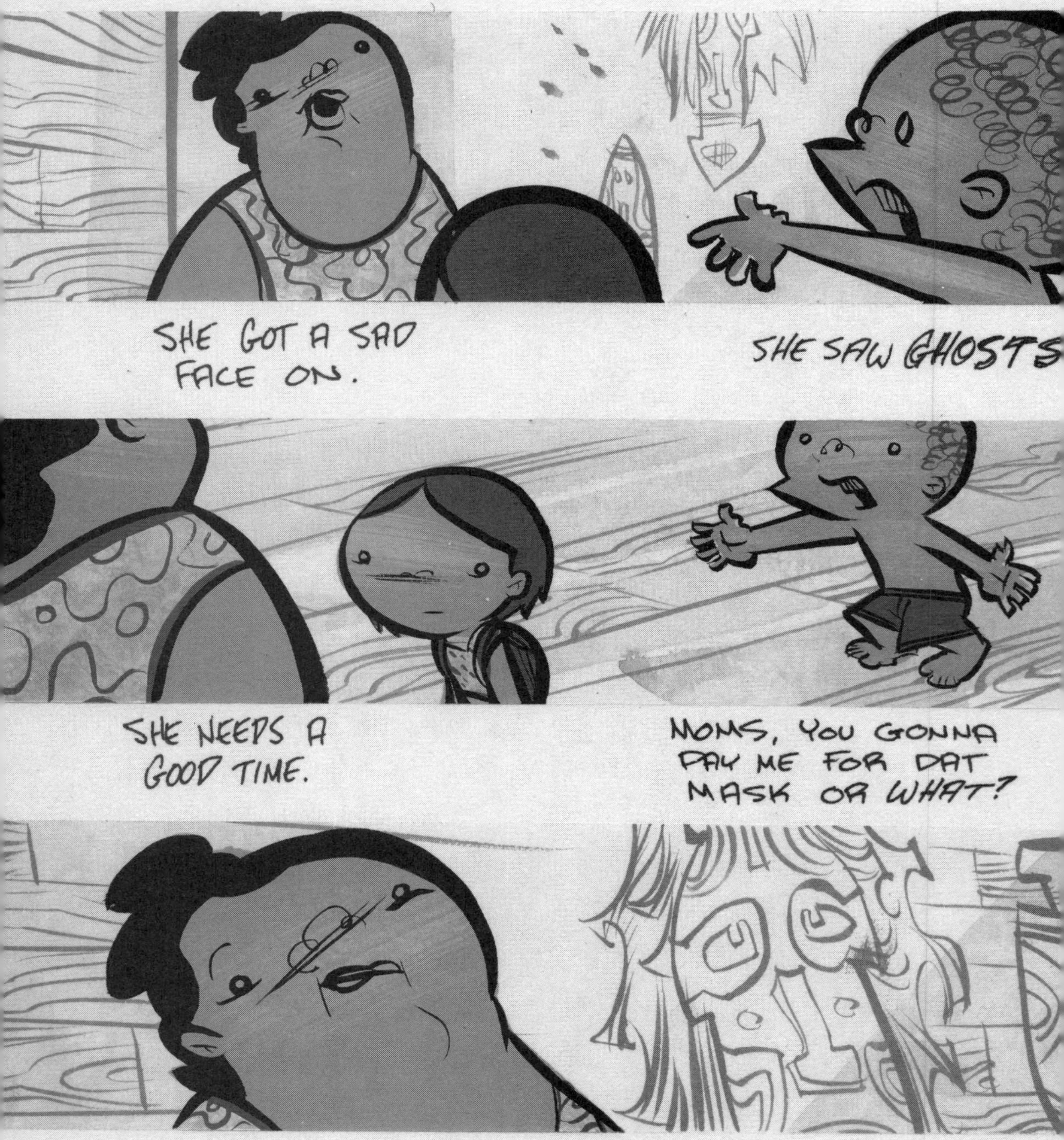
SHE GOT A SAD FACE ON.
SHE SAW GHOSTS
SHE NEEDS A GOOD TIME.
MOMS, YOU GONNA PAY ME FOR DAT MASK OR WHAT?

YOU GOTTA TAKE DAT MASK TO YOUR UNCLE. HE PAY YOU OUTTA HIS DRAWER.

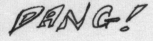

DANG!

'KAY DEN! HERE'S A COUPLA BUCKS ALREADY.

BAM!

SPEN' IT ON DAT
PRETTY GIRL AN'
SHOW HER 'ROUN'.

AN' DON' BE GONE
FROM LONG TIME, YEAH?

WHA?

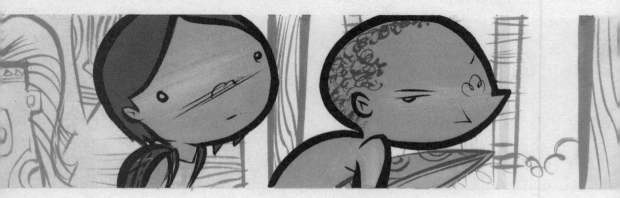

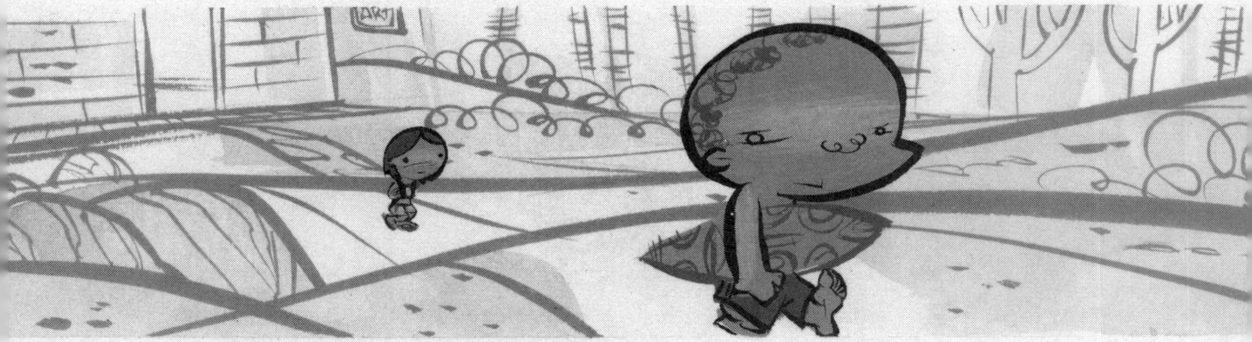

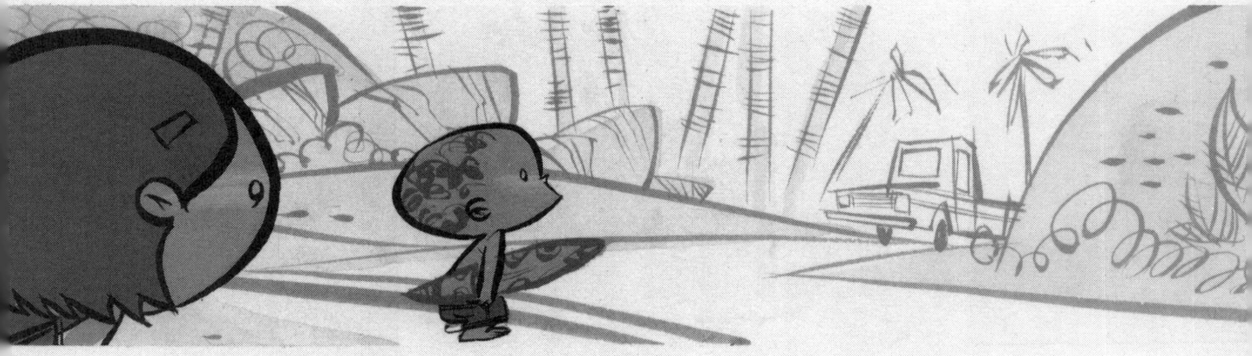

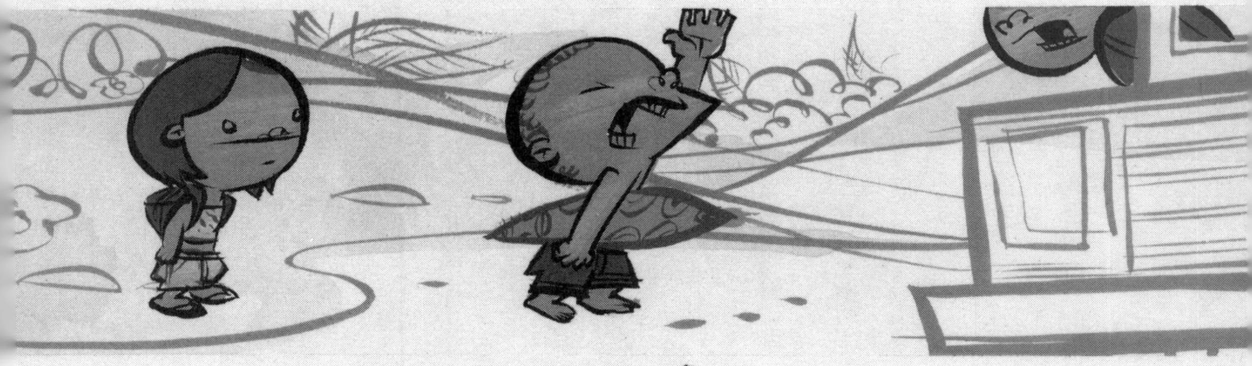

HEY BRAH! HOWZIT?

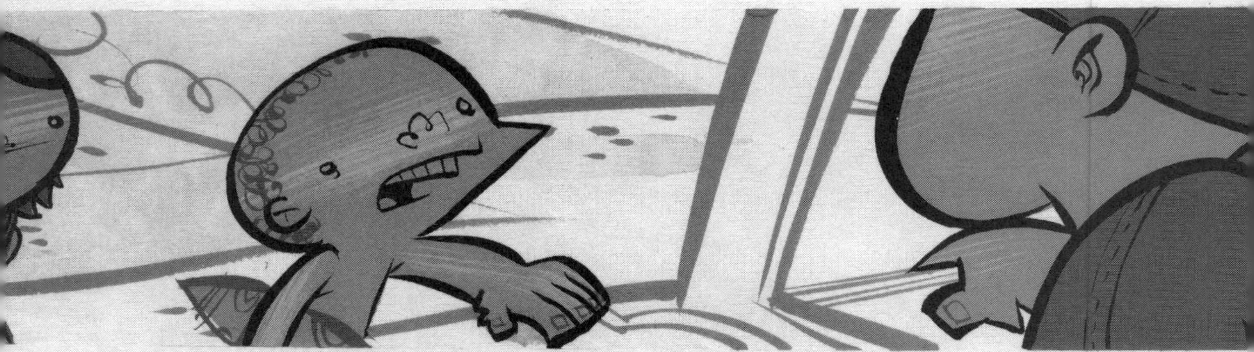
HEY, YOU GO BY MY UNCLE LANI'S? YOU TAKE ME?

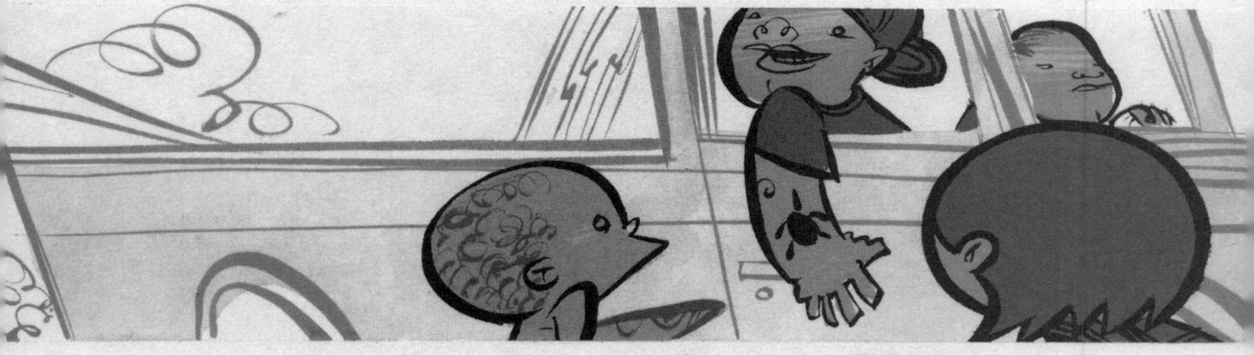
YEAH, WE DROP YOU. HOP IN, YEAH?

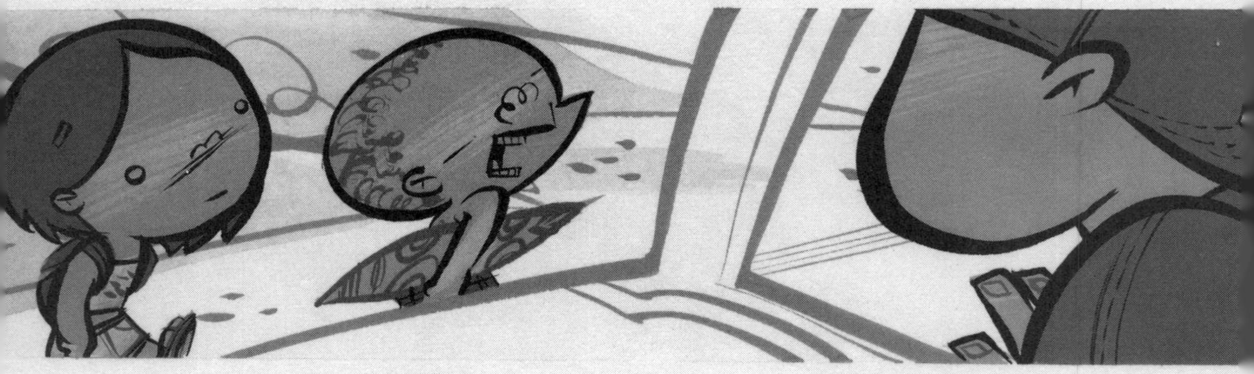
SWEET.
HEY, WHO'S YOUR GIRLIE?

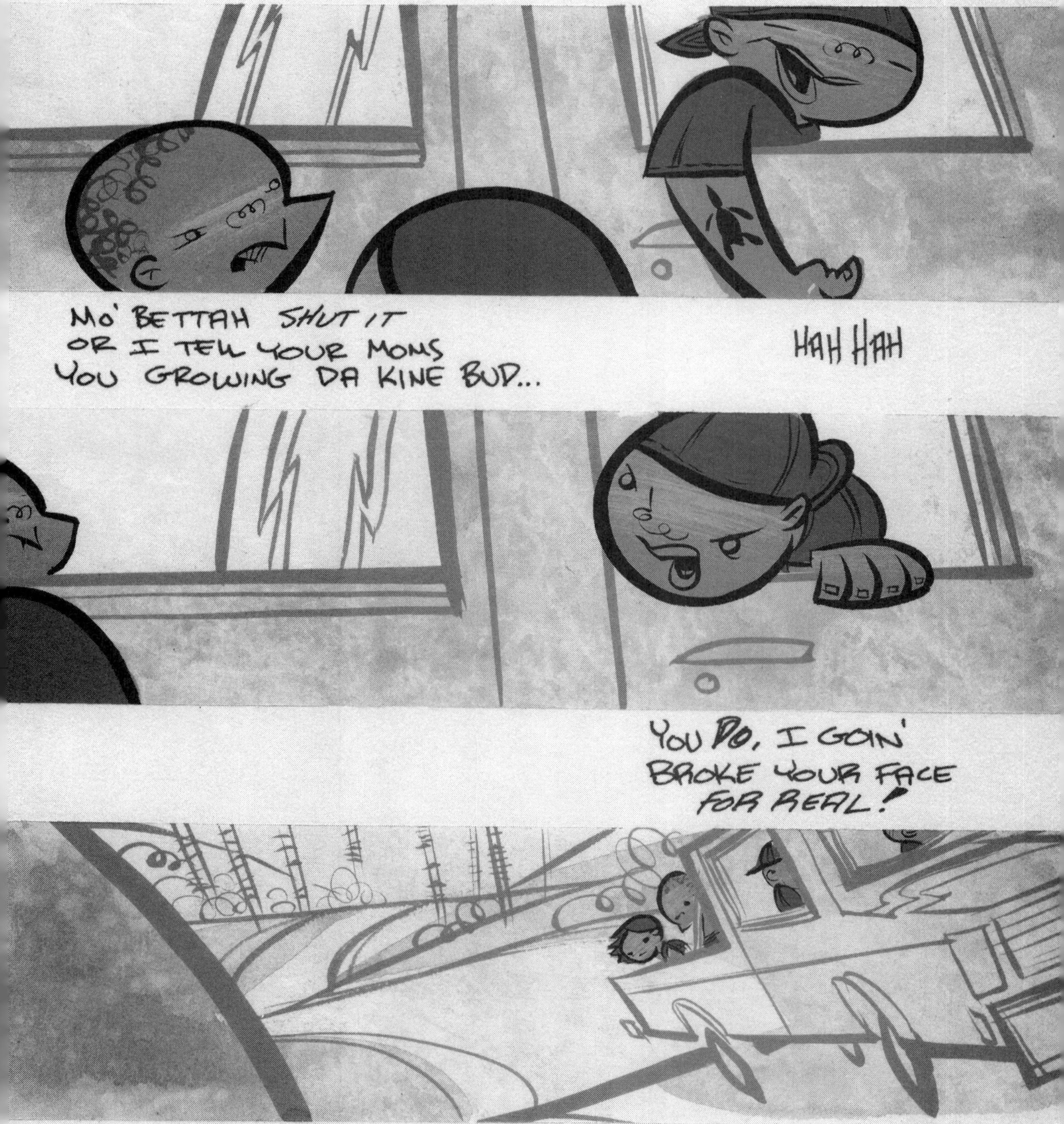
MO' BETTAH SHUT IT OR I TELL YOUR MOMS YOU GROWING DA KINE BUD...
HAH HAH
YOU DO, I GOIN' BROKE YOUR FACE FOR REAL!

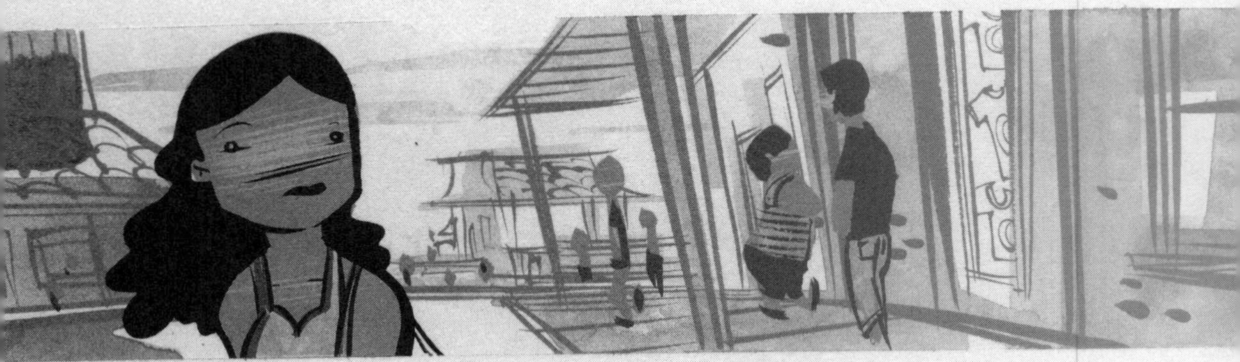

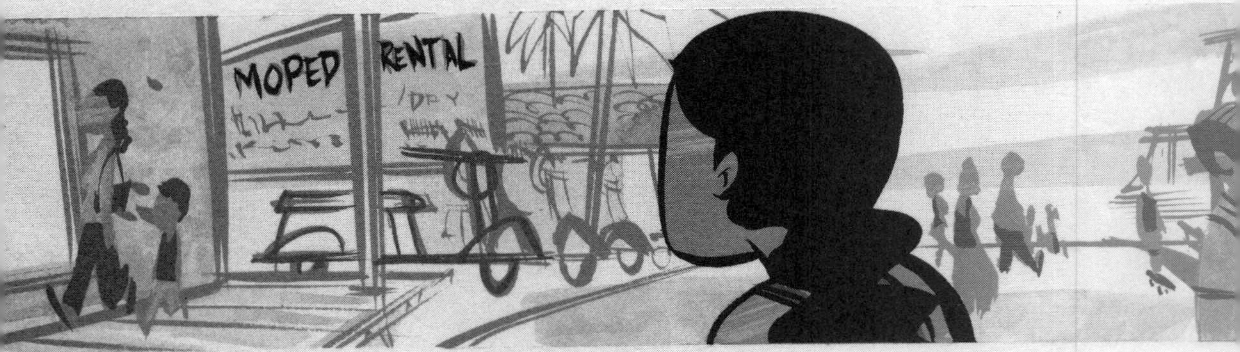
MOPED RENTAL

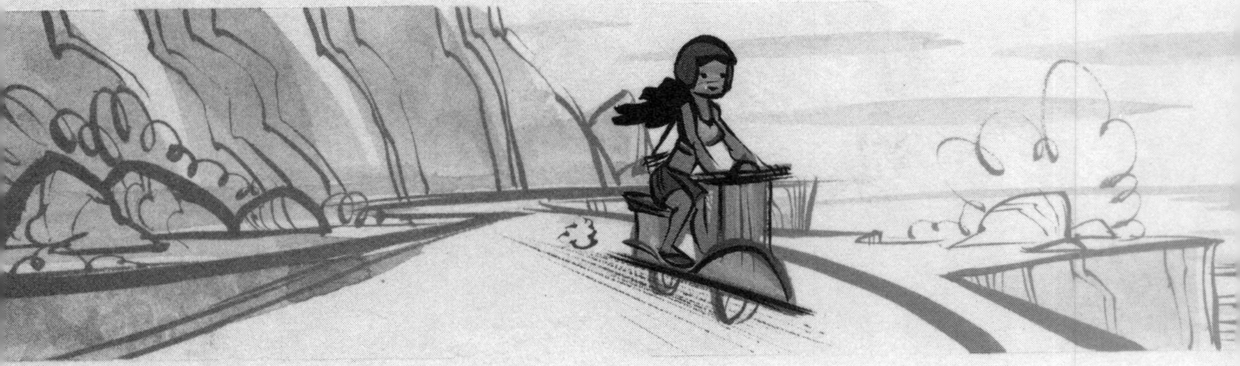

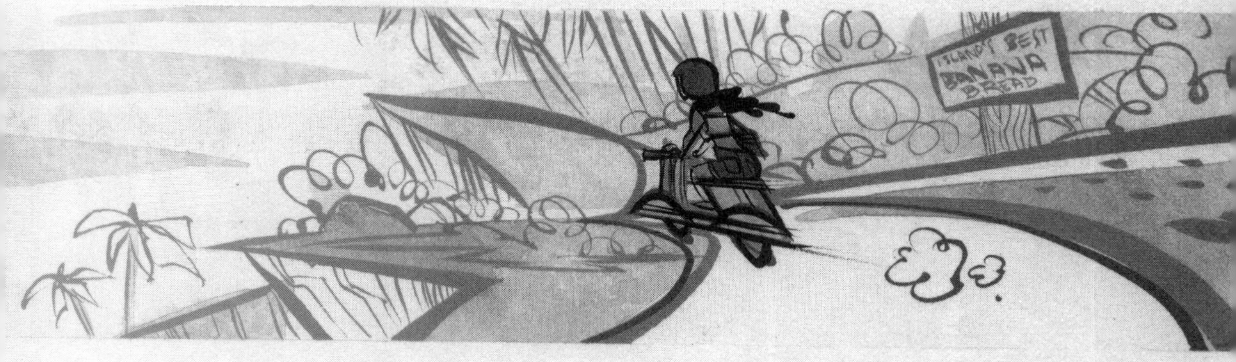
ISLAND'S BEST
BANANA
BREAD

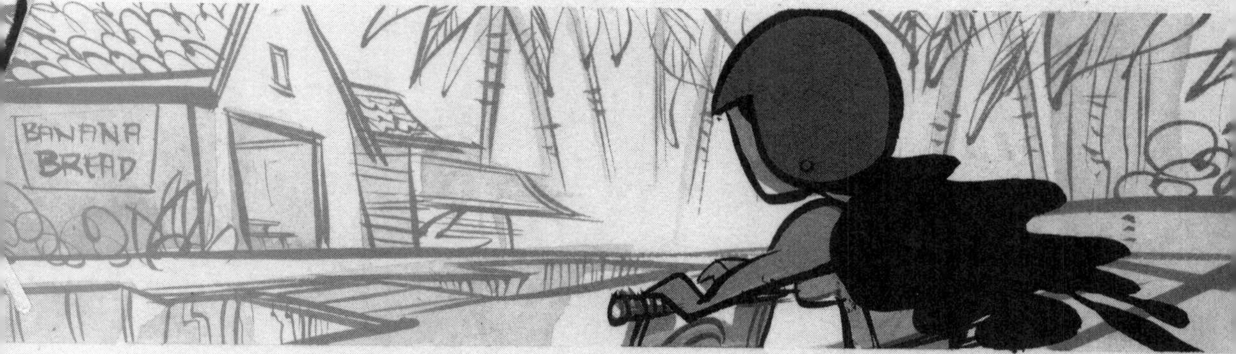
BANANA
BREAD

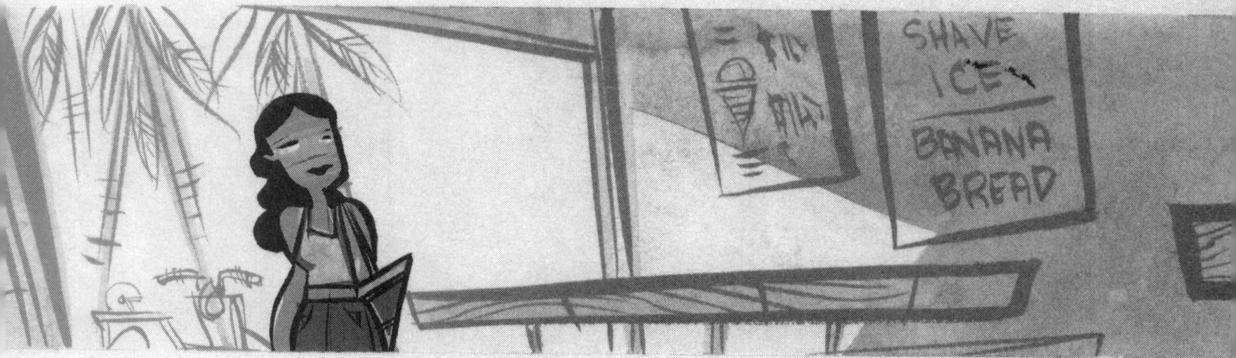
SHAVE
ICE
BANANA
BREAD

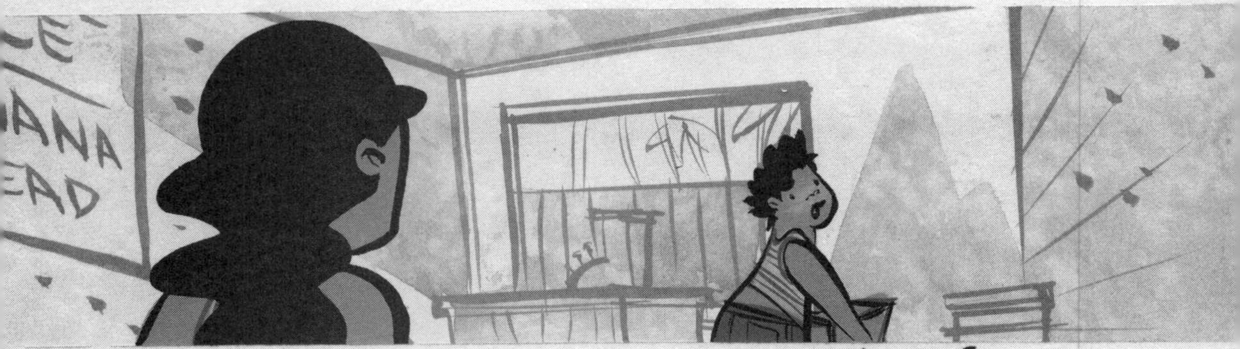

HELLO HELLO!
I GET YOU SAIMIN?

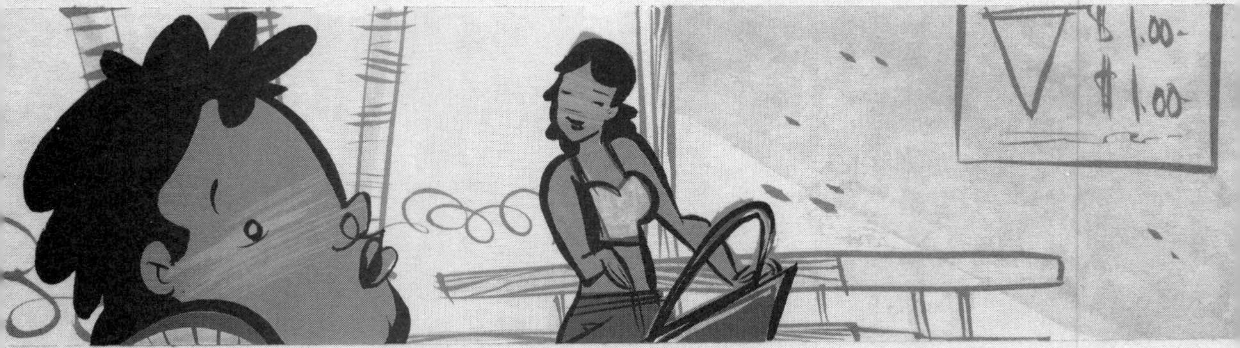
$1.00
$1.00

CAN I GET A
BUBBLEGUM
SHAVE ICE?

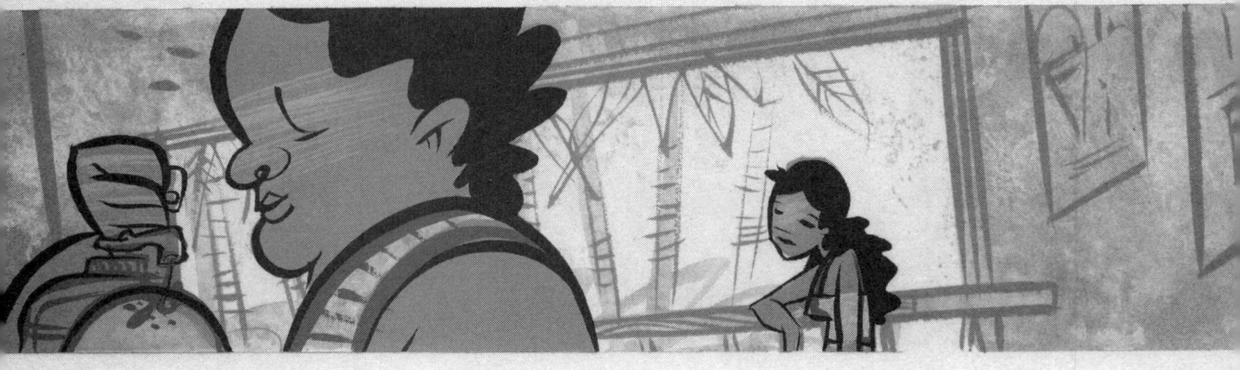

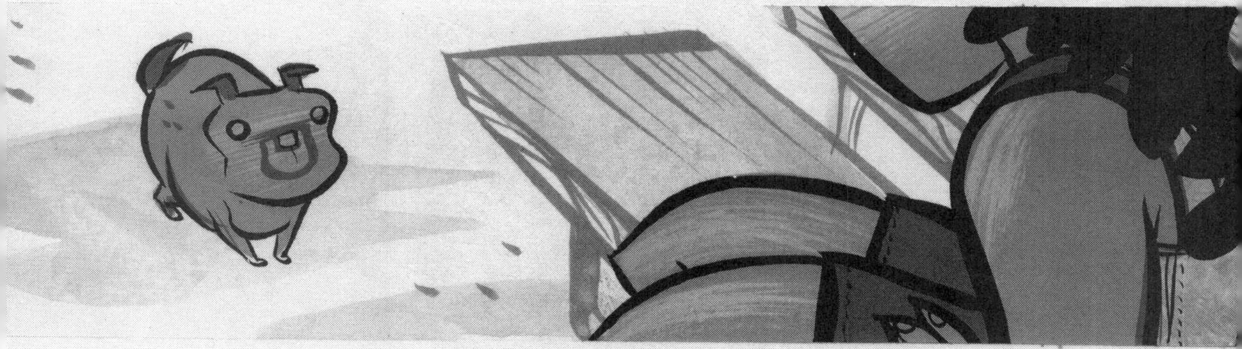

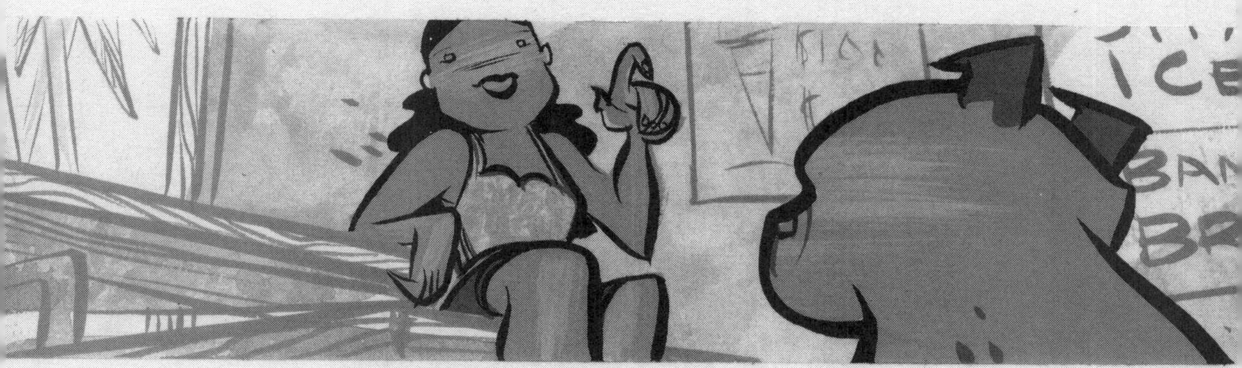

HEY, LIL' GUY.

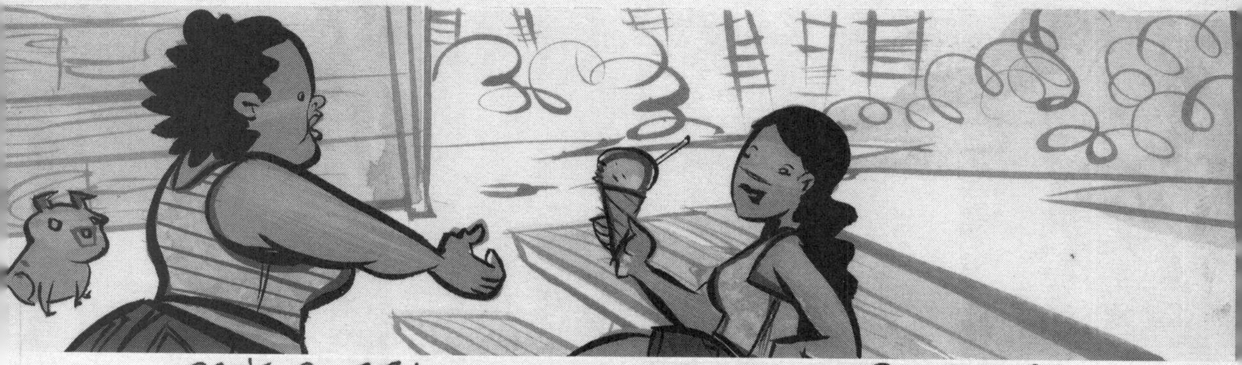

DAT'S A GIRL.
I CALL HER
ILIO MAI.

ILLEO MY? CUTE!
WHAT'S THAT MEAN?

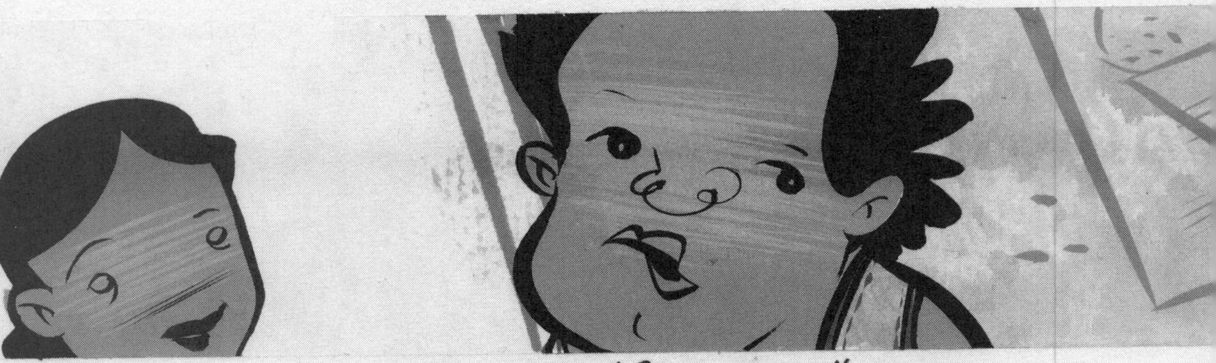

MEANS "COME, DOG." BUT
SHE DON' LIKE COME, EVEN
FOR HER PUPPIES.

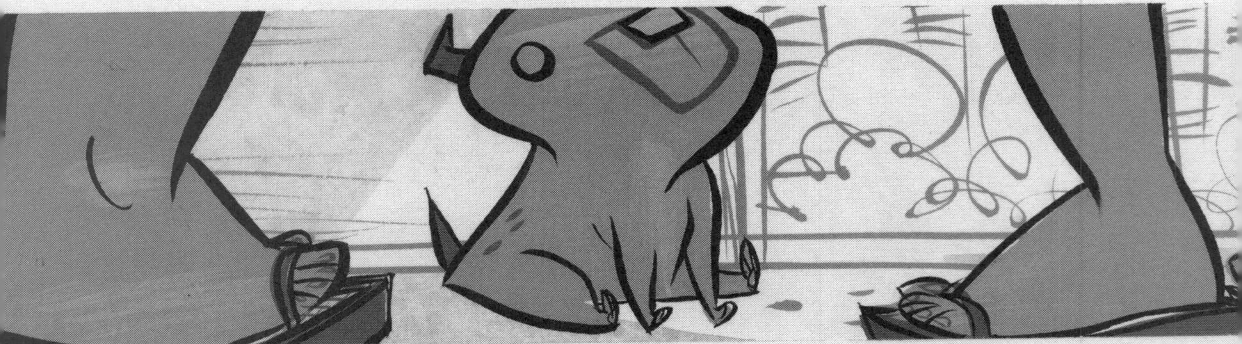

WHAT KIND OF MOMS
LEAVE HER KID, YEAH?
SHE HAD TWO PUPS, BUT SHE ALL SELFISH.

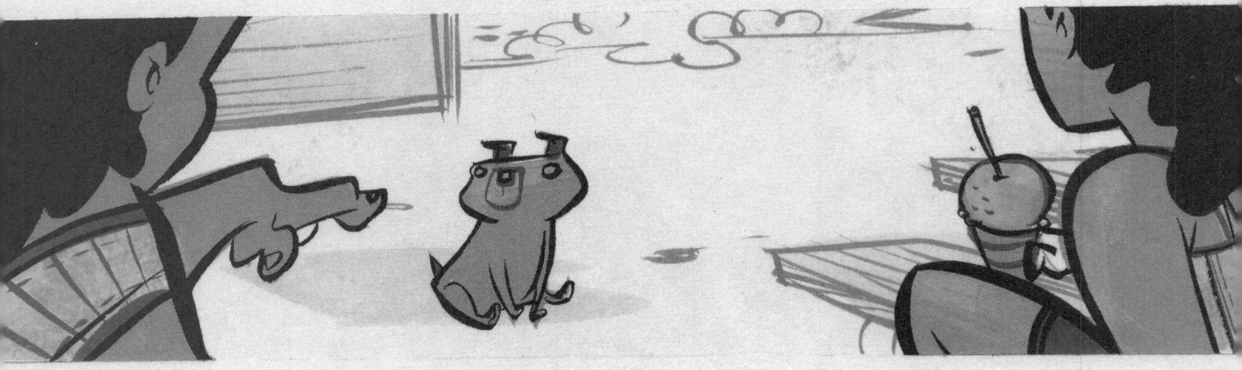

SILLY DOG. NO BEGGING.

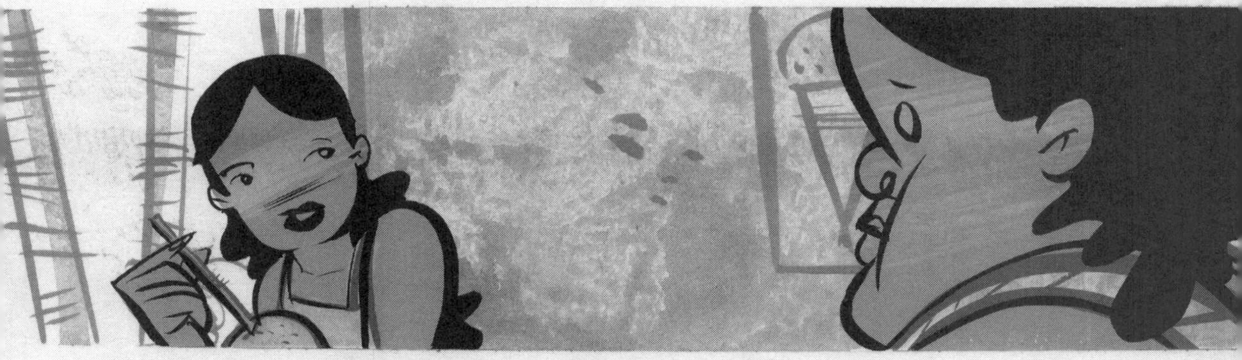

SHE LOOKS SWEET.
WHAT HAPPENED TO
HER PUPS?

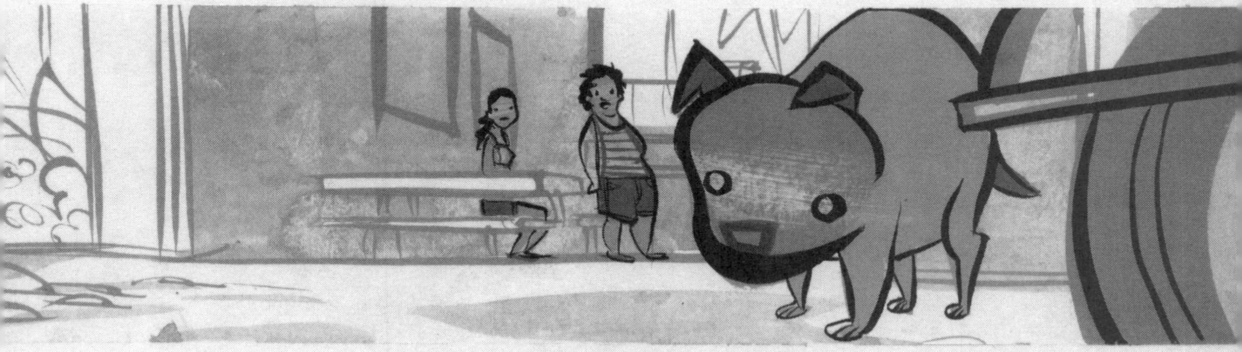

SHE JUST *WATCHED*, AN'
DIS CAR COME *HIT* ONE'A
DEM. IN DA ROAD.

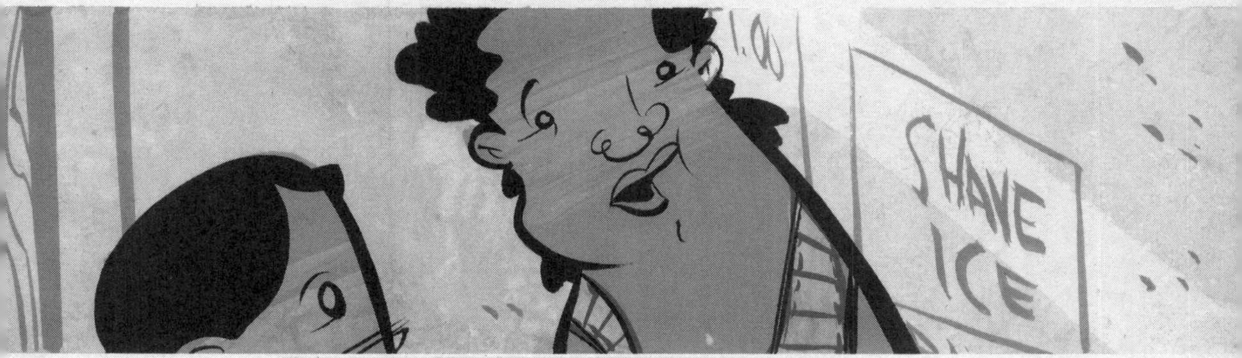
SHAVE ICE

SHE JUST *WATCH*, YEAH?
DON'T TRY TO SAVE IT. SHE SHOULD
MAYBE KNOW SOMETHING *WRONG*, HER
KID IN DA ROAD, YEAH?

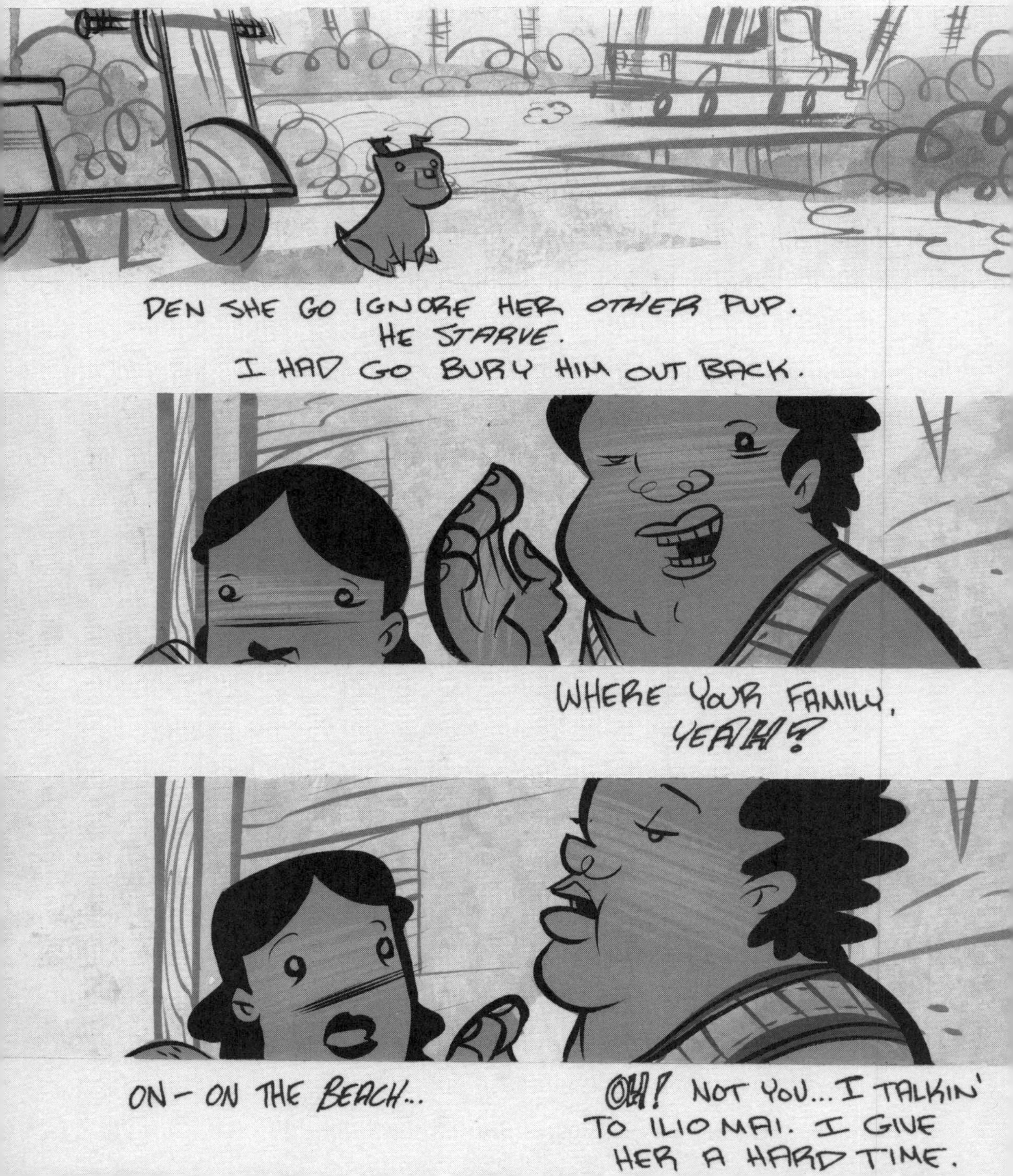
DEN SHE GO IGNORE HER OTHER PUP.
HE STARVE.
I HAD GO BURY HIM OUT BACK.
WHERE YOUR FAMILY, YEAH?
ON- ON THE BEACH...
OH! NOT YOU... I TALKIN' TO ILIOMAI. I GIVE HER A HARD TIME.

ICE SHAVE
IS TWO BUCKS,
YEAH?

OH! RIGHT...

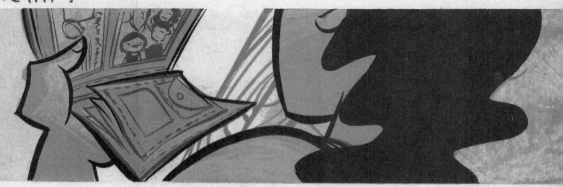

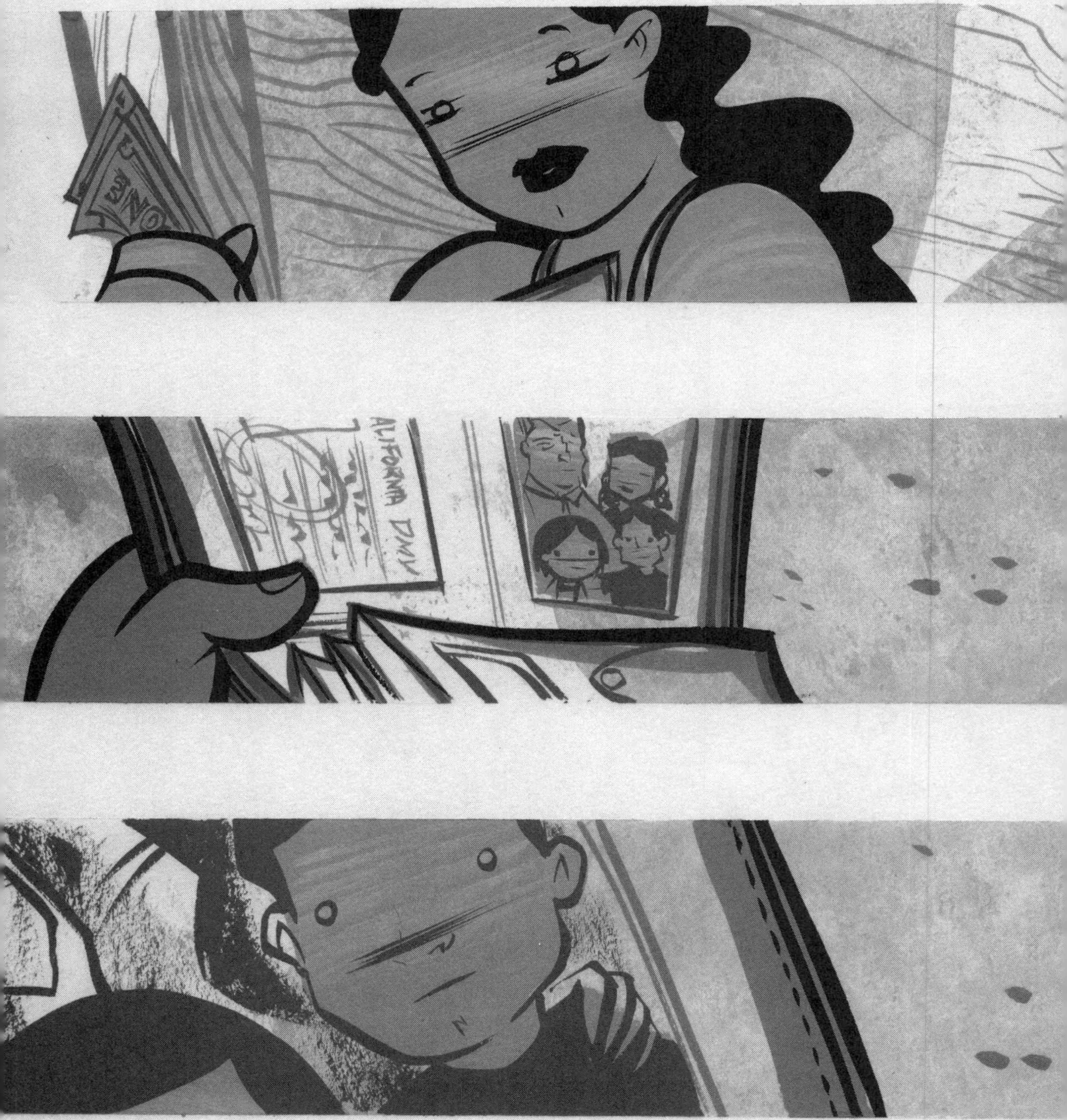
ALIFORNIA DMV

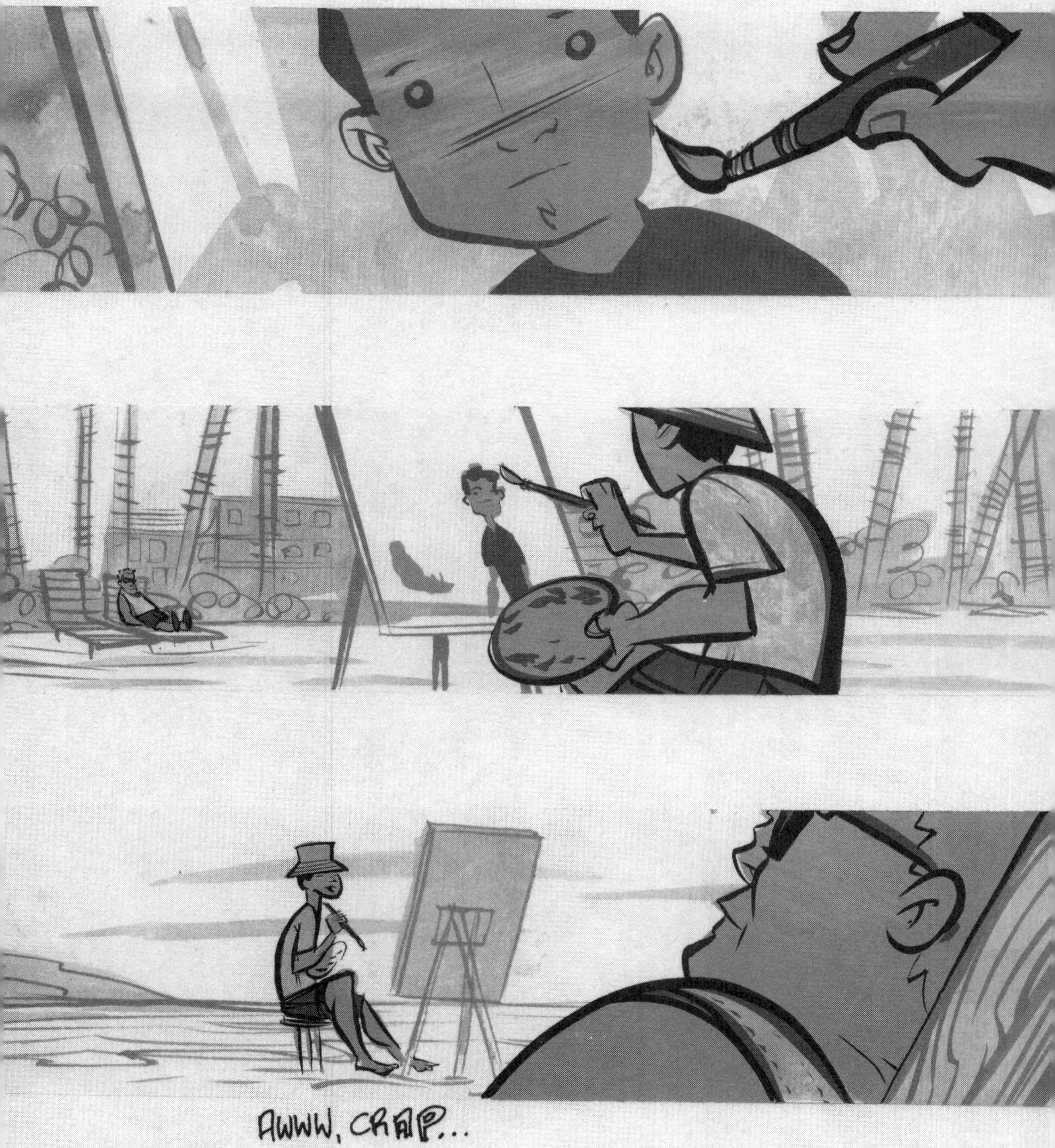
AWWW, CRAP...

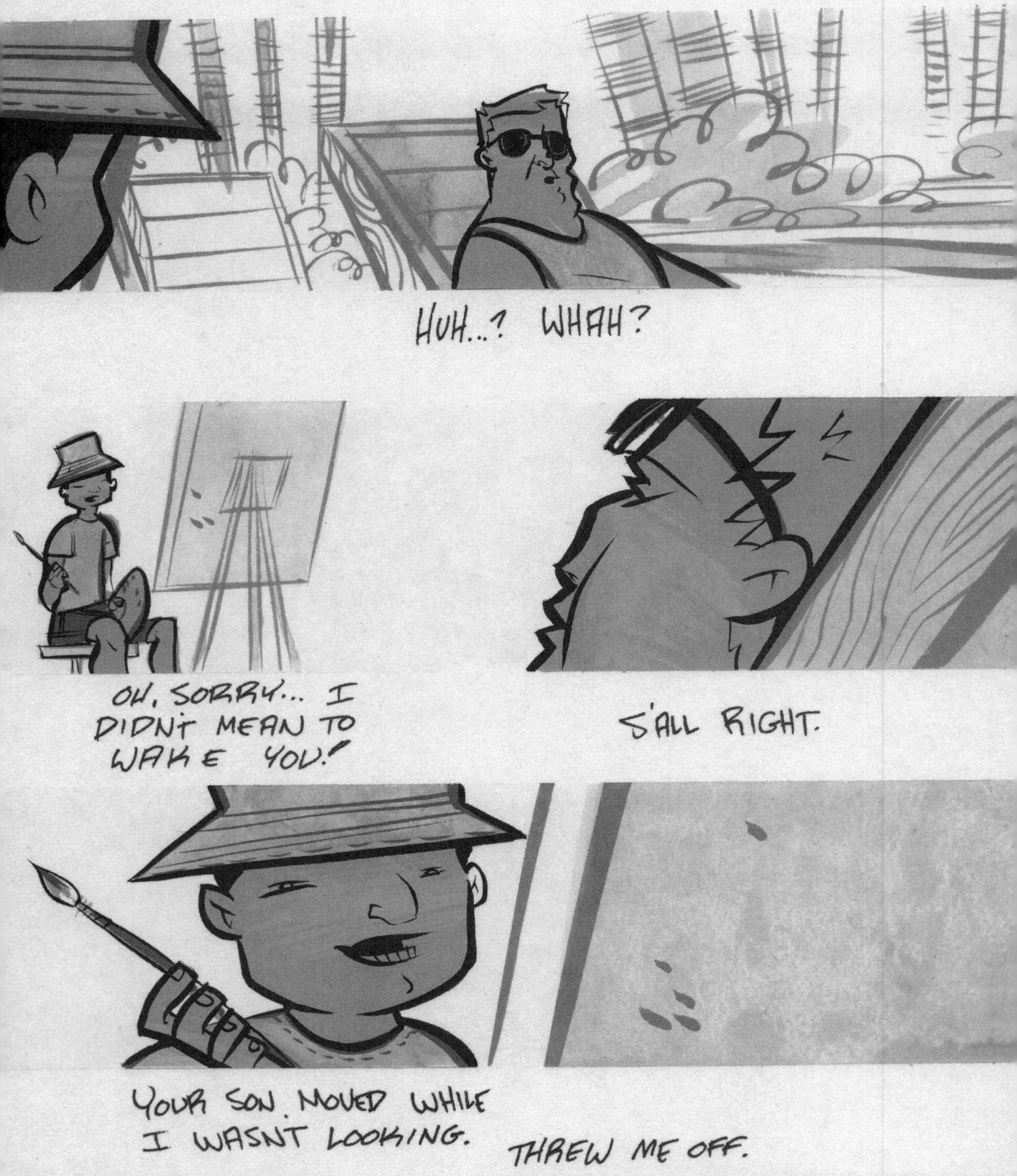
HUH...? WHAH?
OH, SORRY... I DIDN'T MEAN TO WAKE YOU!
S'ALL RIGHT.
YOUR SON MOVED WHILE I WASN'T LOOKING.
THREW ME OFF.

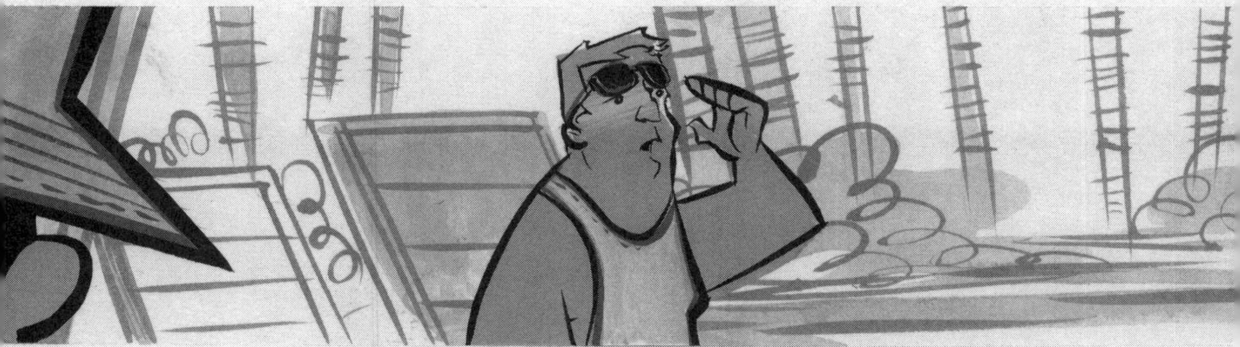

THE SUN?

YEAH, I GUESS IT DID MOVE.

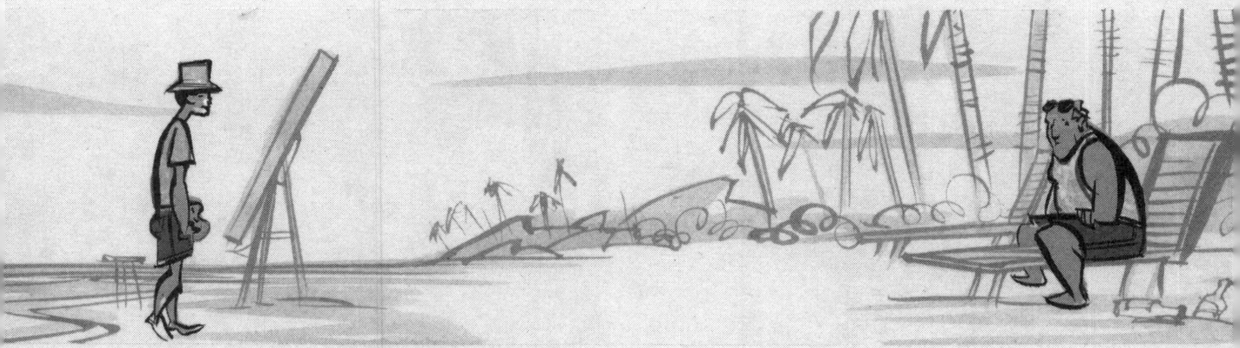

NO, NO... YOUR BOY.

I WAS PAINTING THE BOTH OF YOU.

HOW'S THAT?

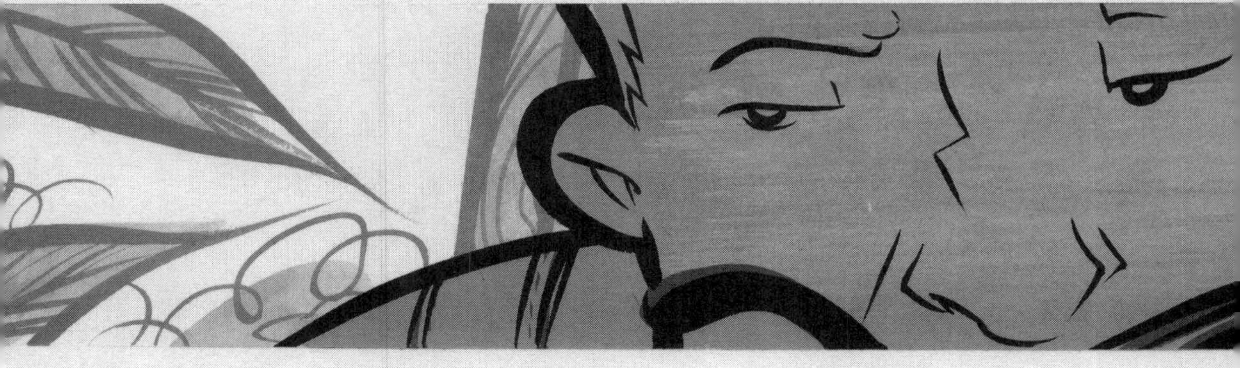

I SAID, YOUR BOY, HE–

I HEARD YOU.

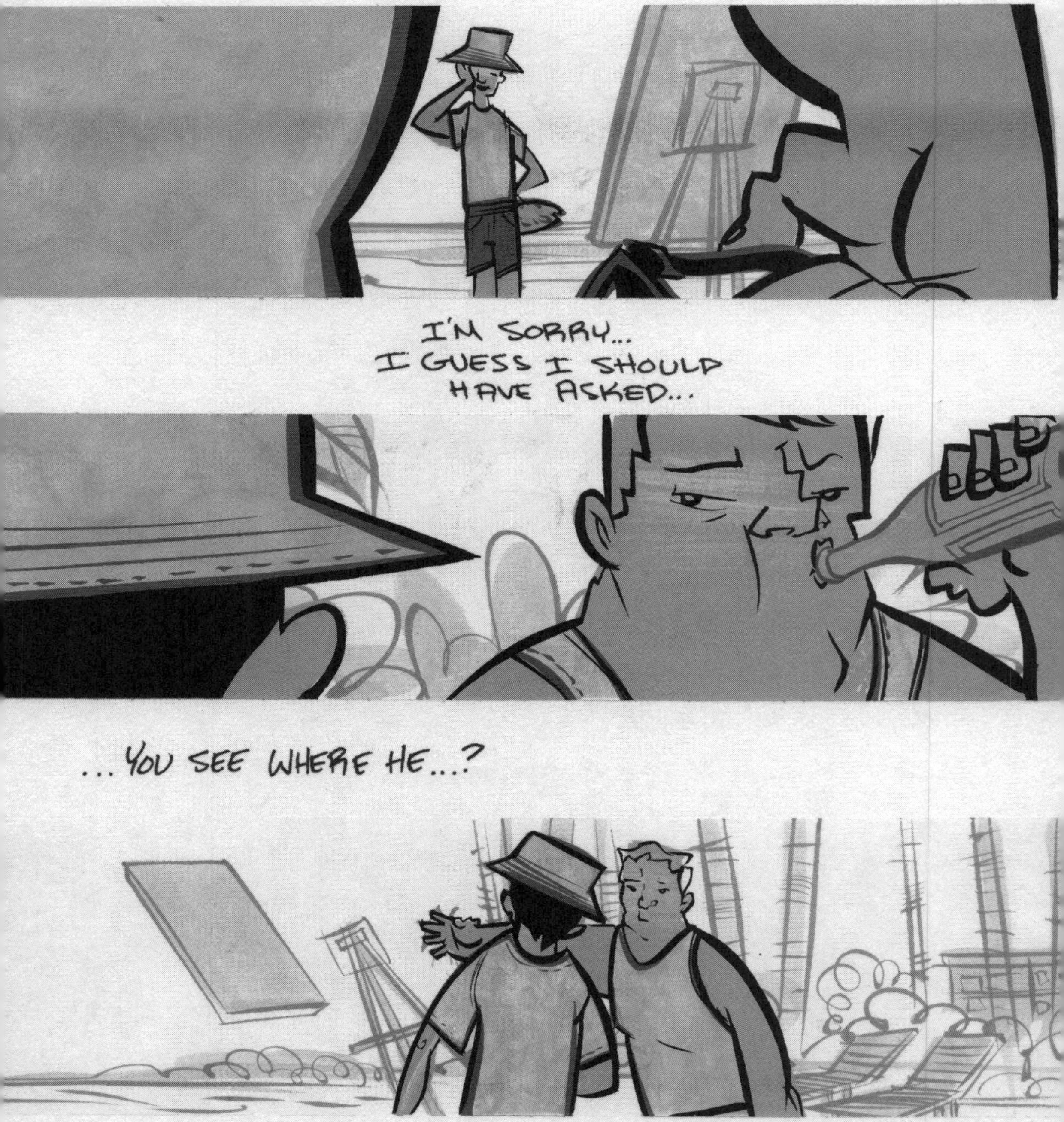
I'M SORRY... I GUESS I SHOULD HAVE ASKED...
...YOU SEE WHERE HE...?

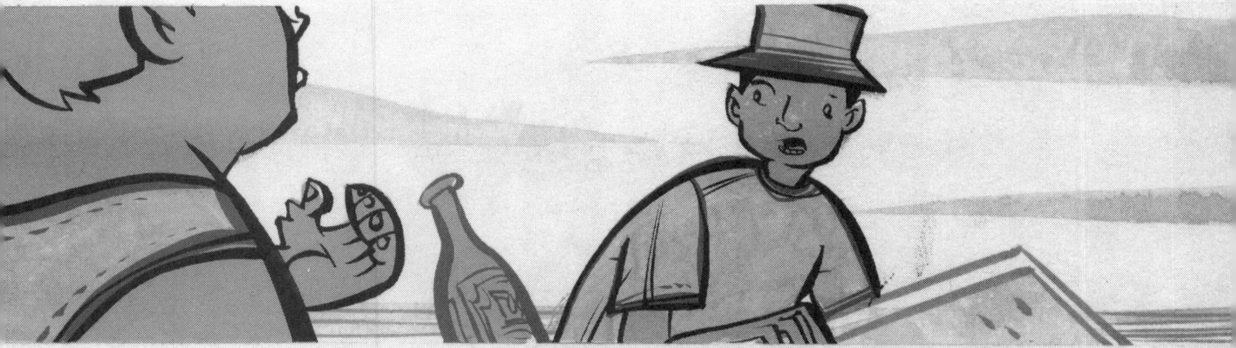
HEY, MAN... WHAT TH' HELL?
YOU DONT GOTTA BE AN ASS ABOUT IT...

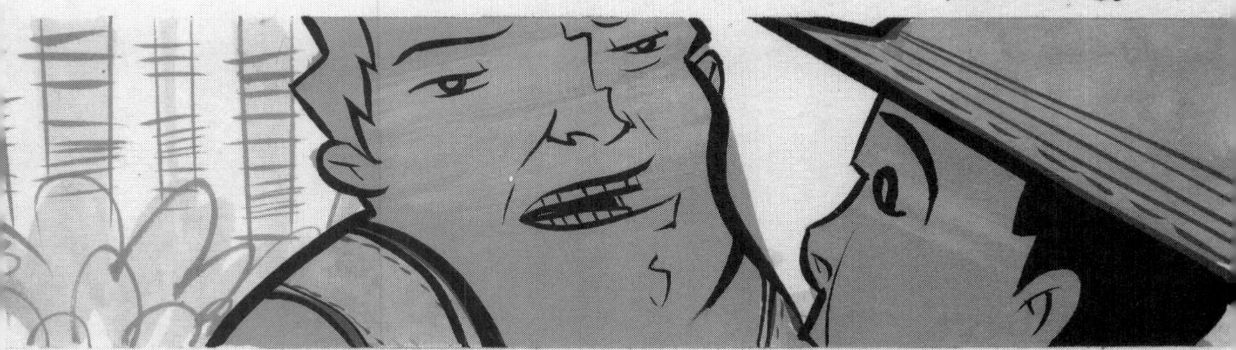
MY SON AINT AROUND NO MORE.

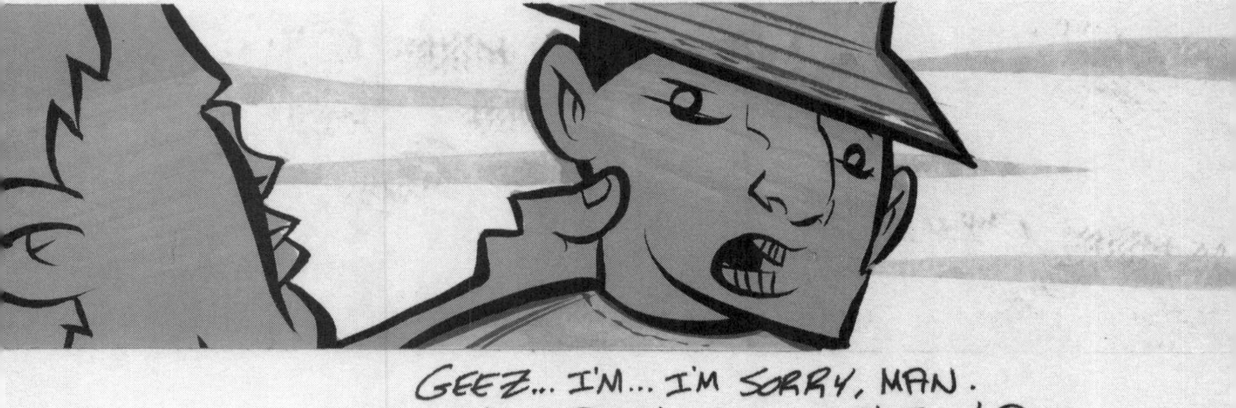
GEEZ... I'M... I'M SORRY, MAN.
MUST'VE BEEN SOME OTHER KID...
...LOOKED JUST LIKE YOU, MAN...

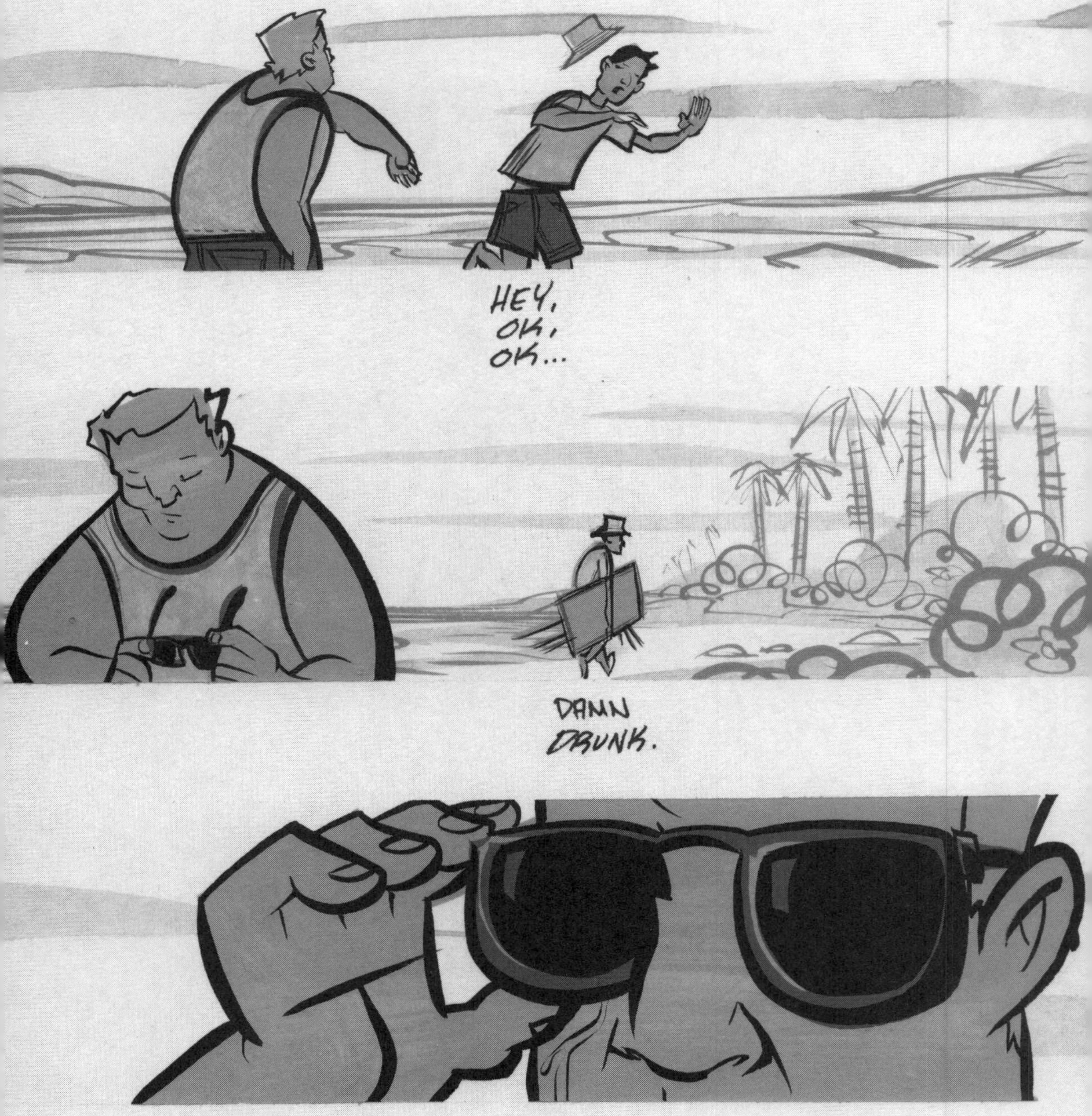
HEY, OK, OK...
DAMN DRUNK.

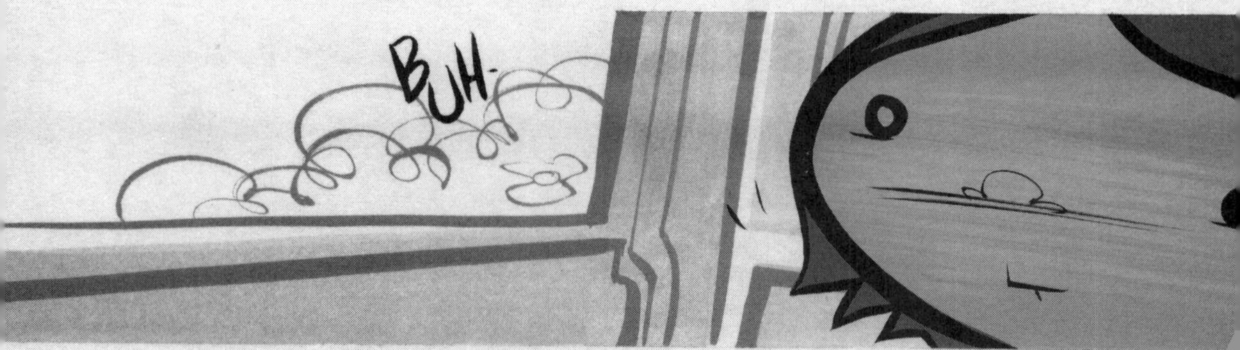
BUH-

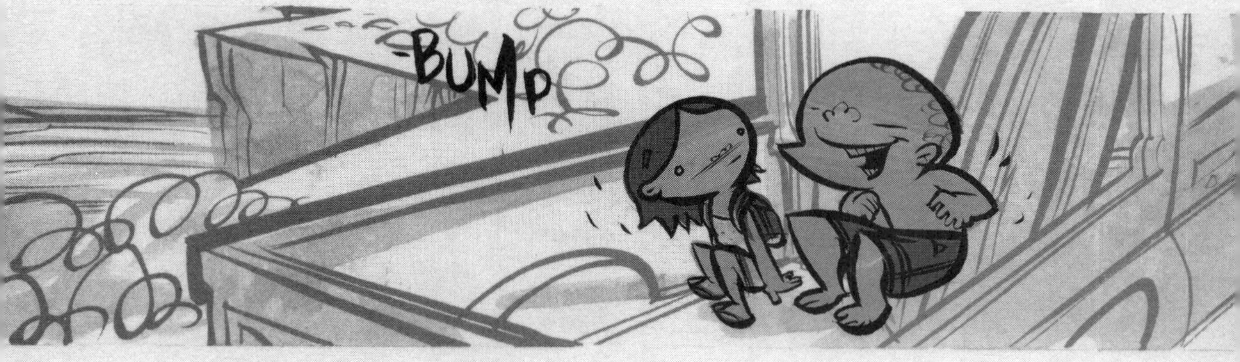
-BUMP

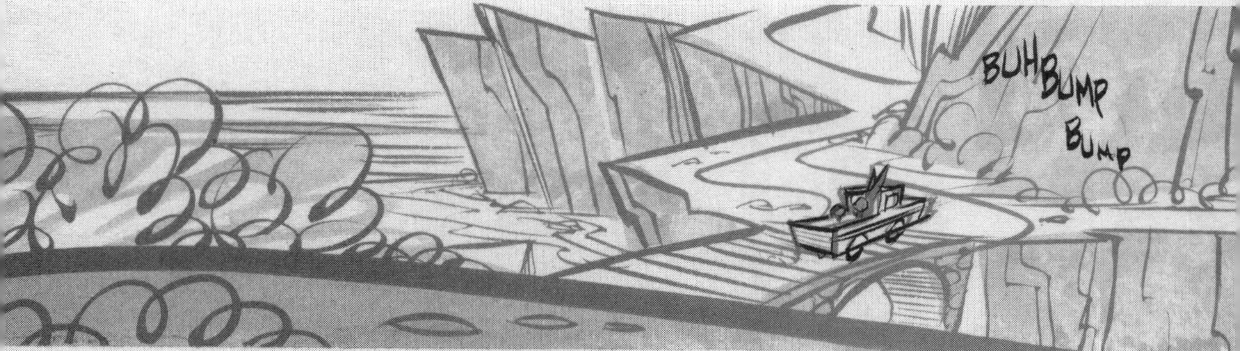
BUHBUMP
BUMP

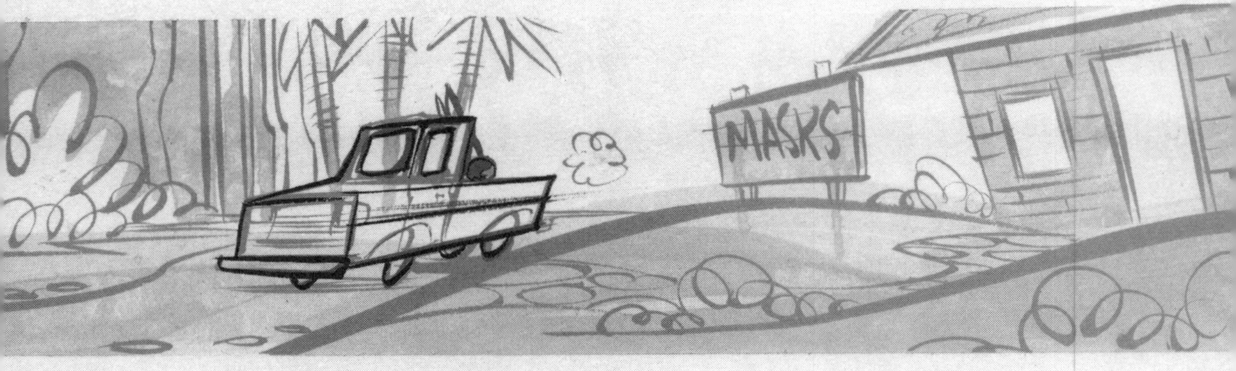
MASKS

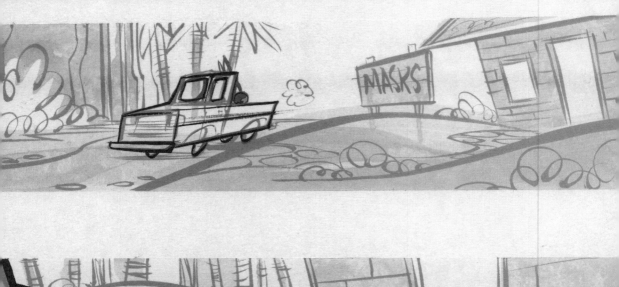

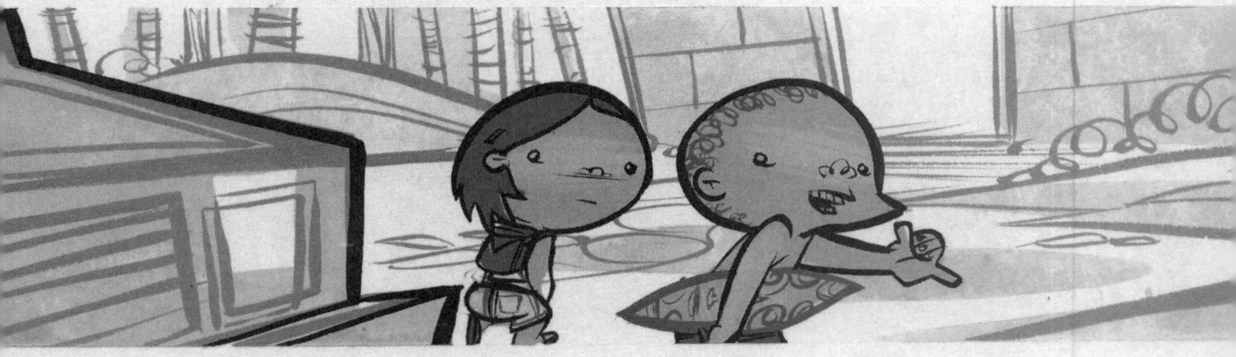
T'ANKS, EH?

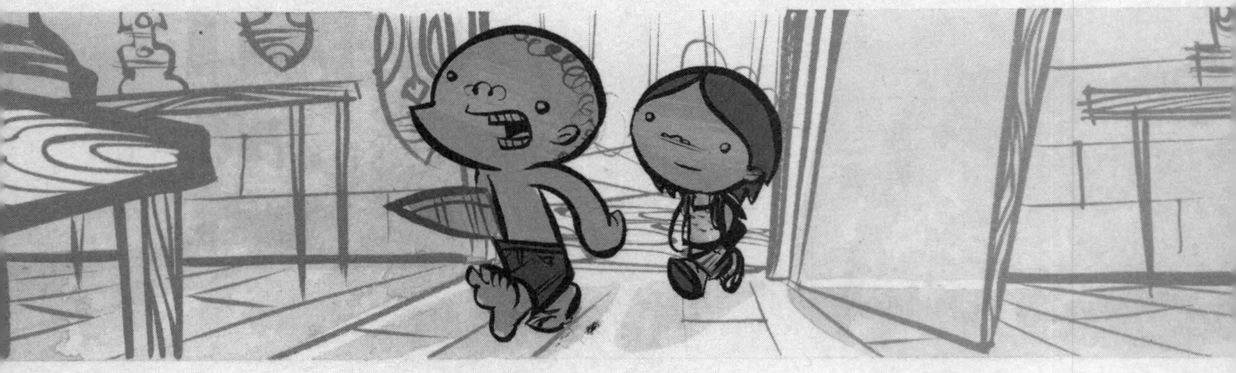
'SUP,
UNCLE LANI?

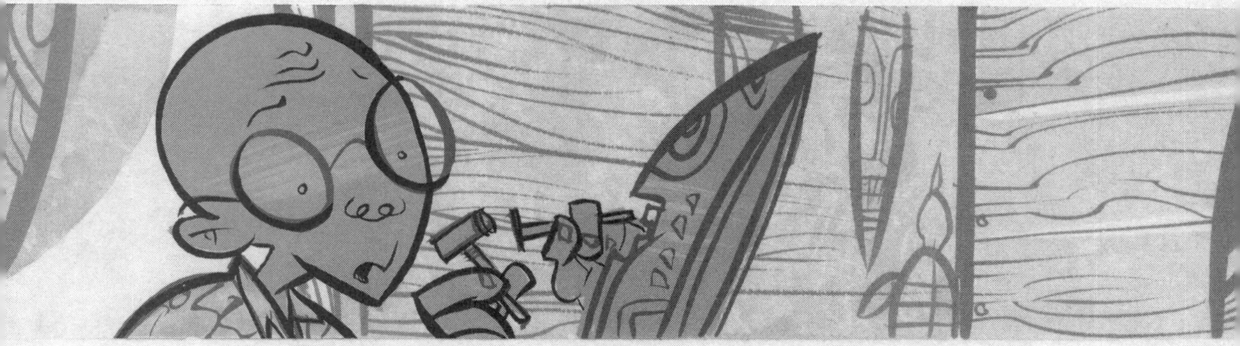

WHA?
OH OH...

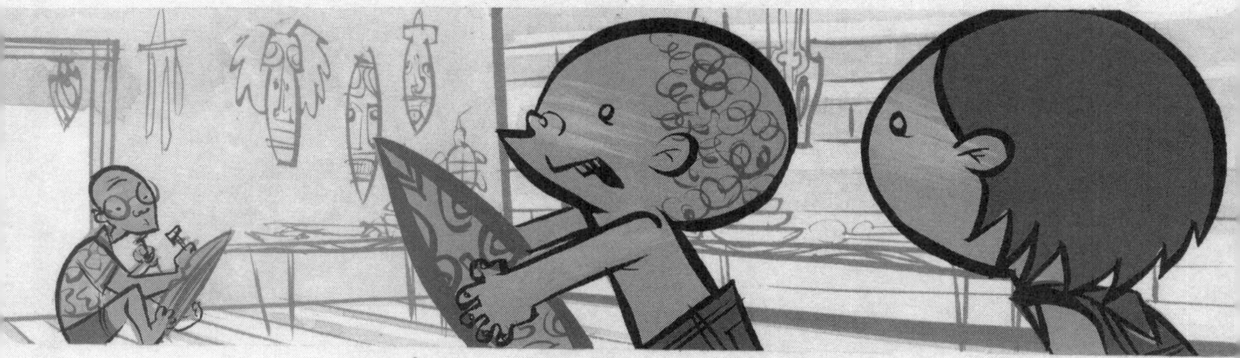

HEY, I MAKE ONE NEW
ONE GO SELL. MOMS
SAID YOU GIMME MONEY, YEAH?

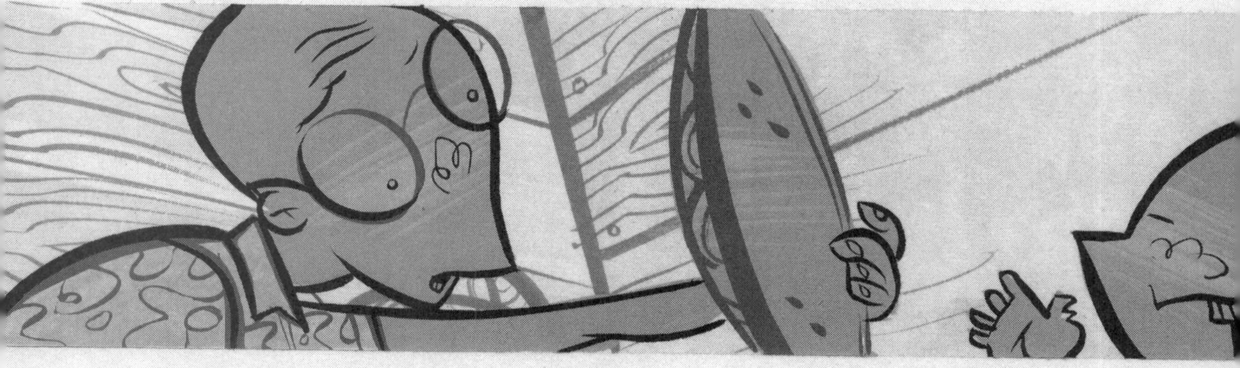

WHA? HUH.

SOME GOOD, YEAH?

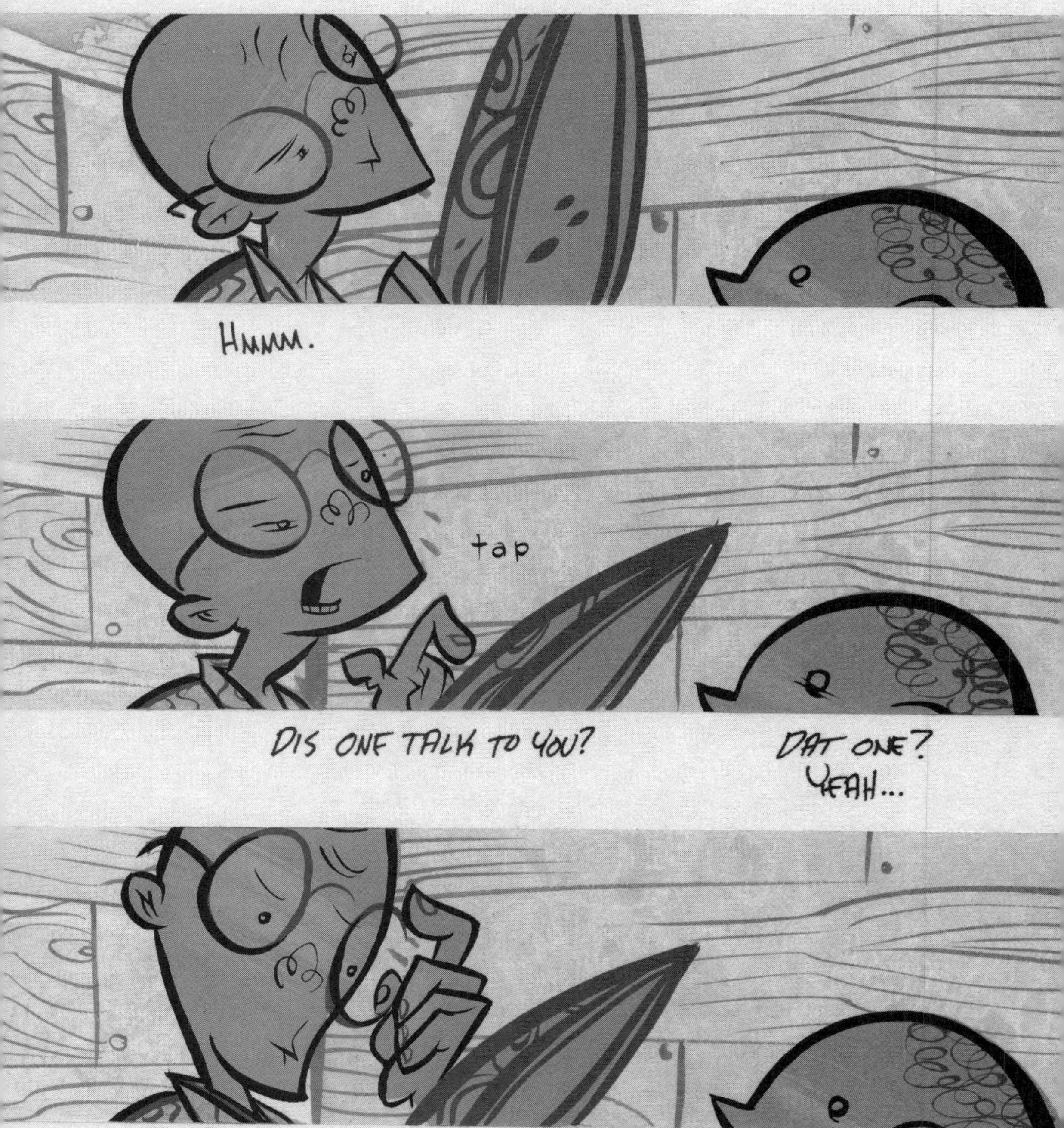
HMMM.
tap
DIS ONE TALK TO YOU?
DAT ONE? YEAH...

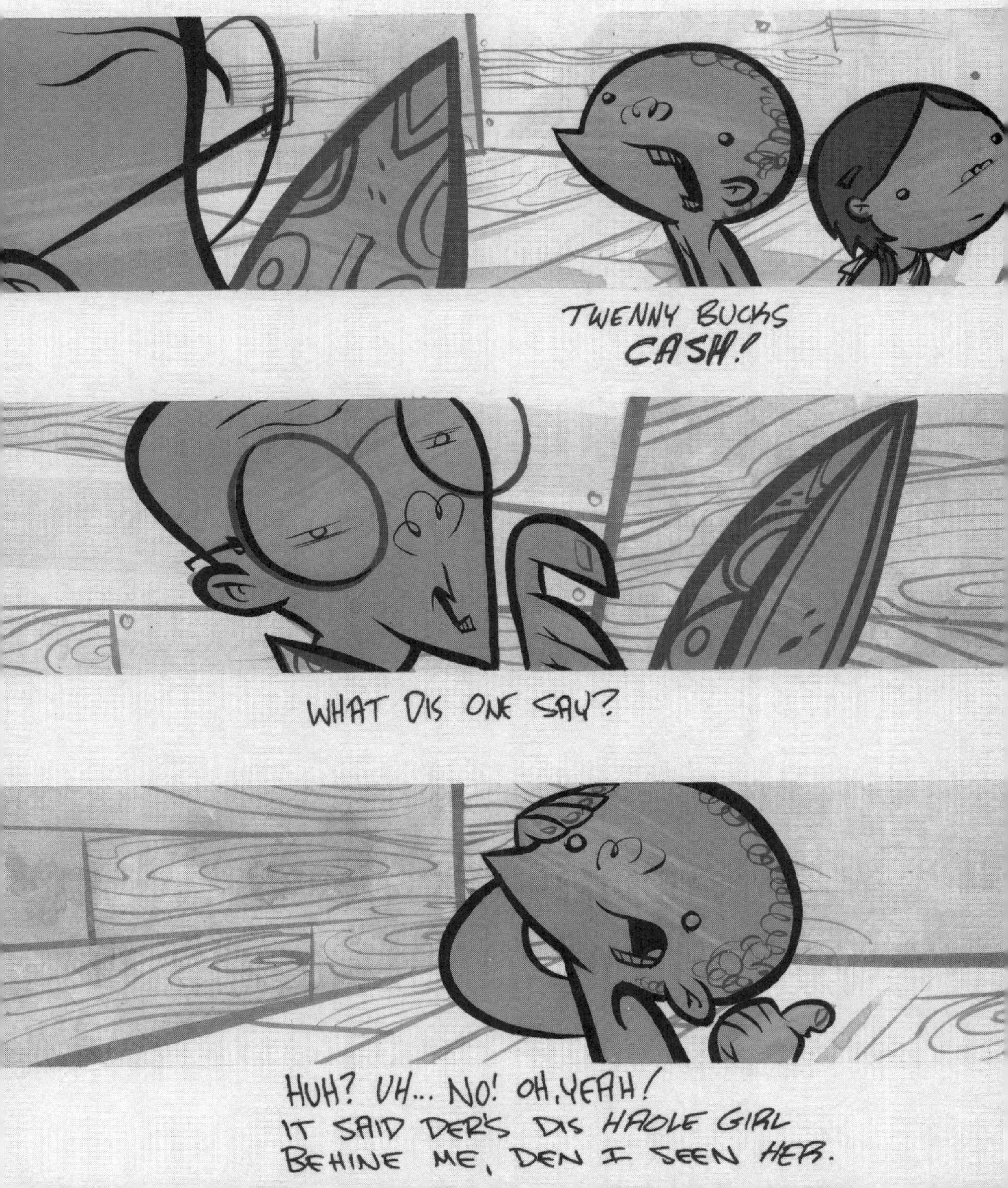
TWENNY BUCKS CASH!
WHAT DIS ONE SAY?
HUH? UH... NO! OH, YEAH! IT SAID DER'S DIS HAOLE GIRL BEHINE ME, DEN I SEEN HER.

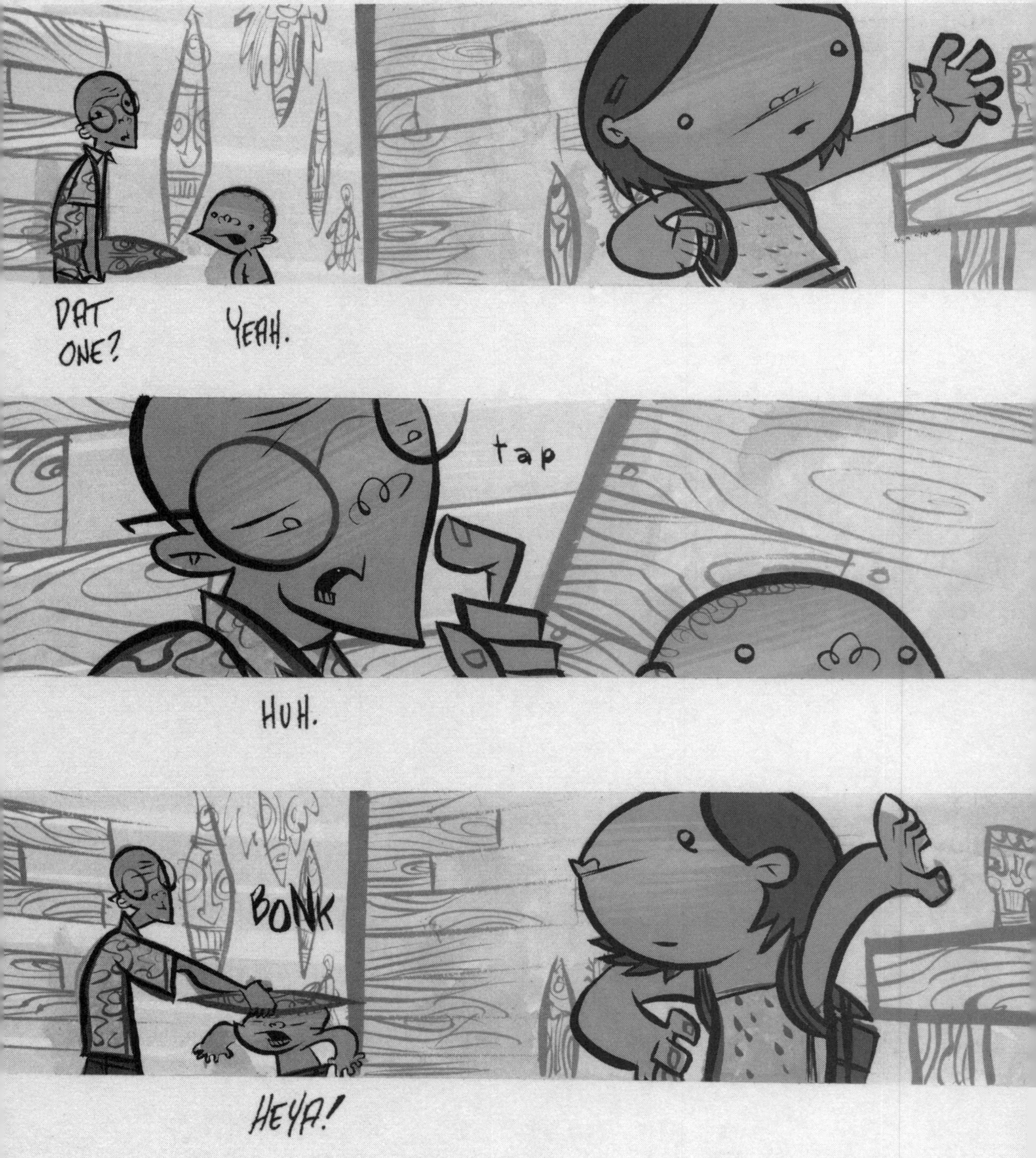
DAT ONE?
YEAH.
tap
HUH.
BONK
HEYA!

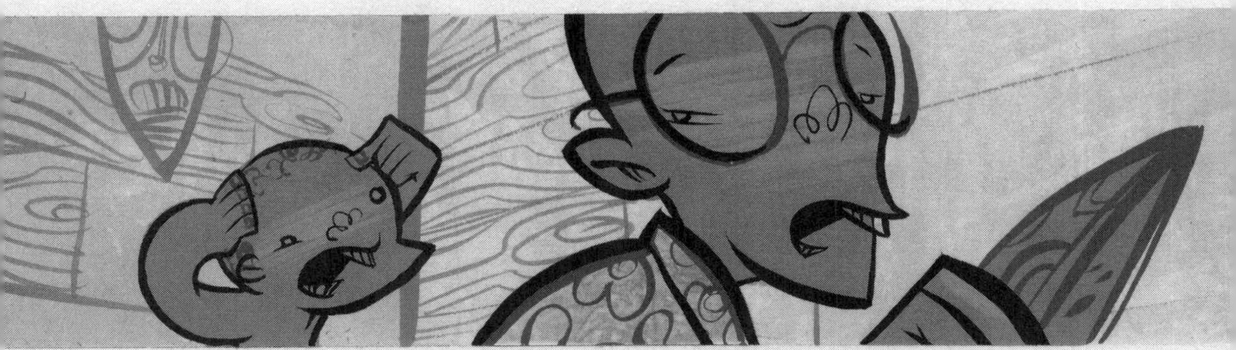

WHAZZAT FOR?!

YOU GOTTA LISSEN *BETTAHS*, YEAH?

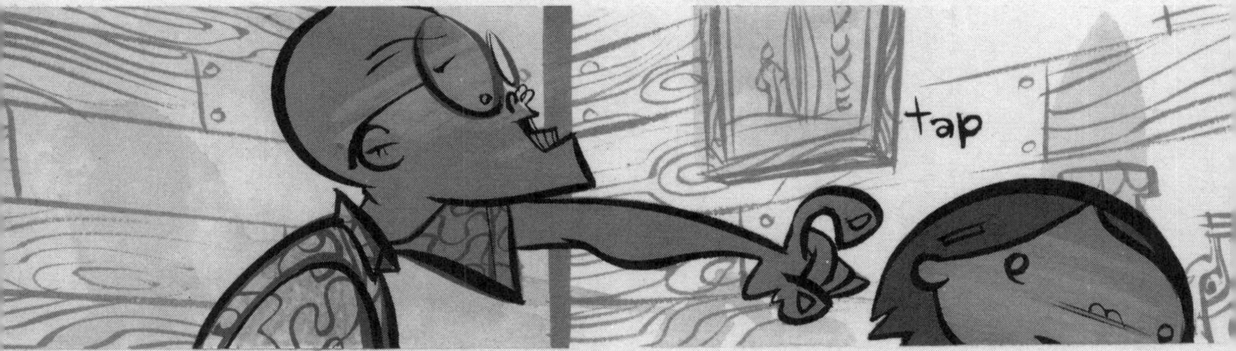
tap

YOU GIRL. HELLO DER.

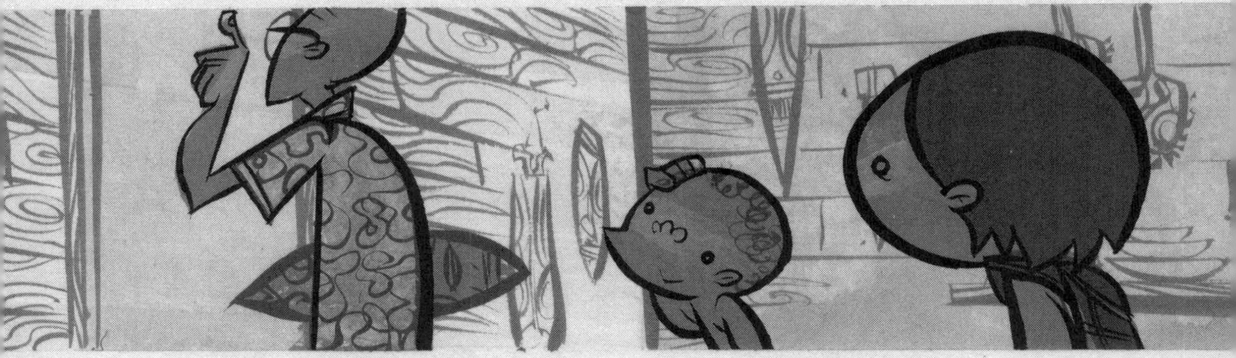

COME WITH ME A MINUTE.

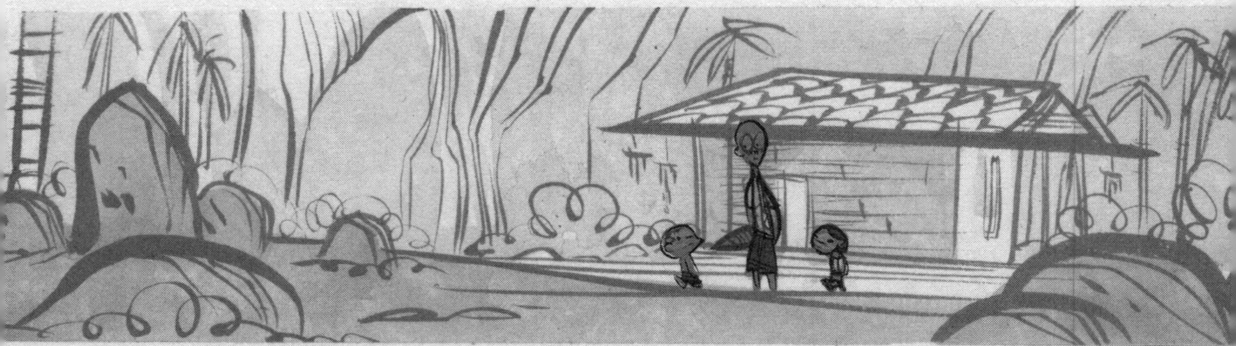

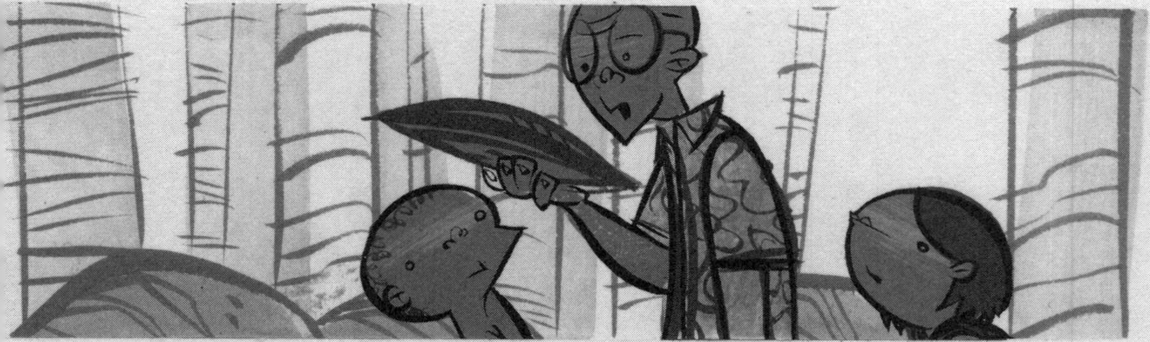

WHA?
mmm hmmm.
I GONNA TALK STORY.

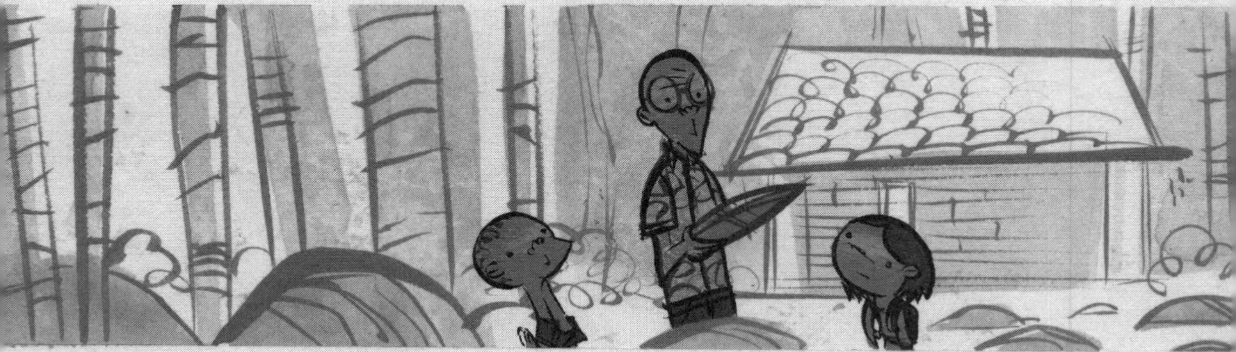

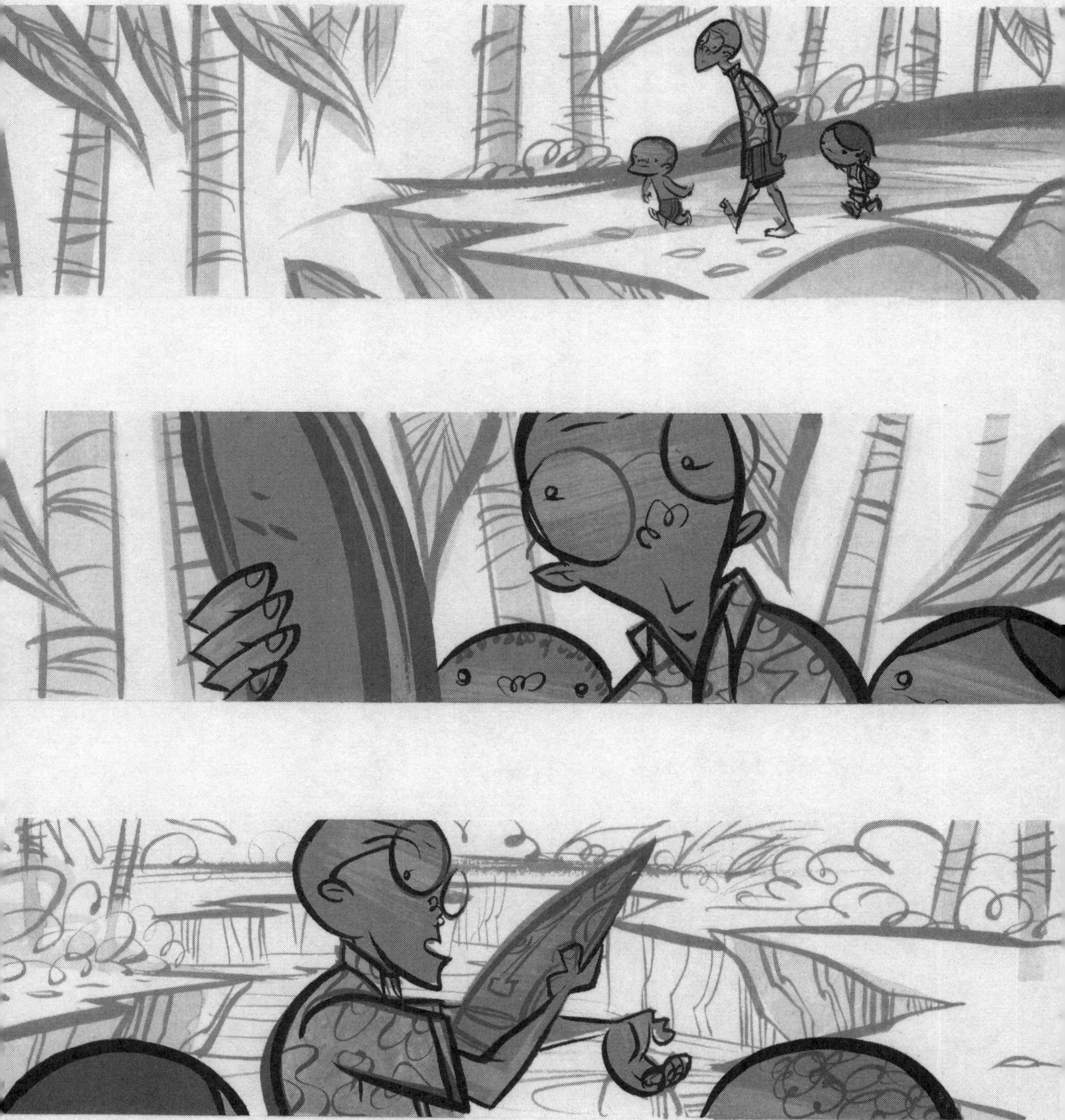

ALRIGHT.
LOOK DOWN.

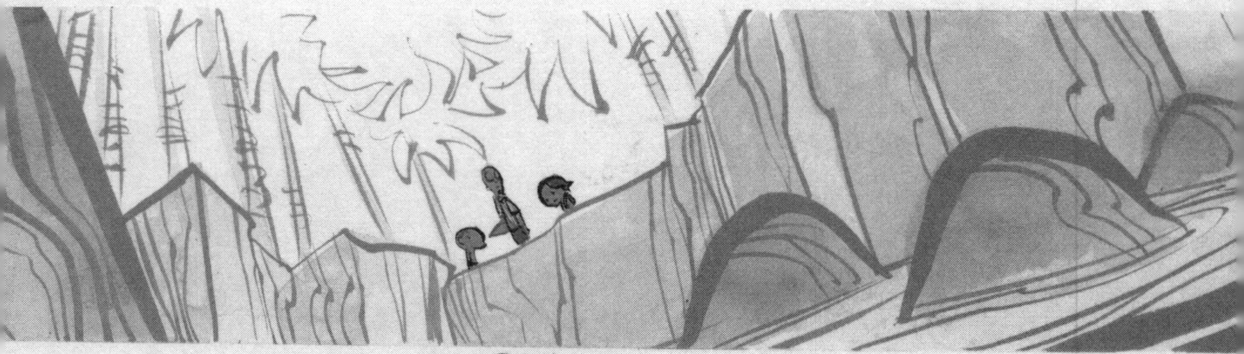

DAT'S A
SAD LITTLE
POND, YEAH?

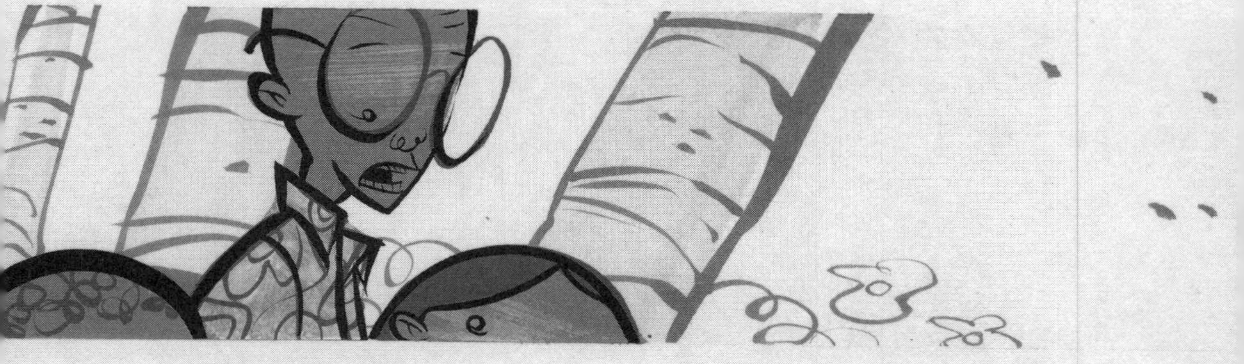

NO GOOD FOR
SWIMMING. NO GOOD FOR *NOTHING*.

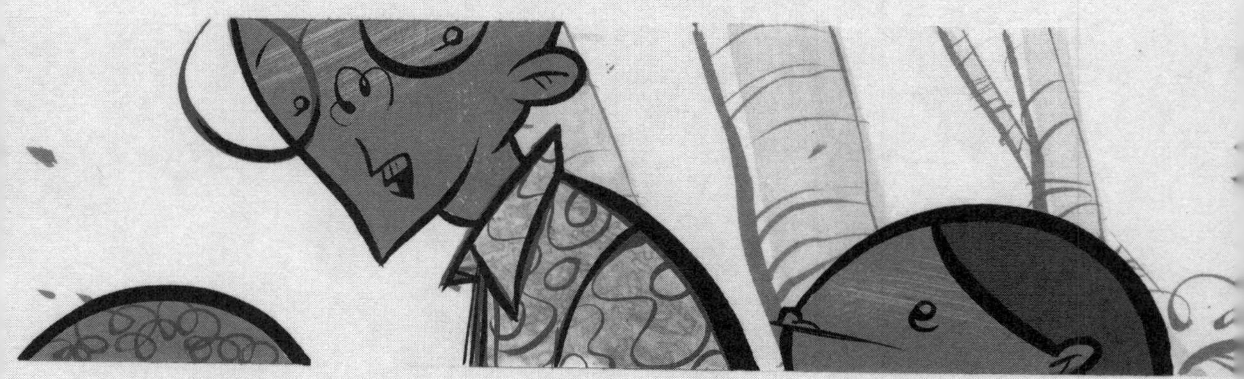

A COUPLE YEARS BACK,
SOME ARCHAEOLOGISTS FIND
SOME BONES IN DER. REAL OLD KINE.

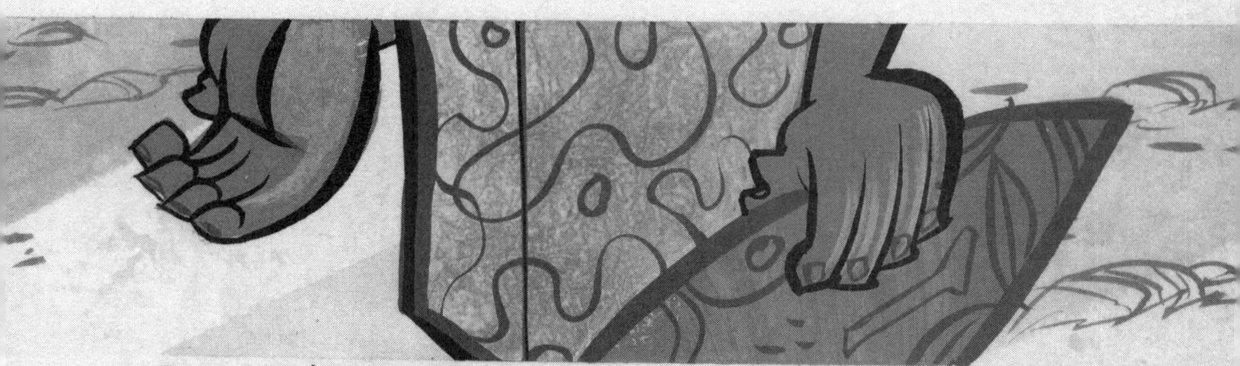

HAWAIIANS SEND DA DEAD OUT TO SEA IN DA OLD TIMES...

...DEM ARCHAEOLOGISTS CONFUSED WHY DEM BONES ALL IN DERE.

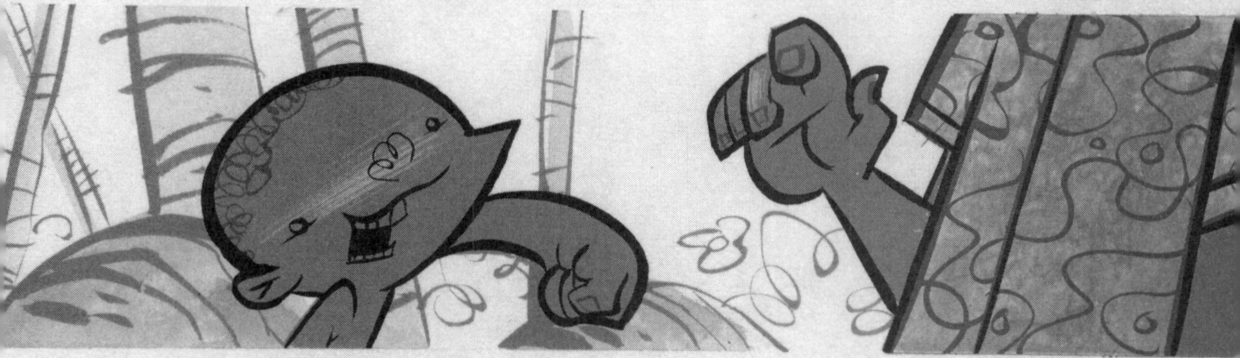

I WANNA SEE DA BONES!

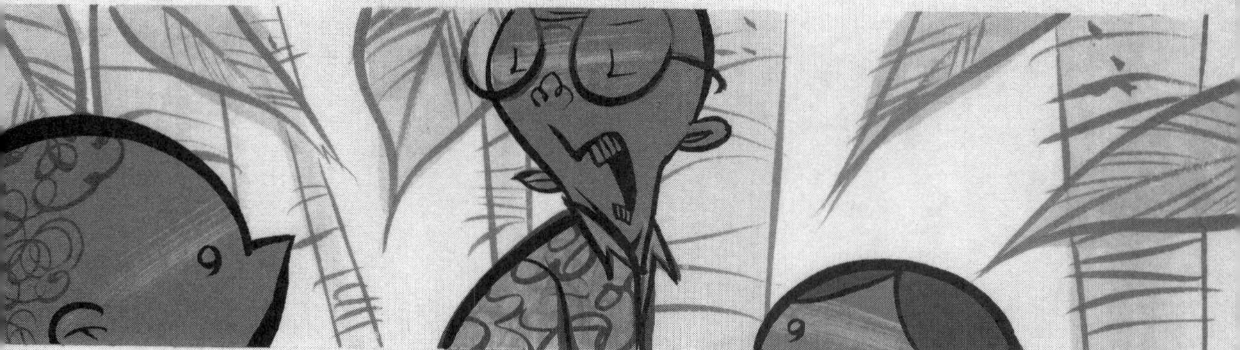

HUSH UP. I TALKIN' STORY.

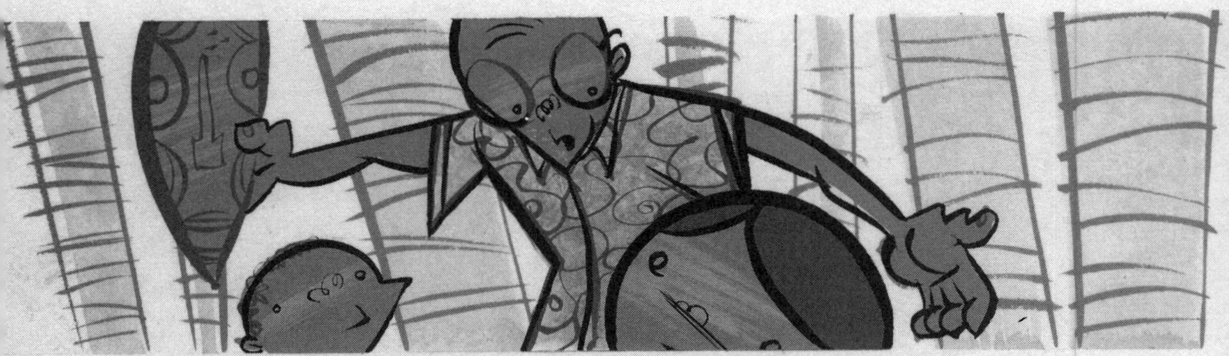

NOW, DAT'S ONE SAD
LITTLE POND.

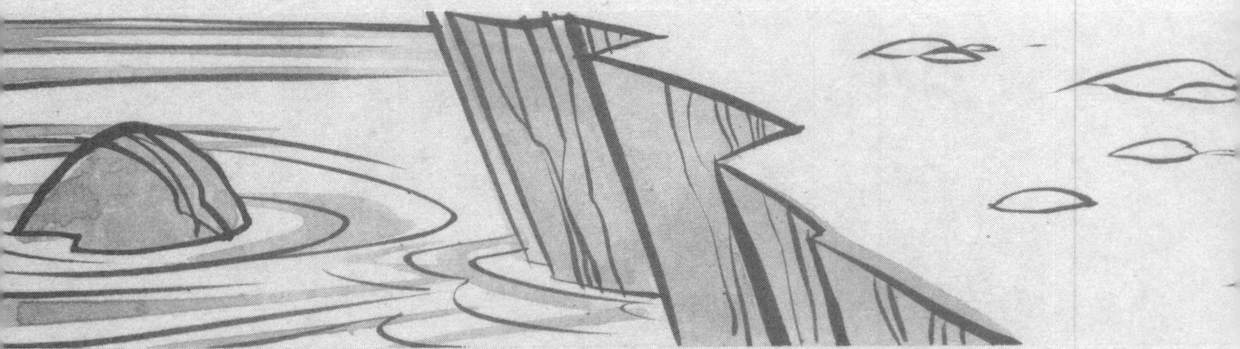

NEVER GETS BIGGER.
AN' IT GOOD FOR *NOTHING*.
ONLY GOT *BIGGER* ONCE.

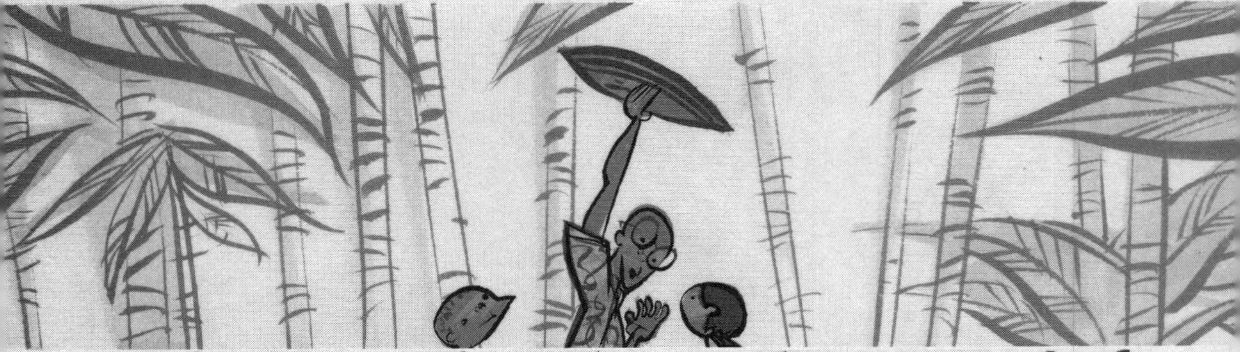

THE ARCHAEOLOGISTS, WHEN THEY TAKE DA BONES OUT, DA POND ALL FLOOD UP AROUND DERE FEET.

THEY DROP DEM BONES BACK INSIDE AND LEAVE, DA POND GO BACK TO NORMAL.

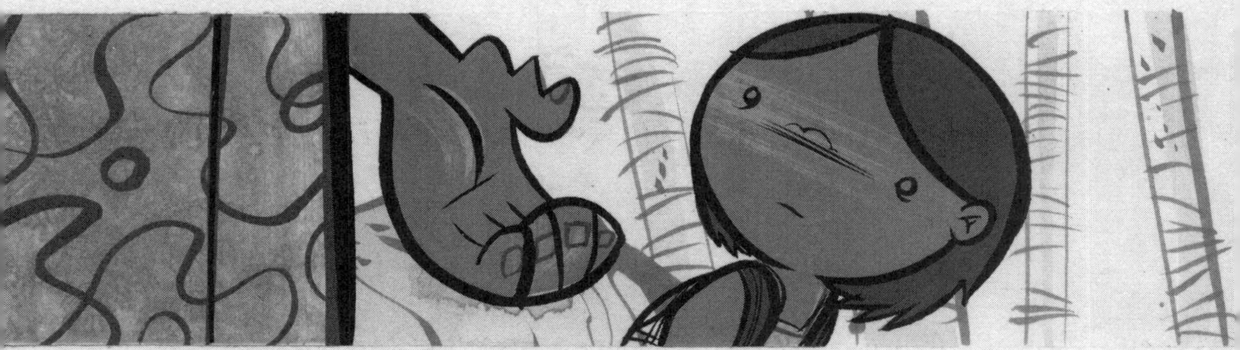

IT JUST DON'T LIKE
LET GO DA DEAD.

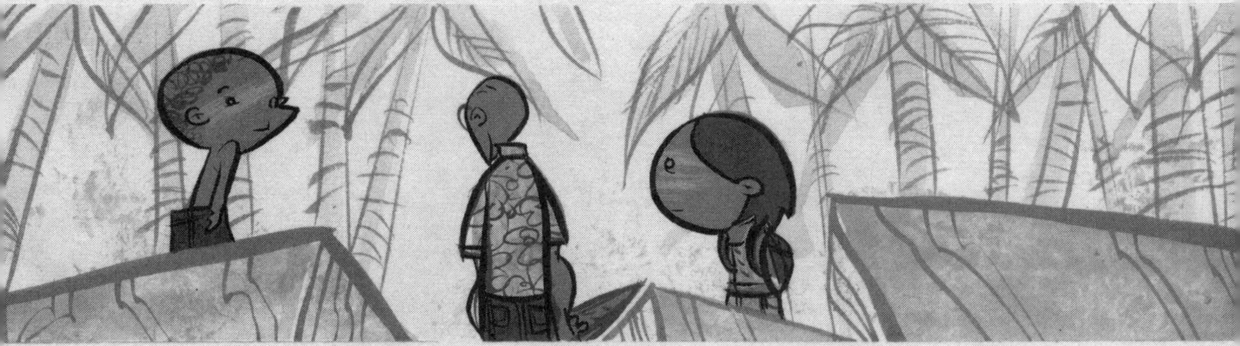

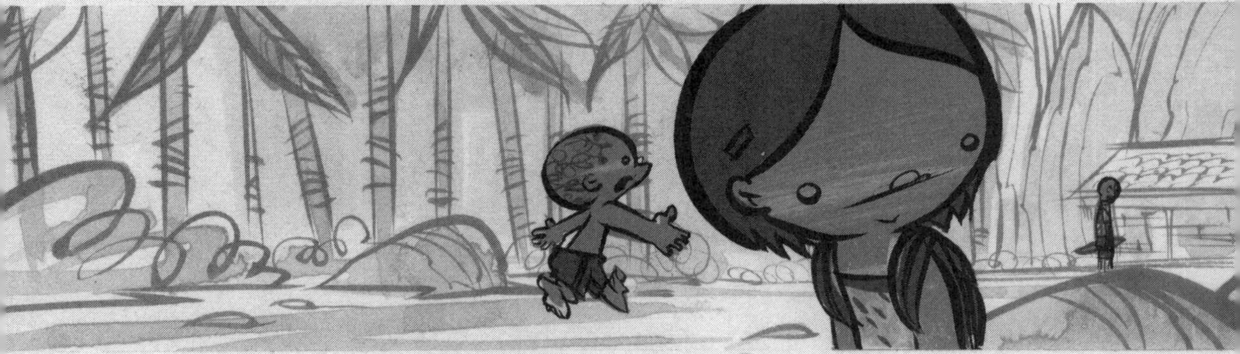

HEY! WAIT UP!

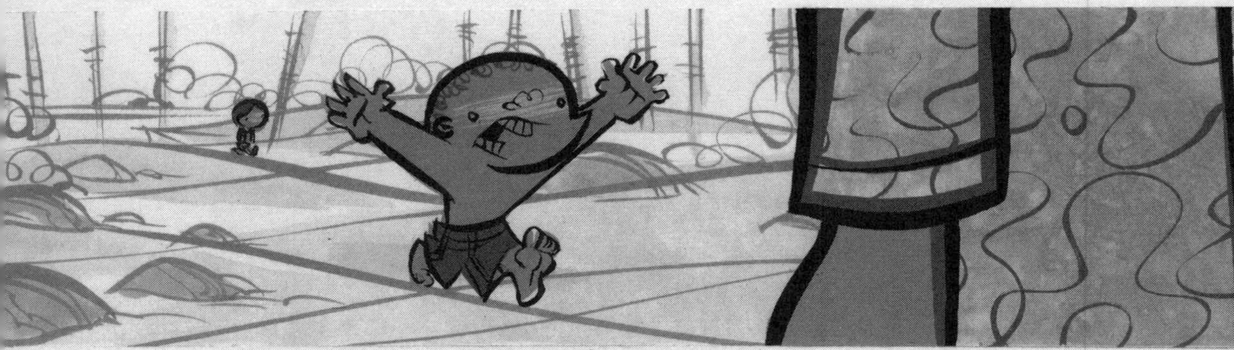

YOU LIKE GOIN' GIMME
MY *MONEY*?

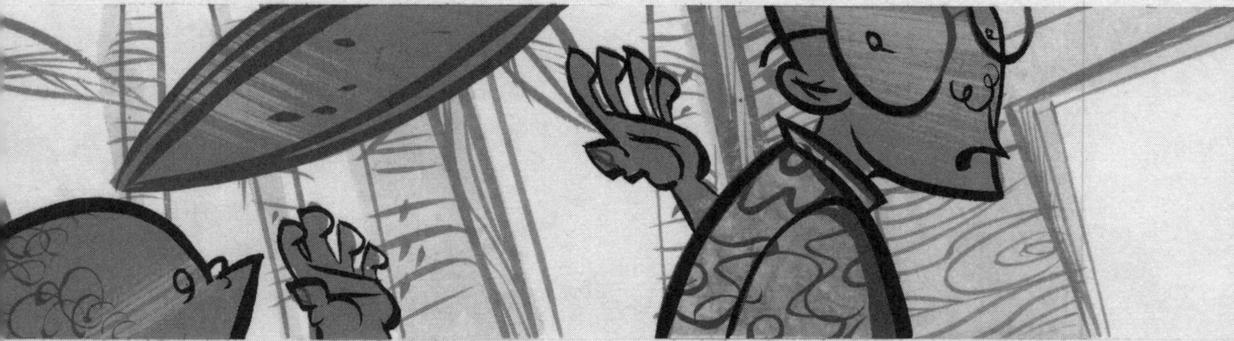

CATCH.

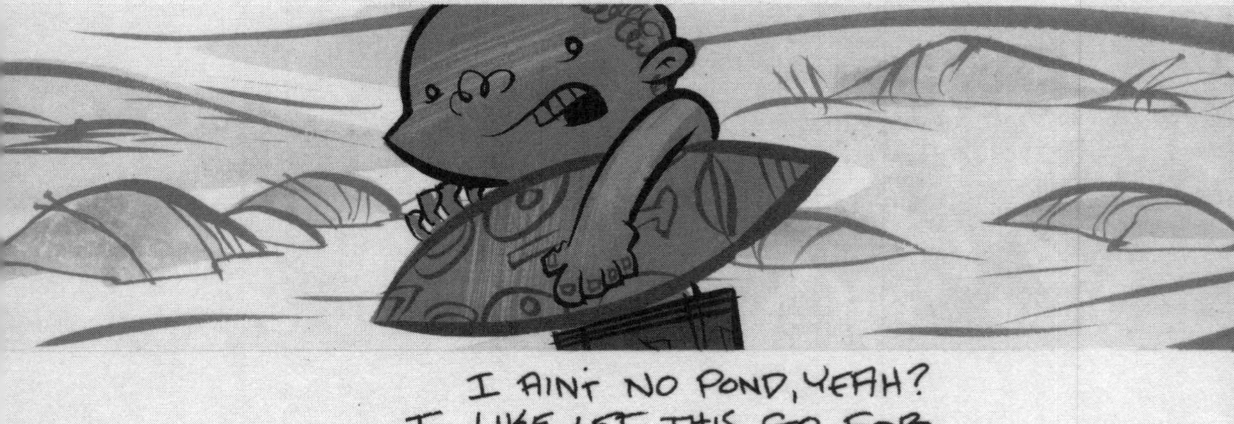

I AIN'T NO POND, YEAH?
I LIKE LET THIS GO FOR
TWENNY BUCKS...

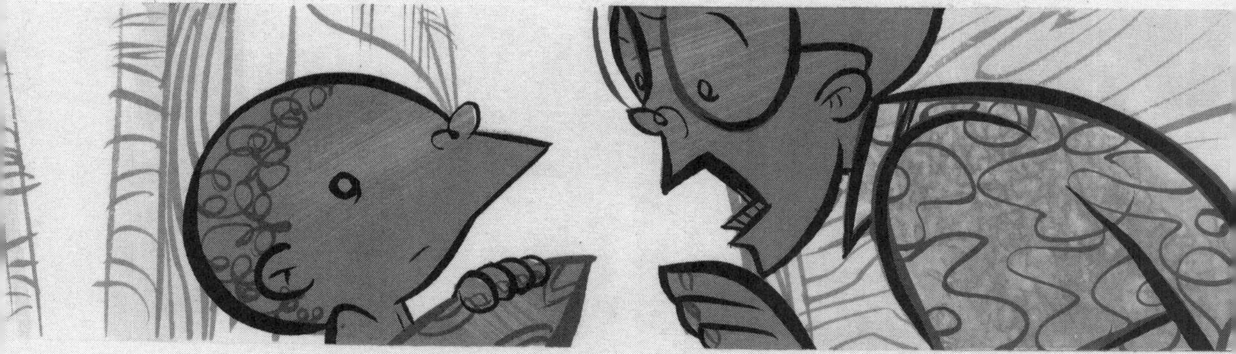

HE AIN'T YOURS TO
LET GO OF.

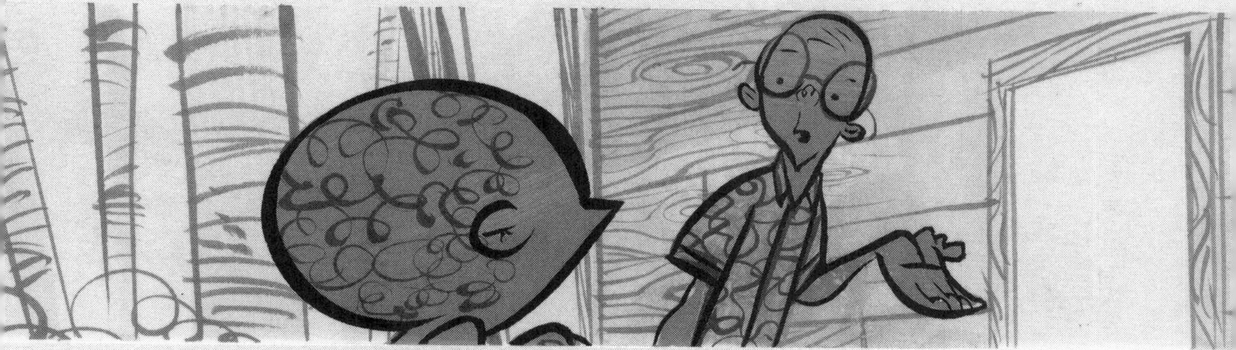

YOU AIN'T DA SAD ONE. YOU AIN'T
GOT SOMETHIN' SNUCK IN YOUR HEART
ALL QUIET, LIKE A SNAKE WIT NO SHOES ON.

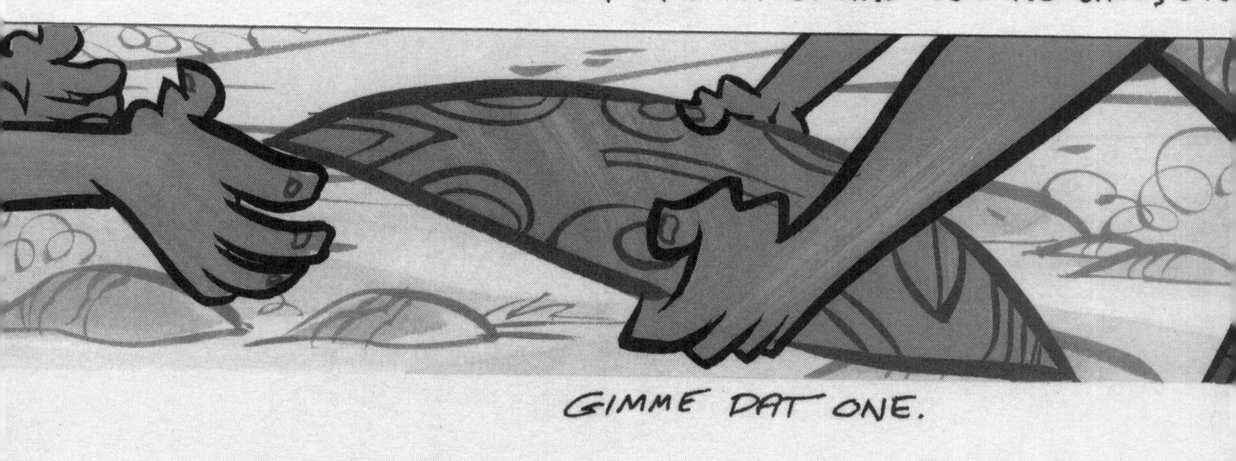

GIMME DAT ONE.

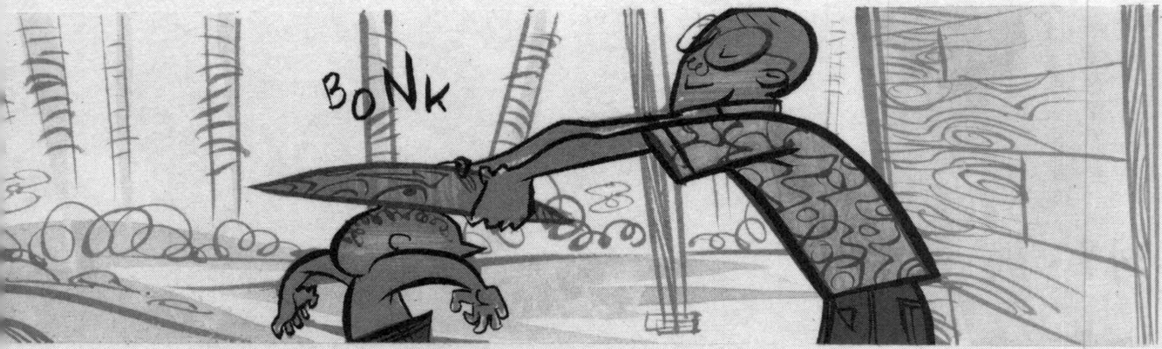
BONK

HEY!

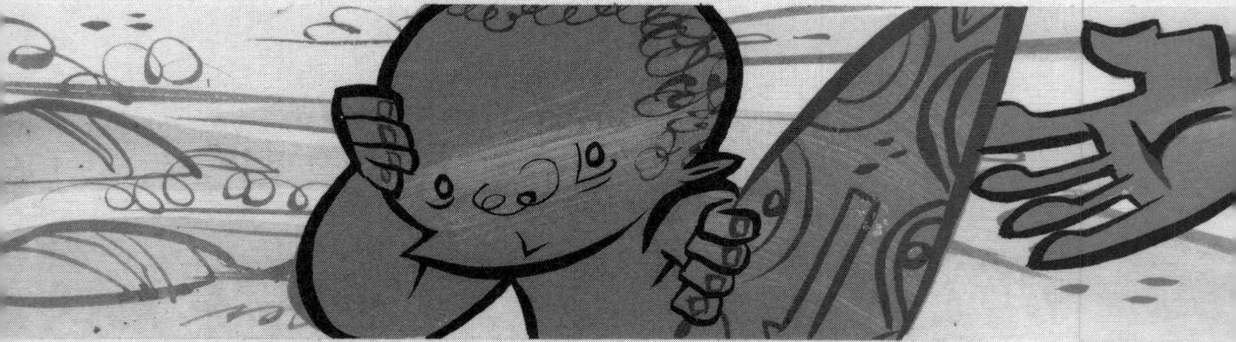

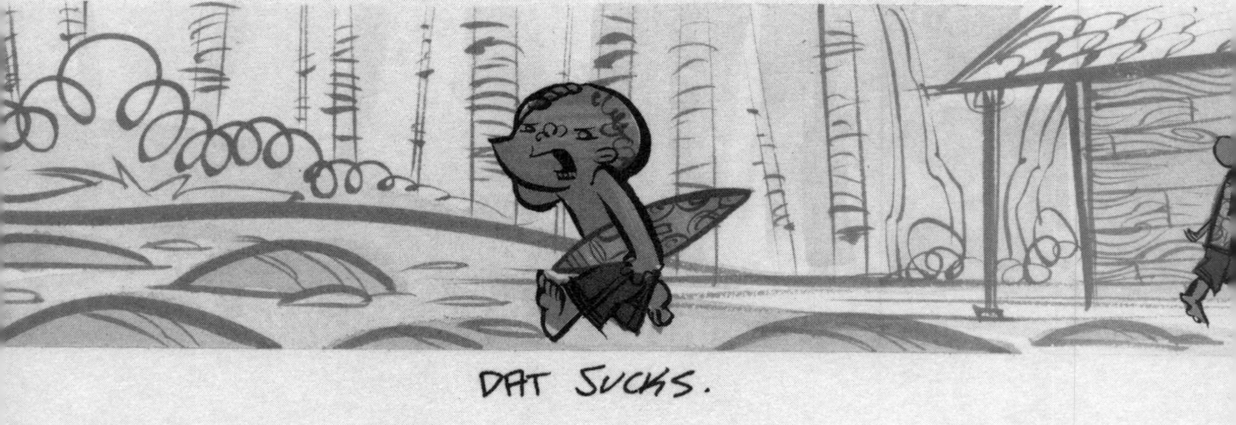

DAT SUCKS.

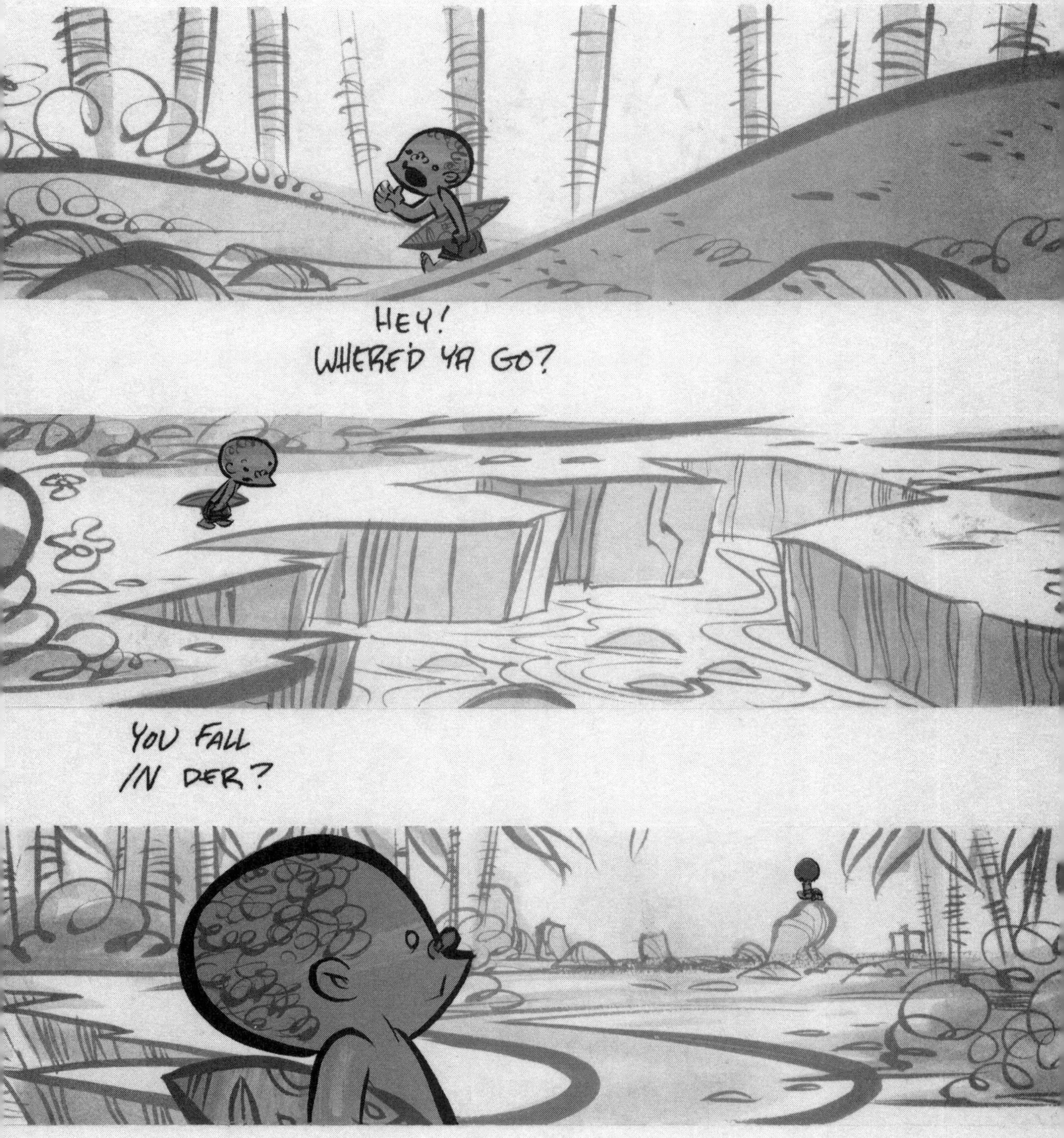
HEY!
WHERE'D YA GO?
YOU FALL
IN DER?

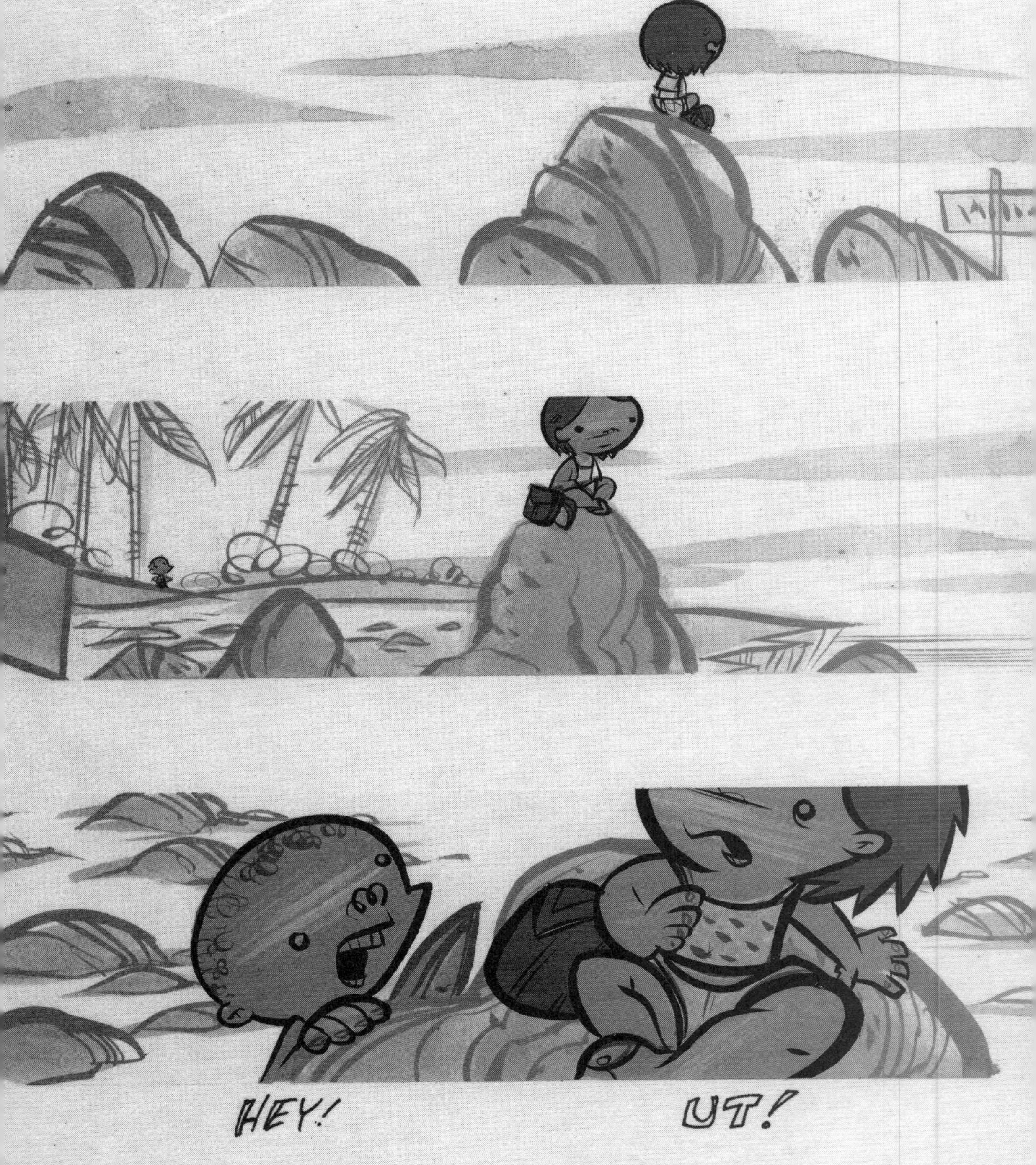
HEY!
UT!

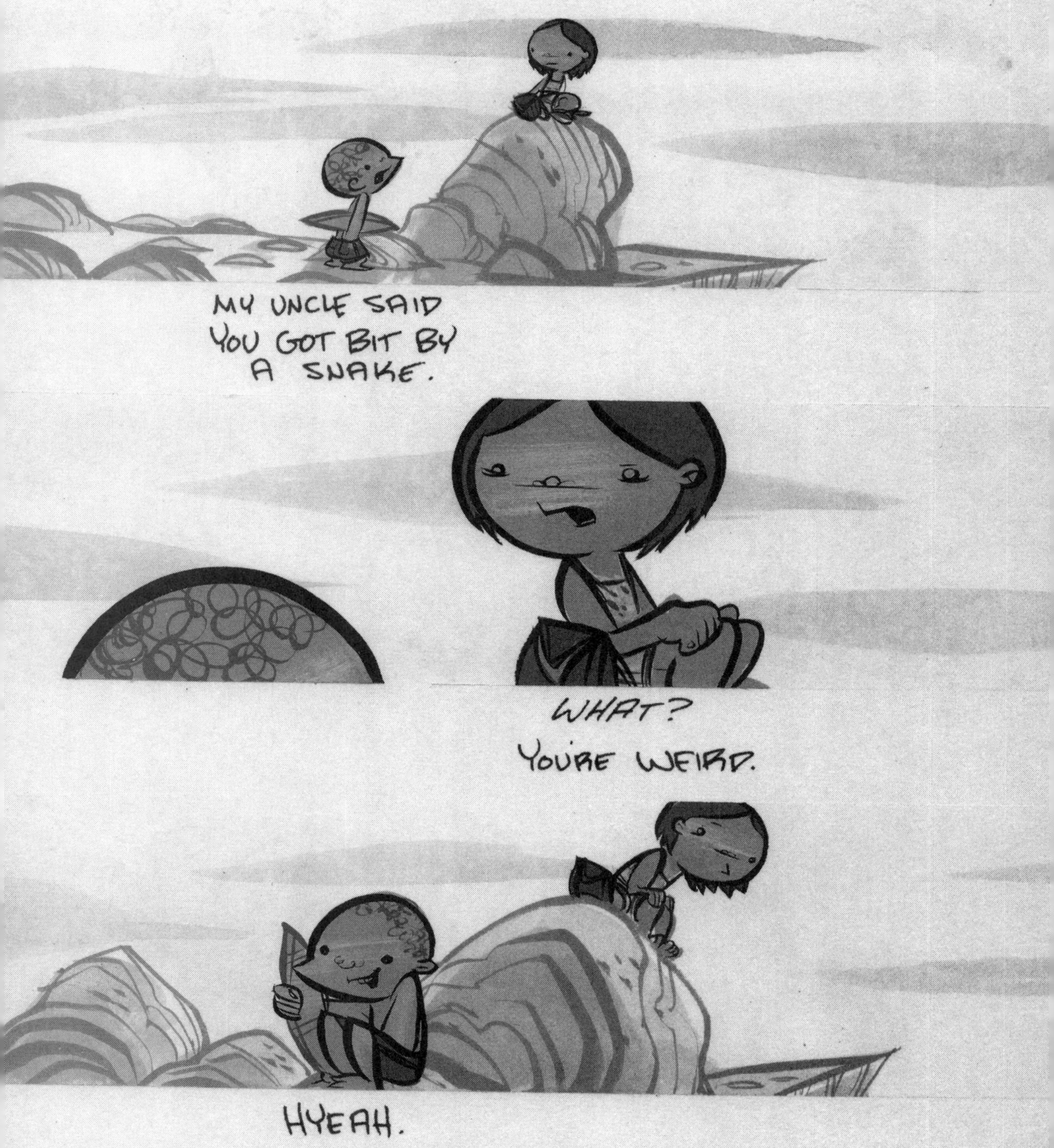
MY UNCLE SAID YOU GOT BIT BY A SNAKE.
WHAT?
YOU'RE WEIRD.
HYEAH.

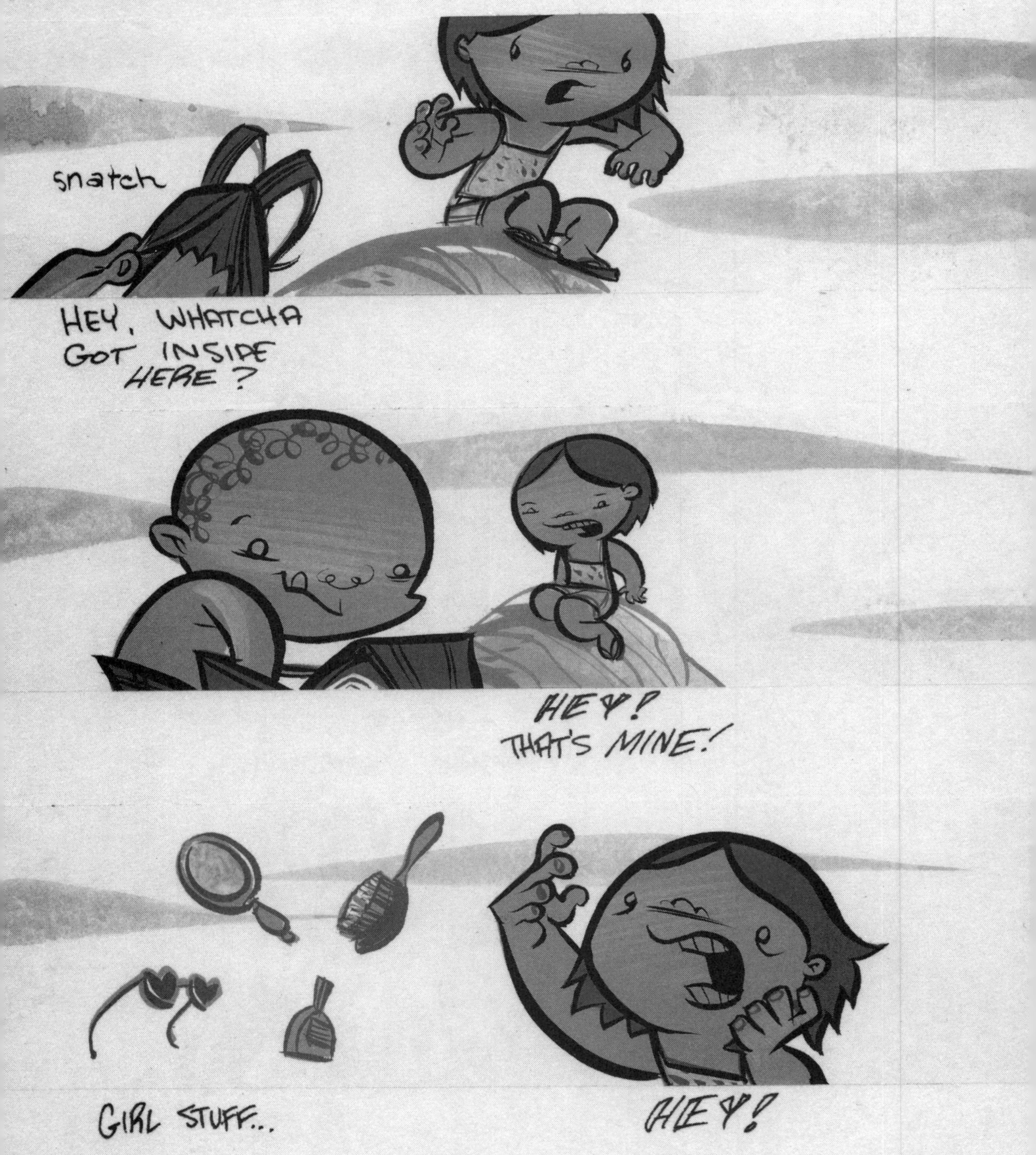

snatch
HEY, WHATCHA GOT INSIDE HERE?
HEY! THAT'S MINE!
GIRL STUFF...
HEY!

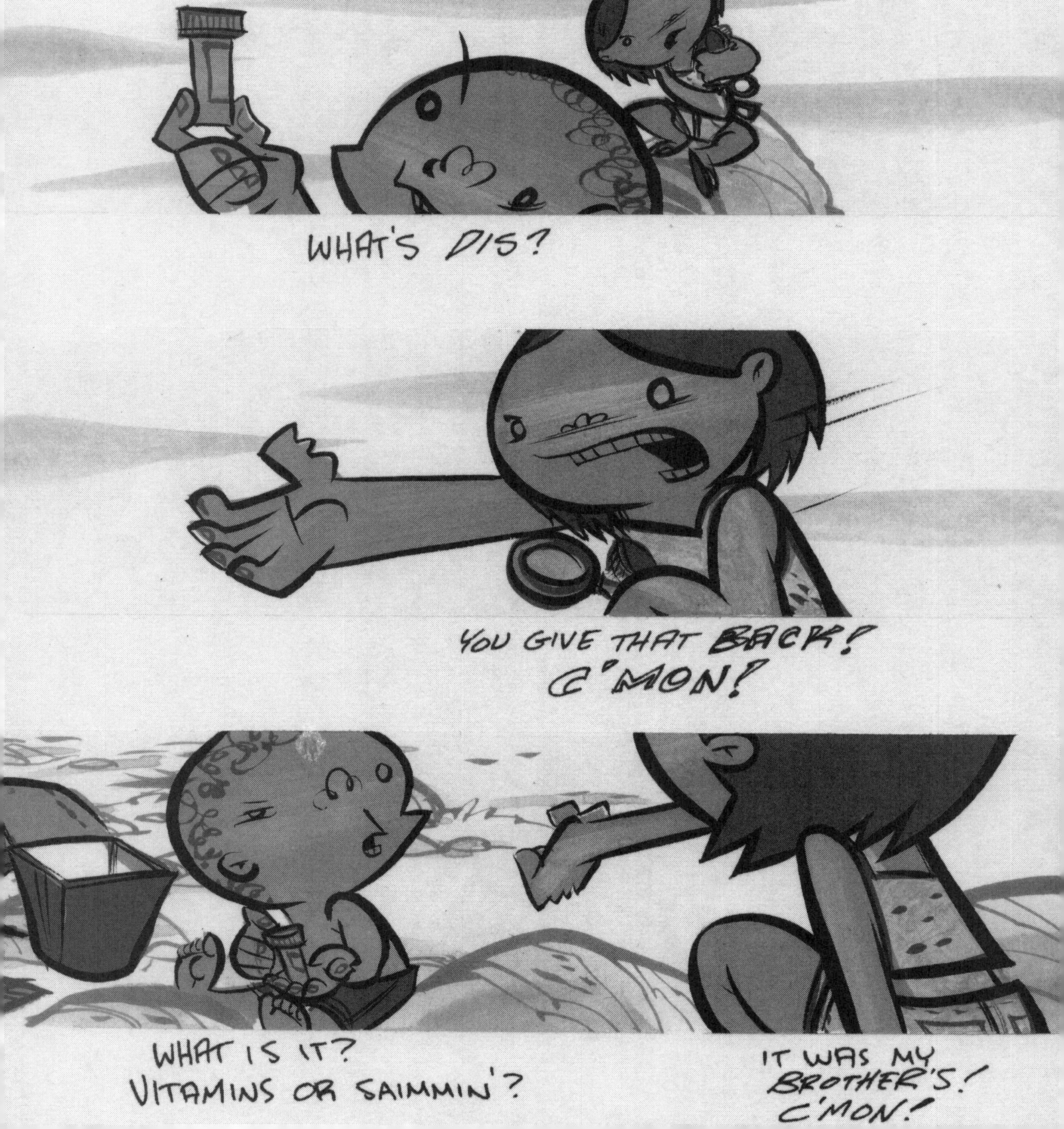
WHAT'S DIS?
YOU GIVE THAT BACK! C'MON!
WHAT IS IT? VITAMINS OR SAIMMIN'?
IT WAS MY BROTHER'S! C'MON!

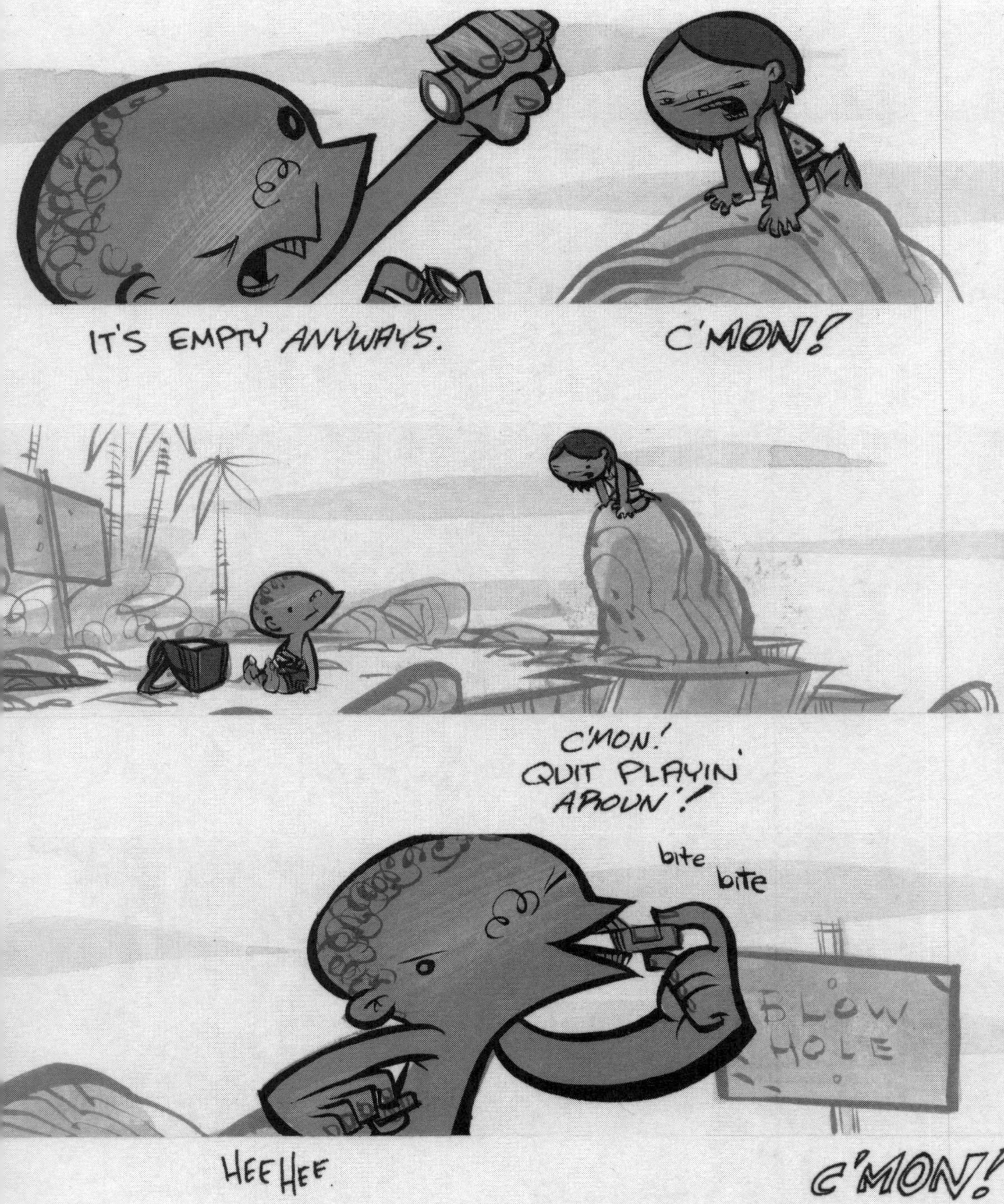
IT'S EMPTY ANYWAYS.
C'MON!
C'MON! QUIT PLAYIN AROUN'!
bite
bite
BLOW HOLE
HEEHEE.
C'MON!

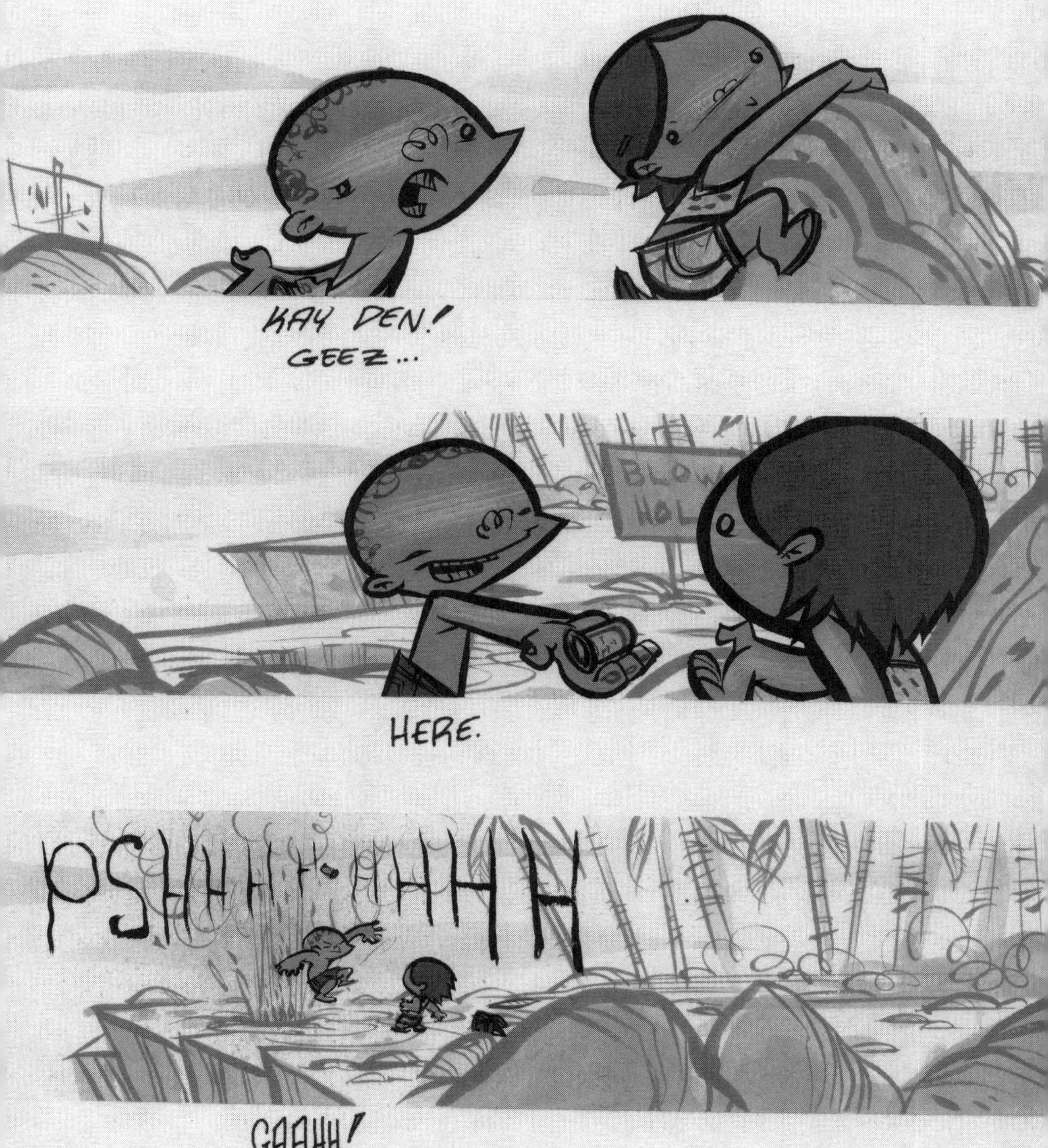
KAY DEN!
GEEZ...
BLOW HOL
HERE.
PSHHHHHHHH
GAAHH!

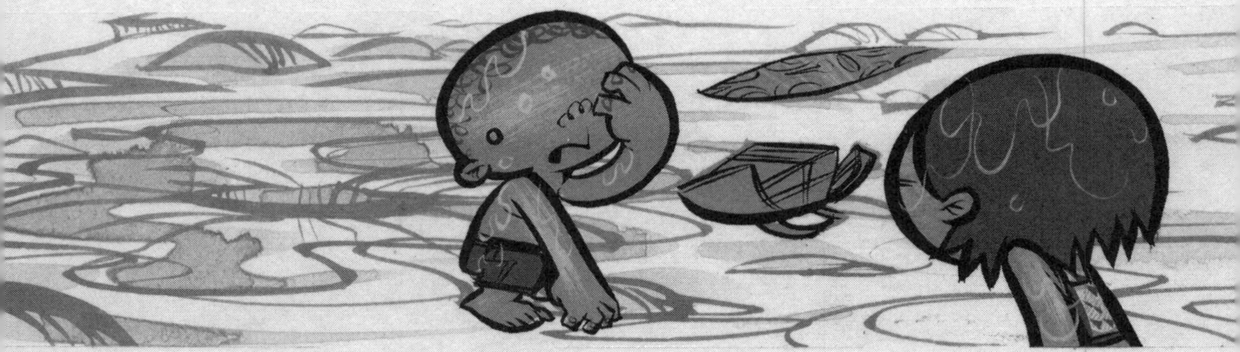

OH YEAH.
DER'S A *BLOWHOLE*.
LOOKOUT.

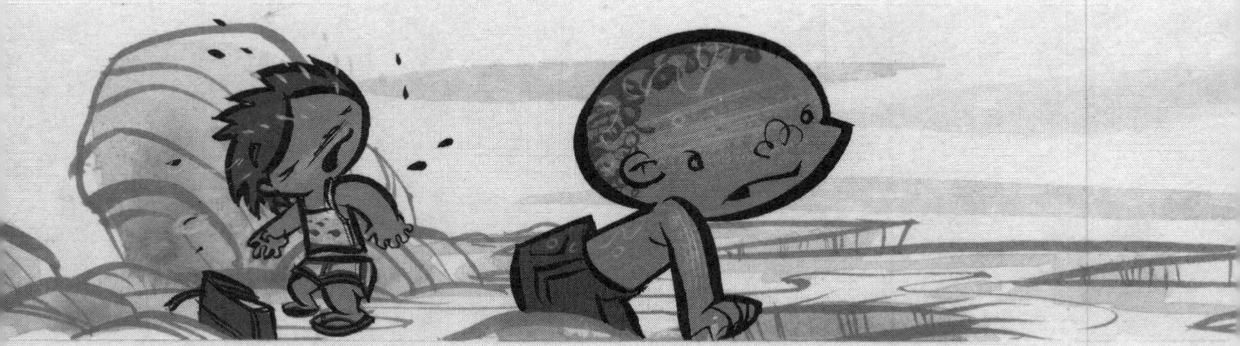

DUMMY.

UH OH.

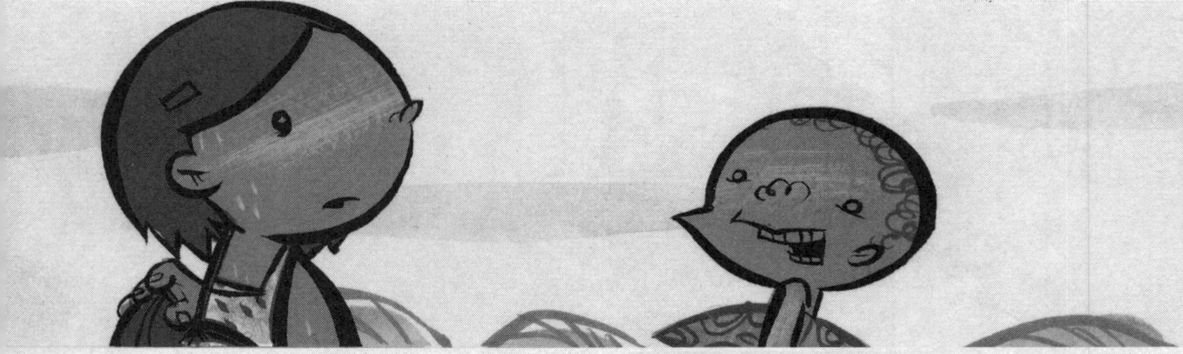

I THINK YOUR
THING DROPPED
INNA HOLE.

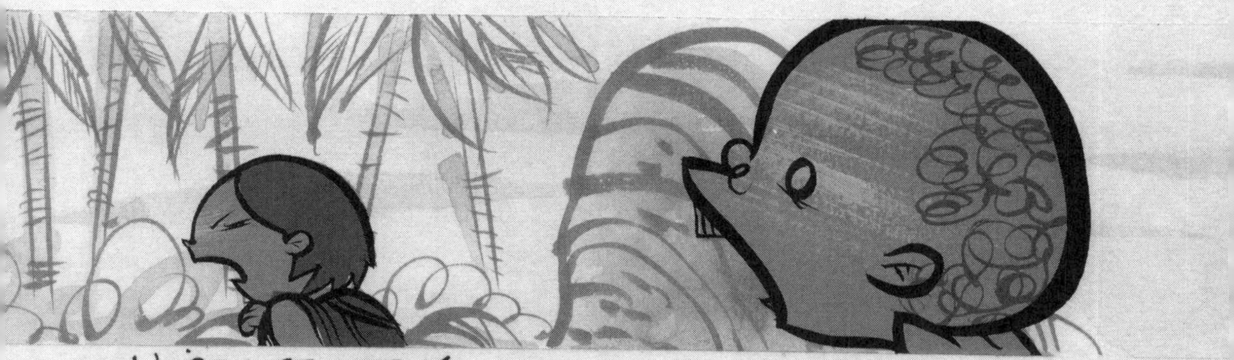

YOU'RE JUST MEAN!
YOU JUST CARE ABOUT
YOUR DUMB MASK.

NAH-HAH!

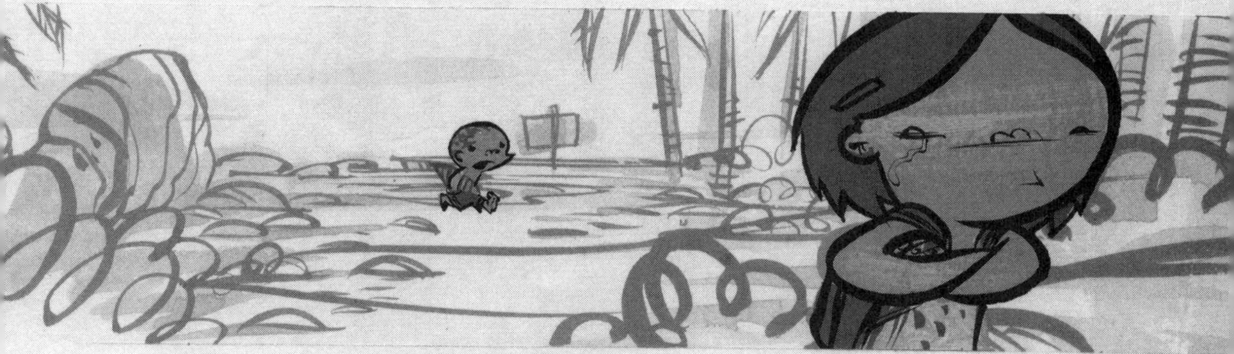

IT WASN'T ON
PURPOSE!
C'MON!

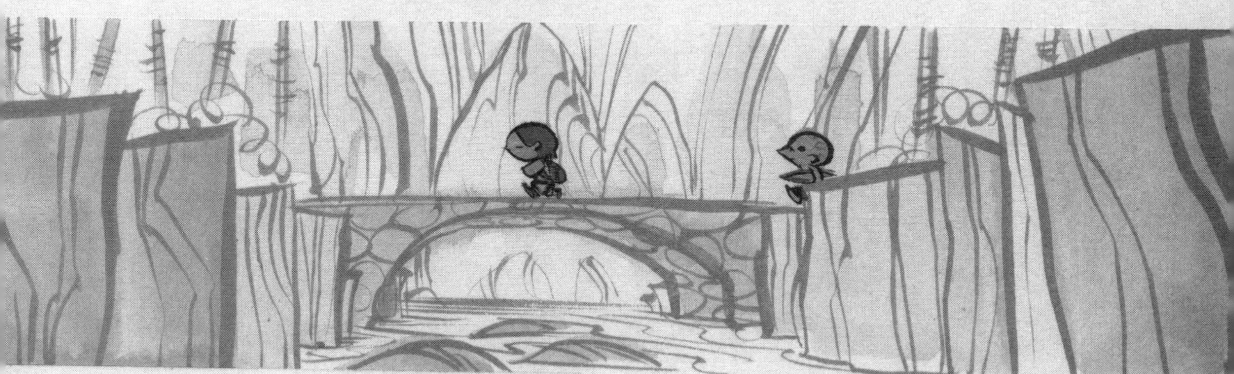

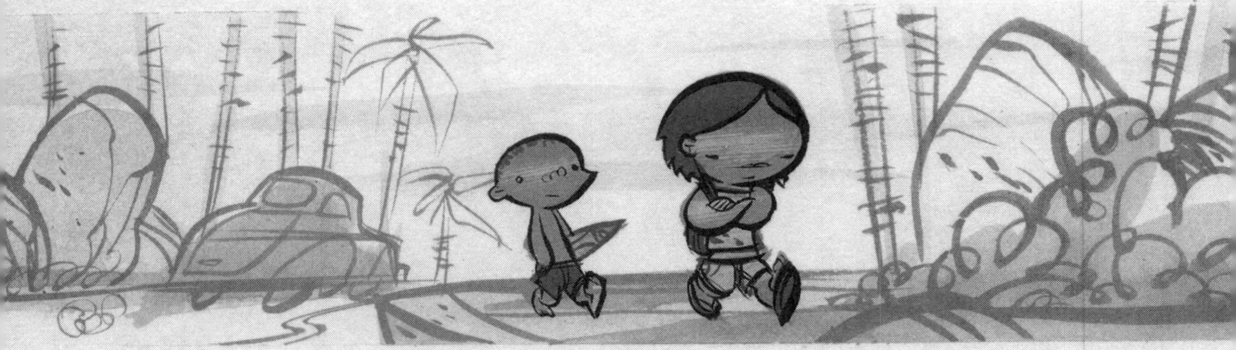

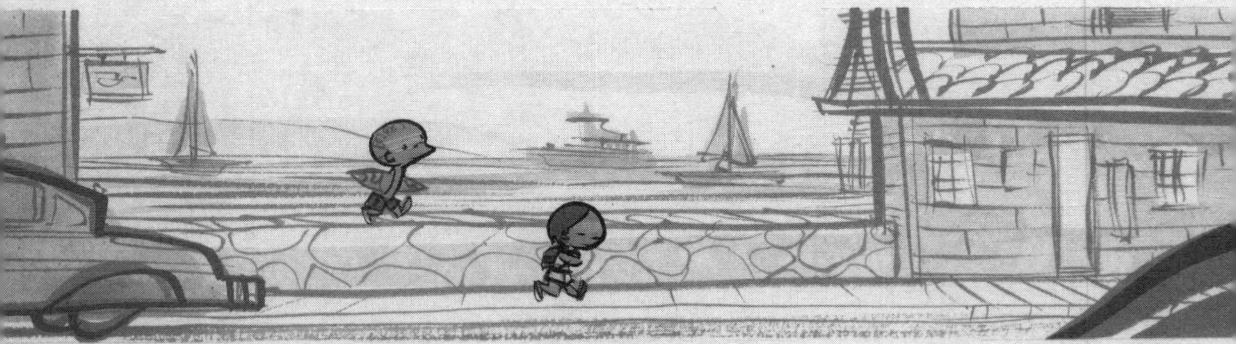

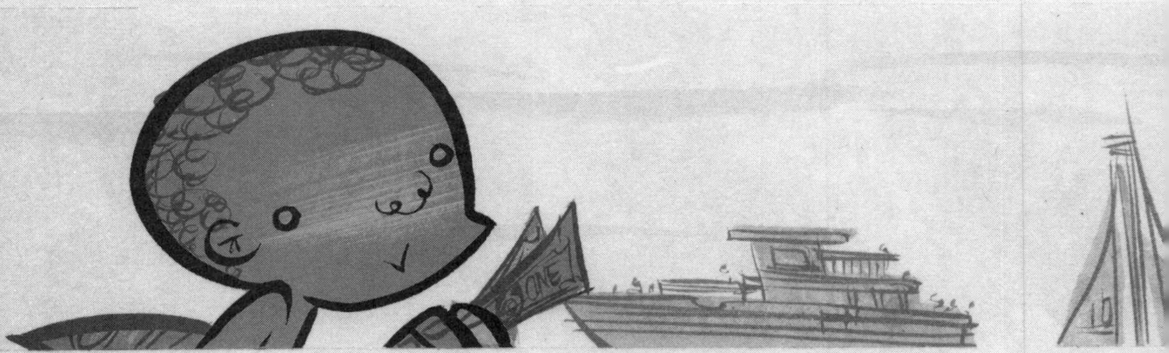
ONE

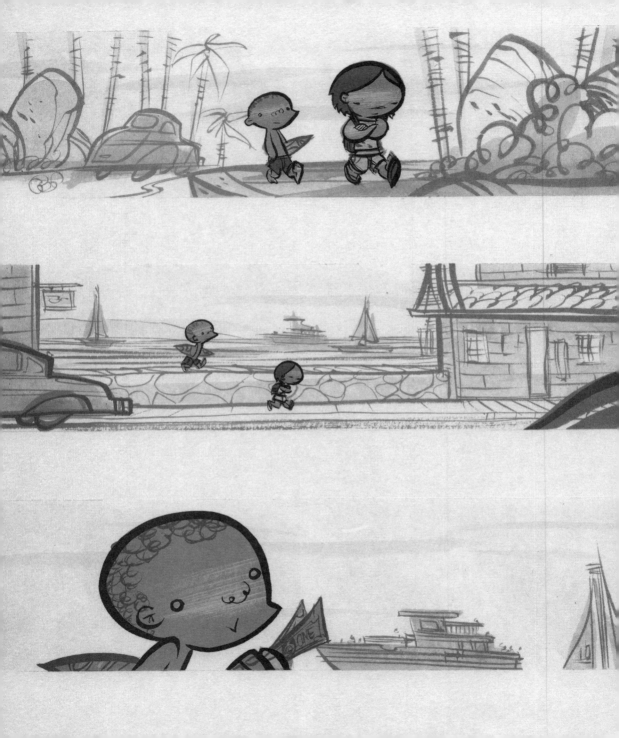

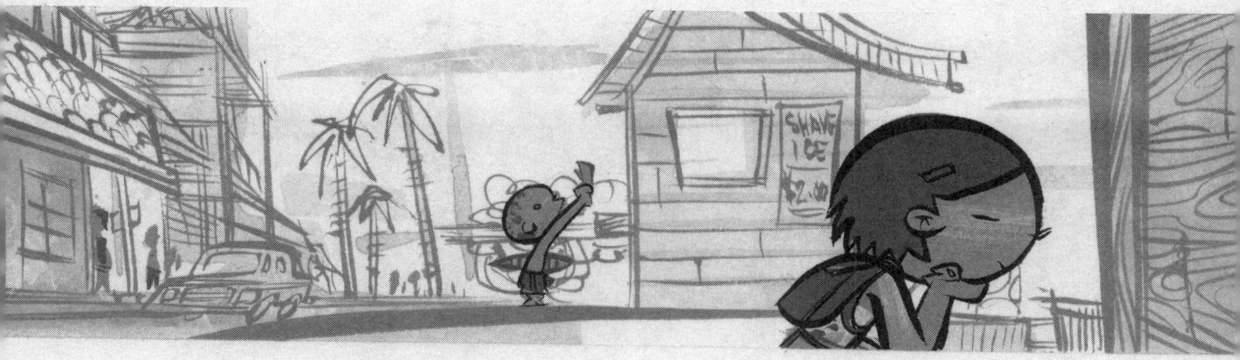
SHAVE
ICE
$2.00

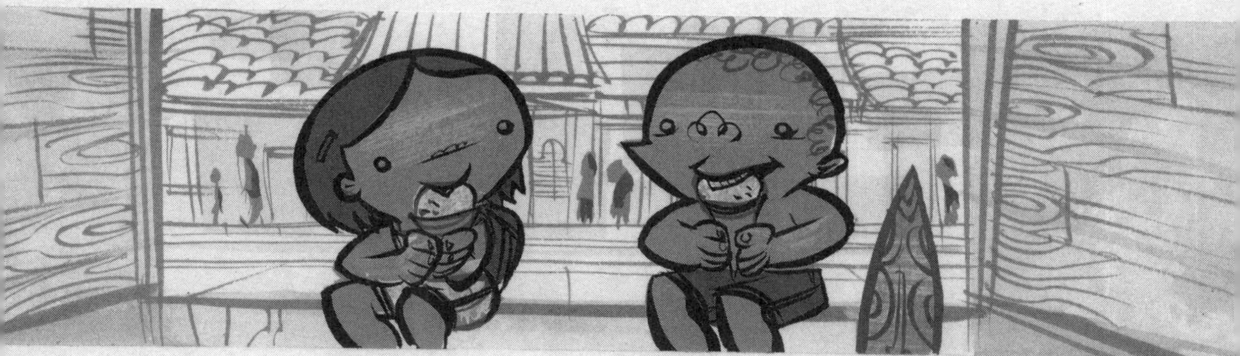

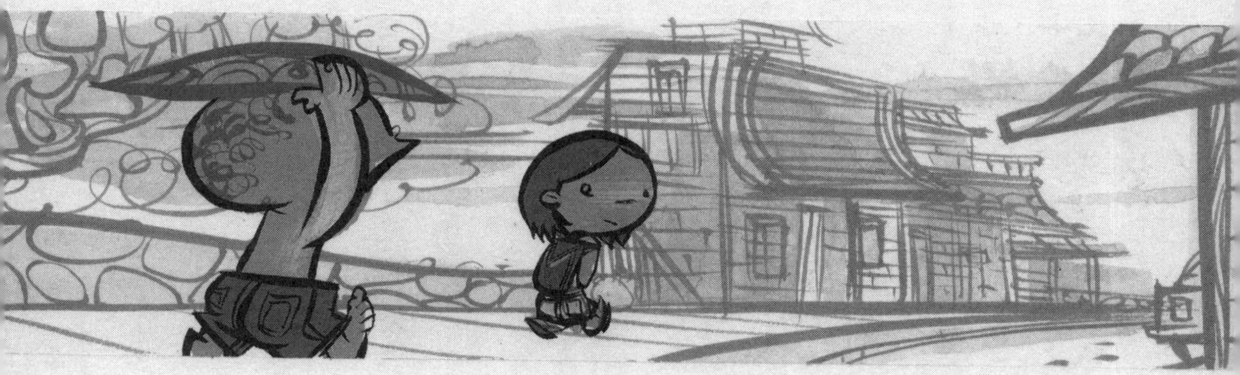

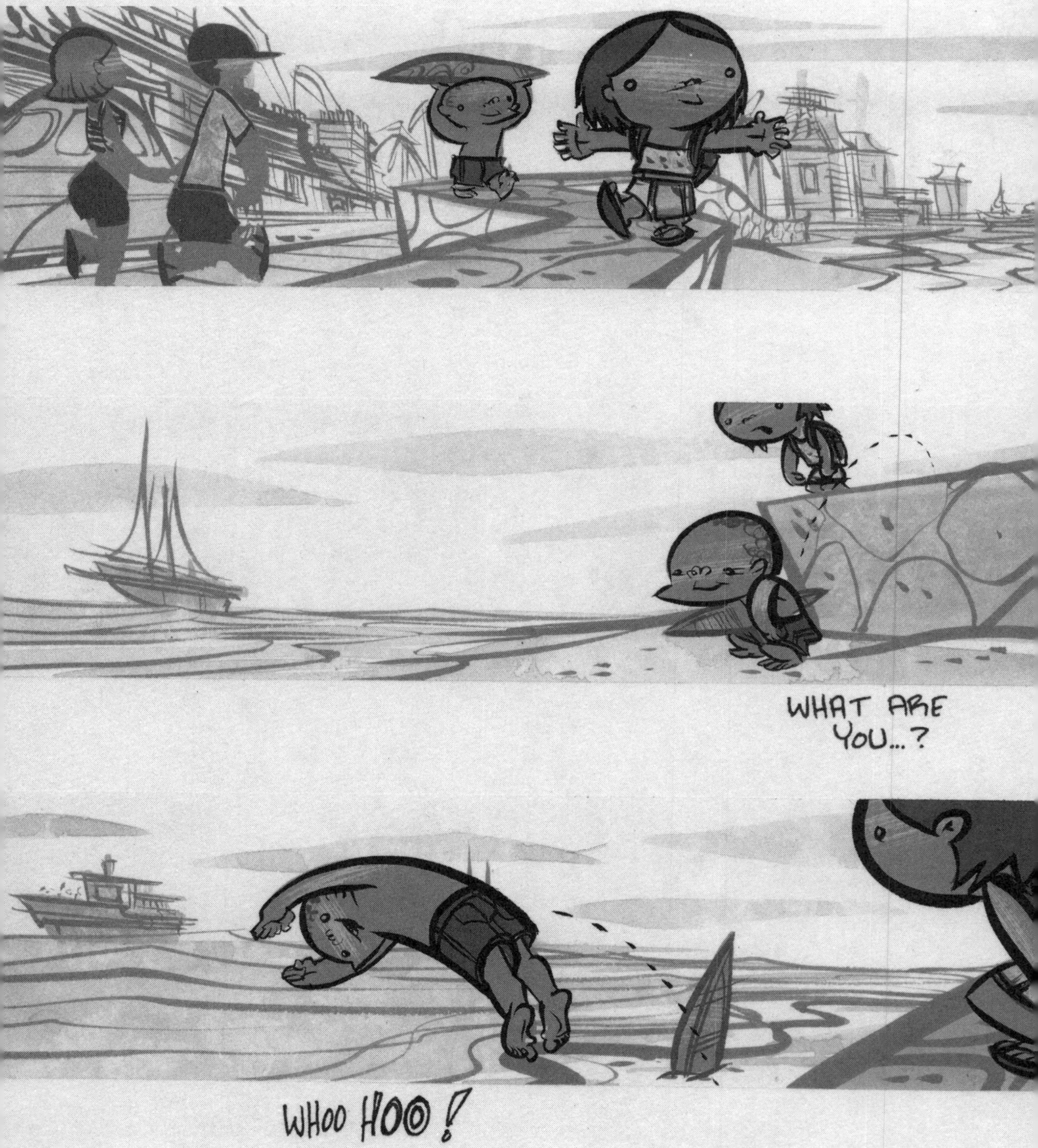
WHAT ARE YOU...?
WHOO HOO!

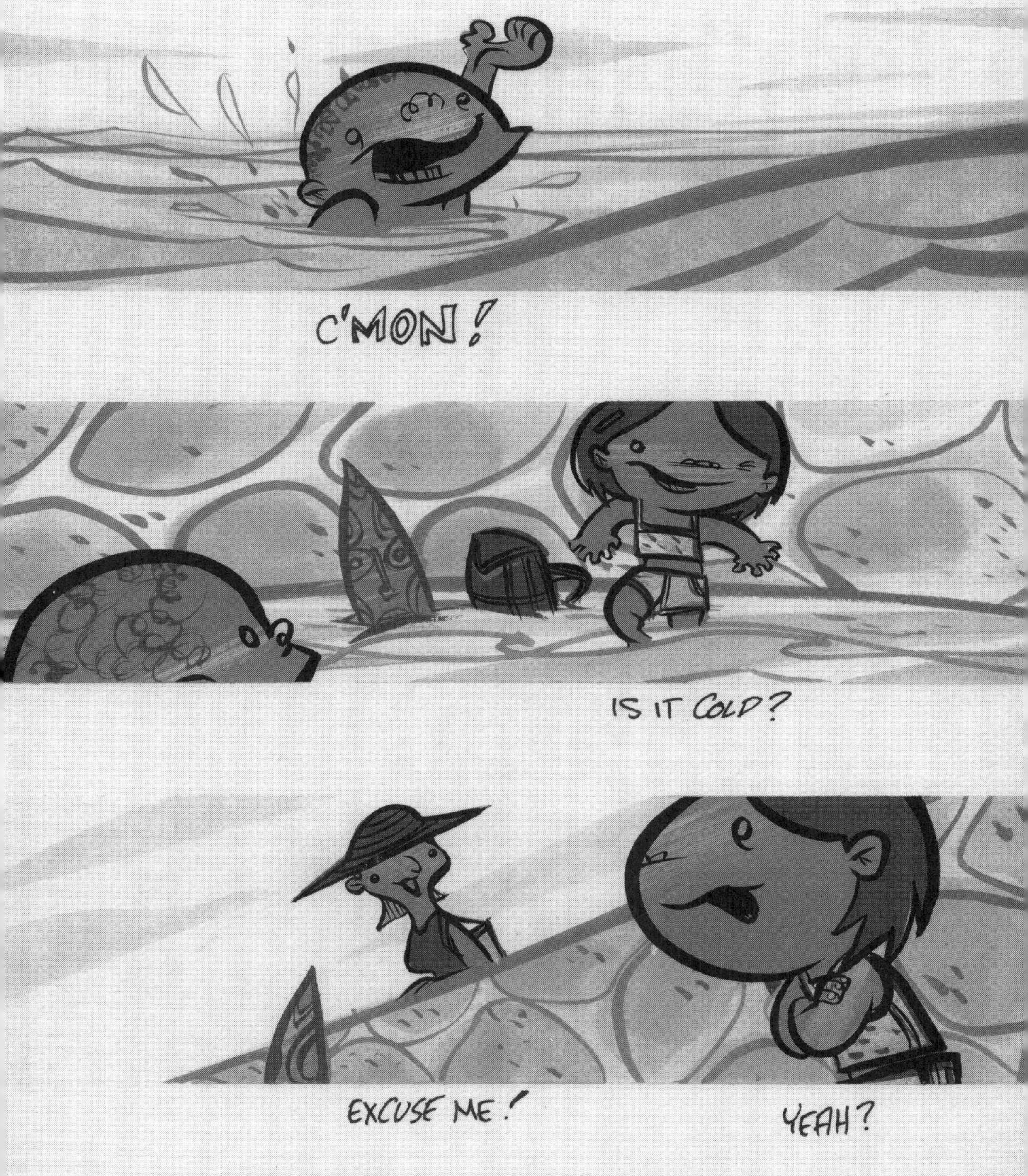
C'MON!
IS IT COLD?
EXCUSE ME!
YEAH?

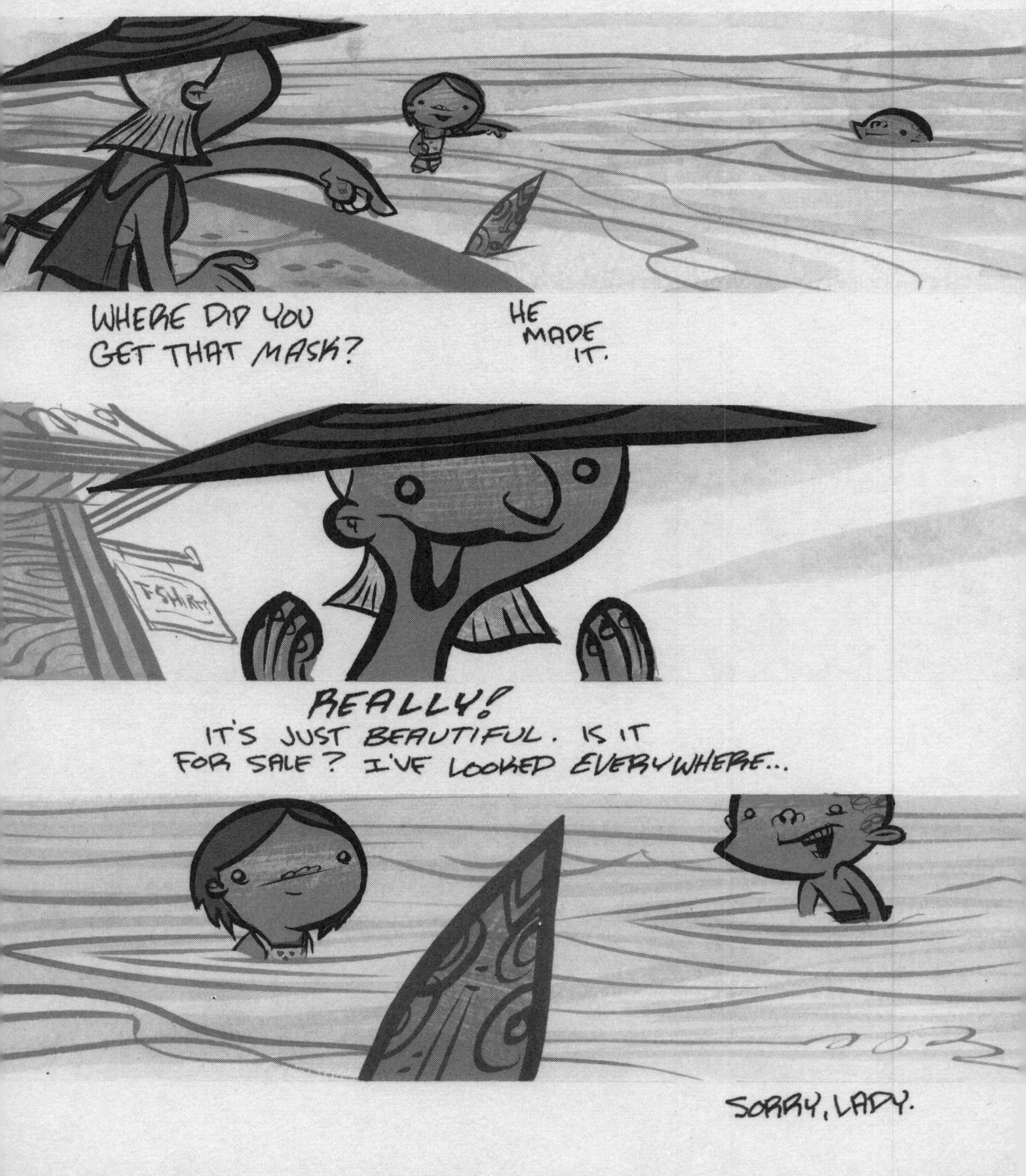
WHERE DID YOU GET THAT MASK?
HE MADE IT.
REALLY!
IT'S JUST BEAUTIFUL. IS IT FOR SALE? I'VE LOOKED EVERYWHERE...
SORRY, LADY.

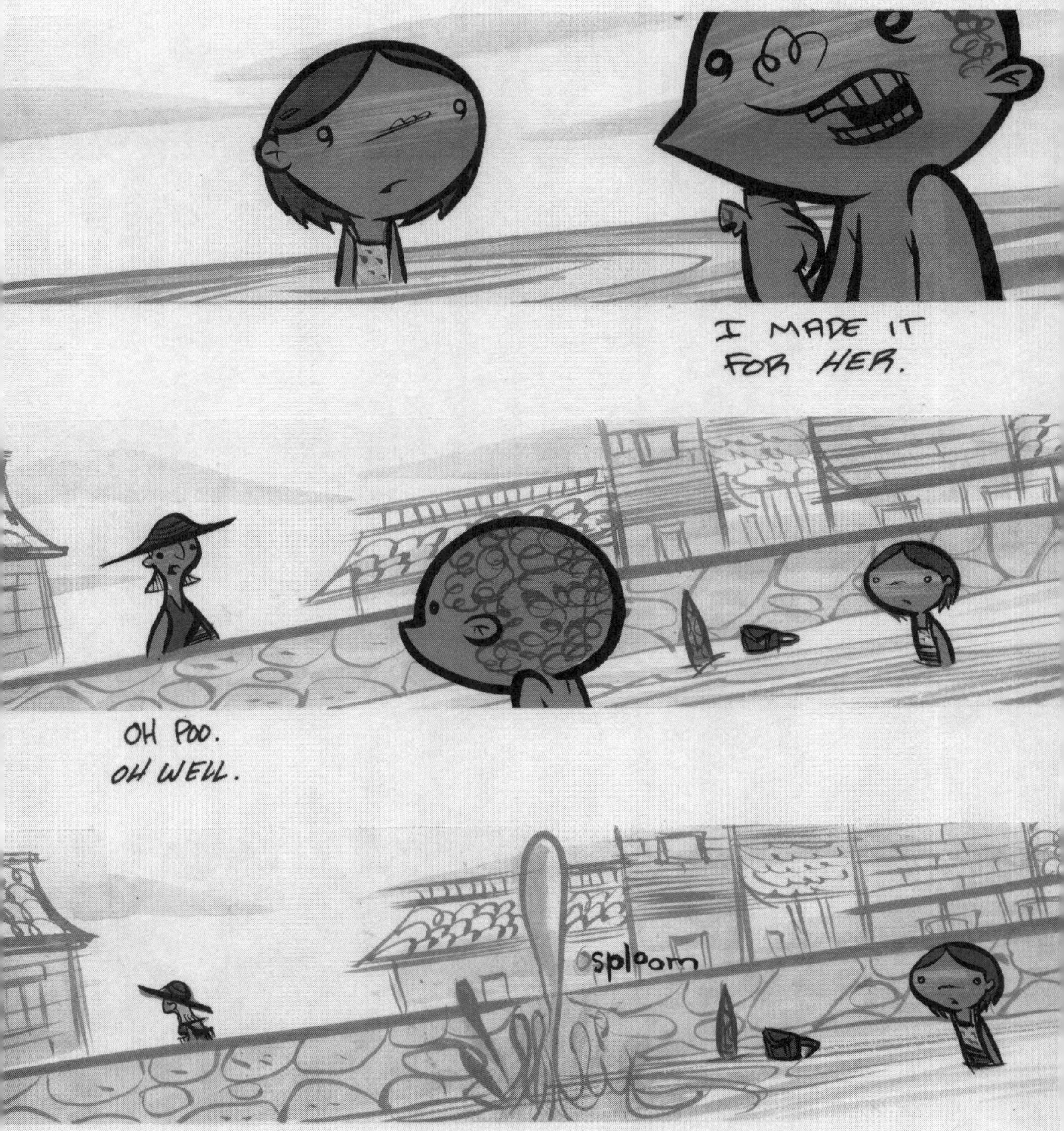
I MADE IT FOR HER.
OH POO. OH WELL.
sploom

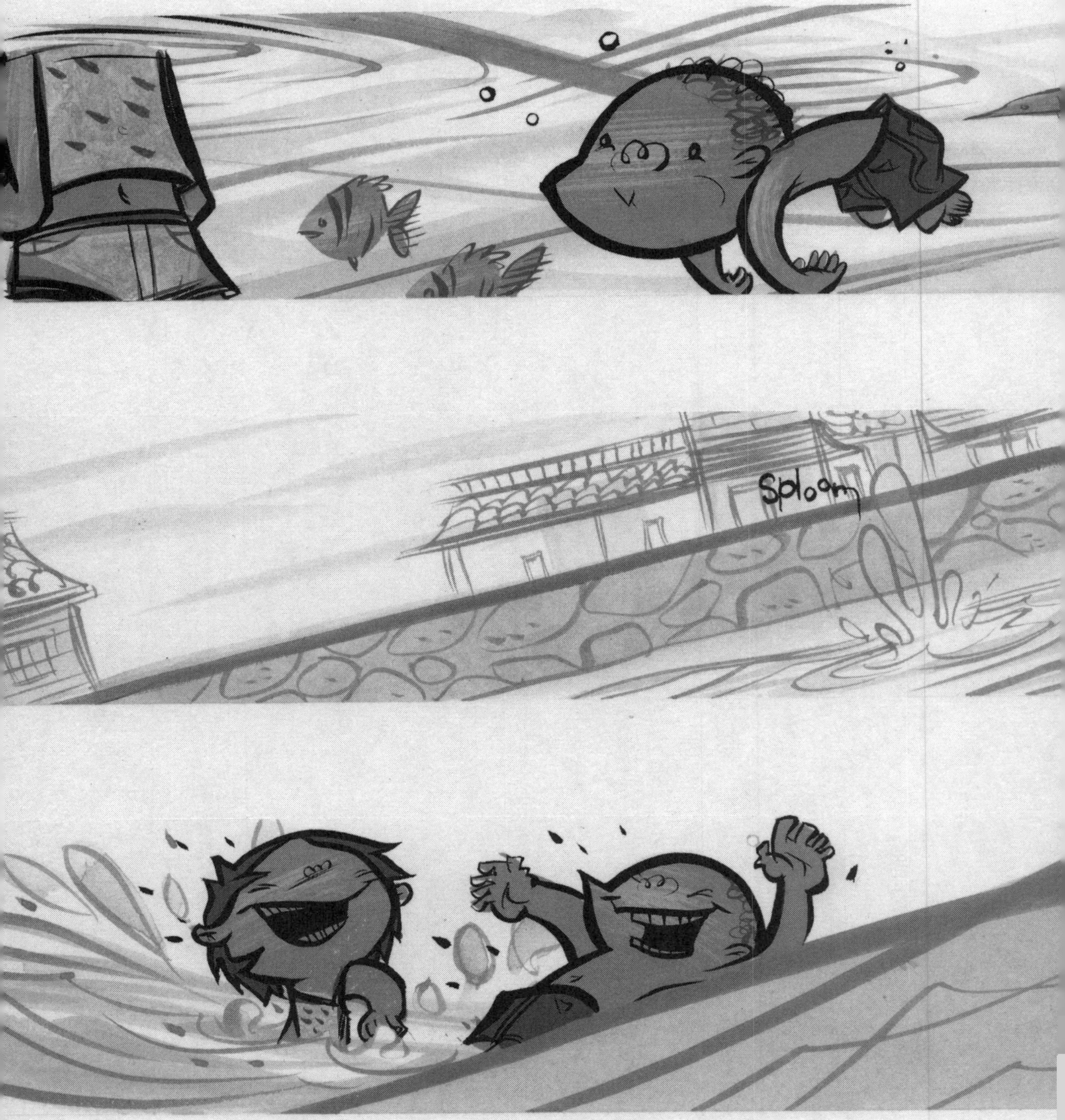
Sploom

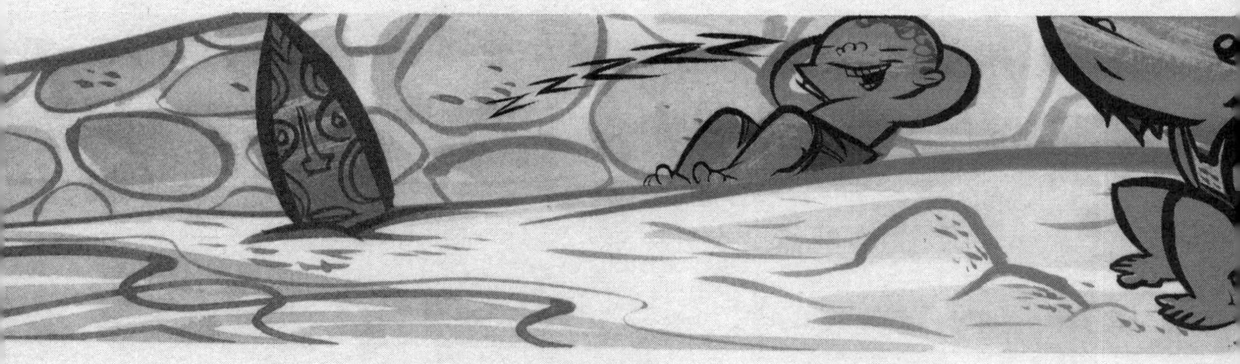

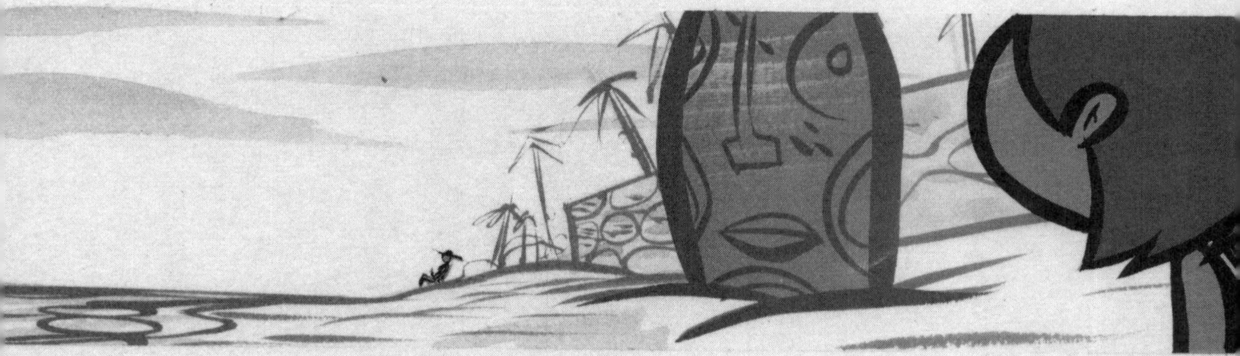

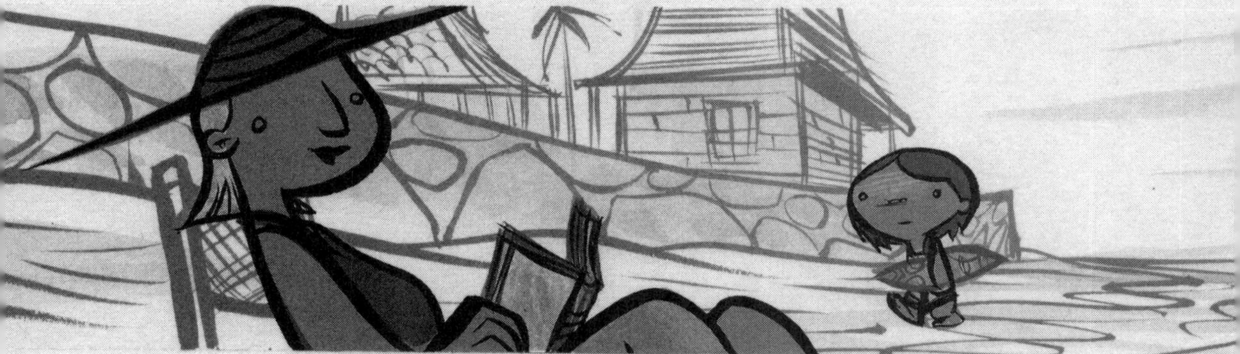

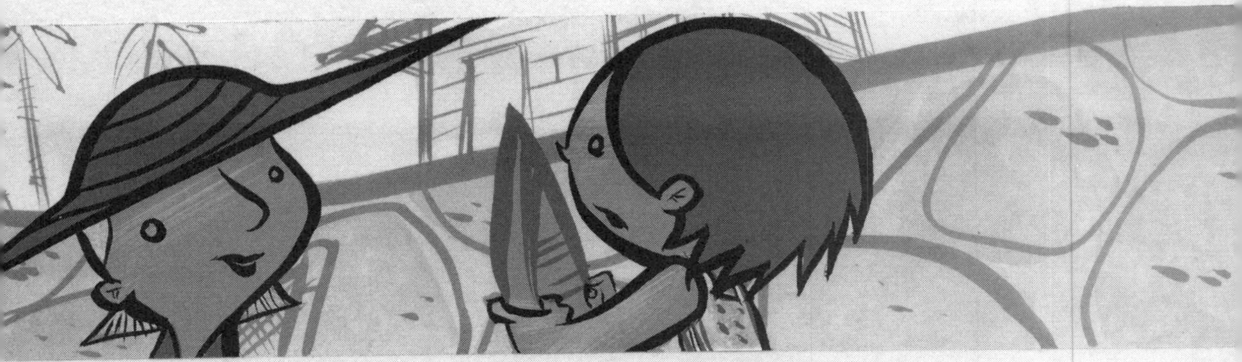

DO YOU REALLY
THINK IT'S BEAUTIFUL?

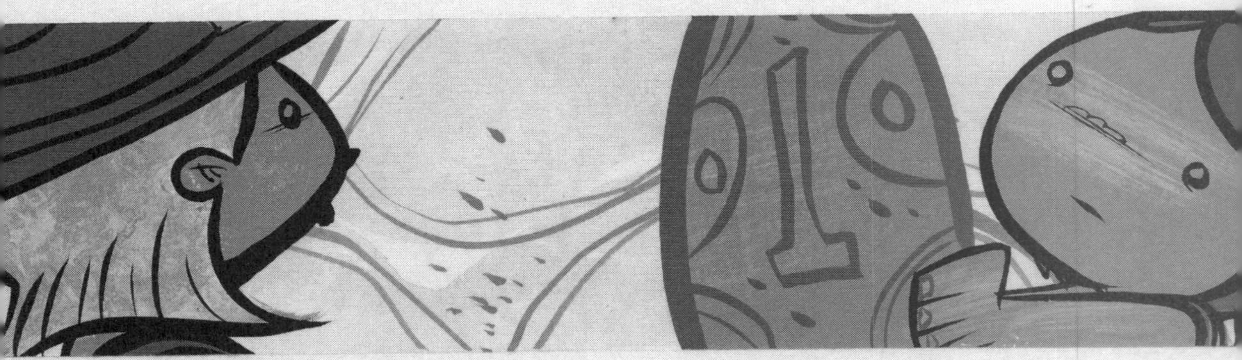

OH, HONEY, I
THINK IT'S PRICELESS.
YOU KNOW...

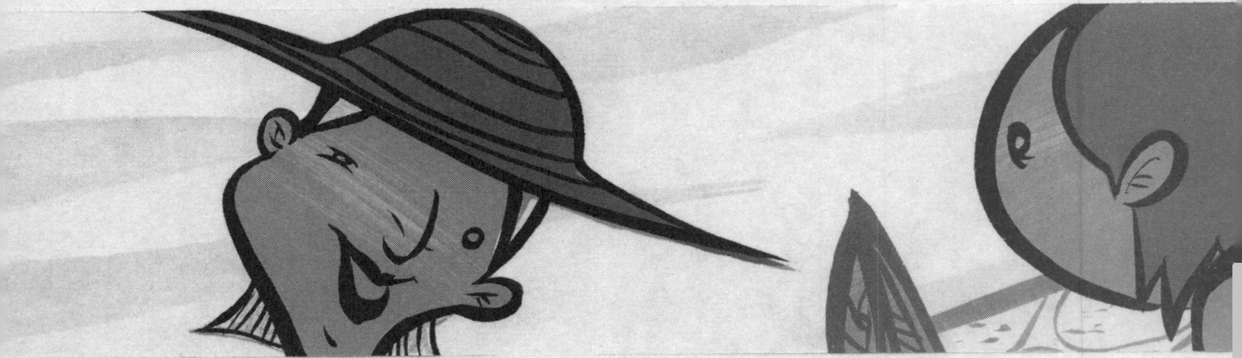

IT KIND OF REMINDS
ME OF MY *BROTHER*.

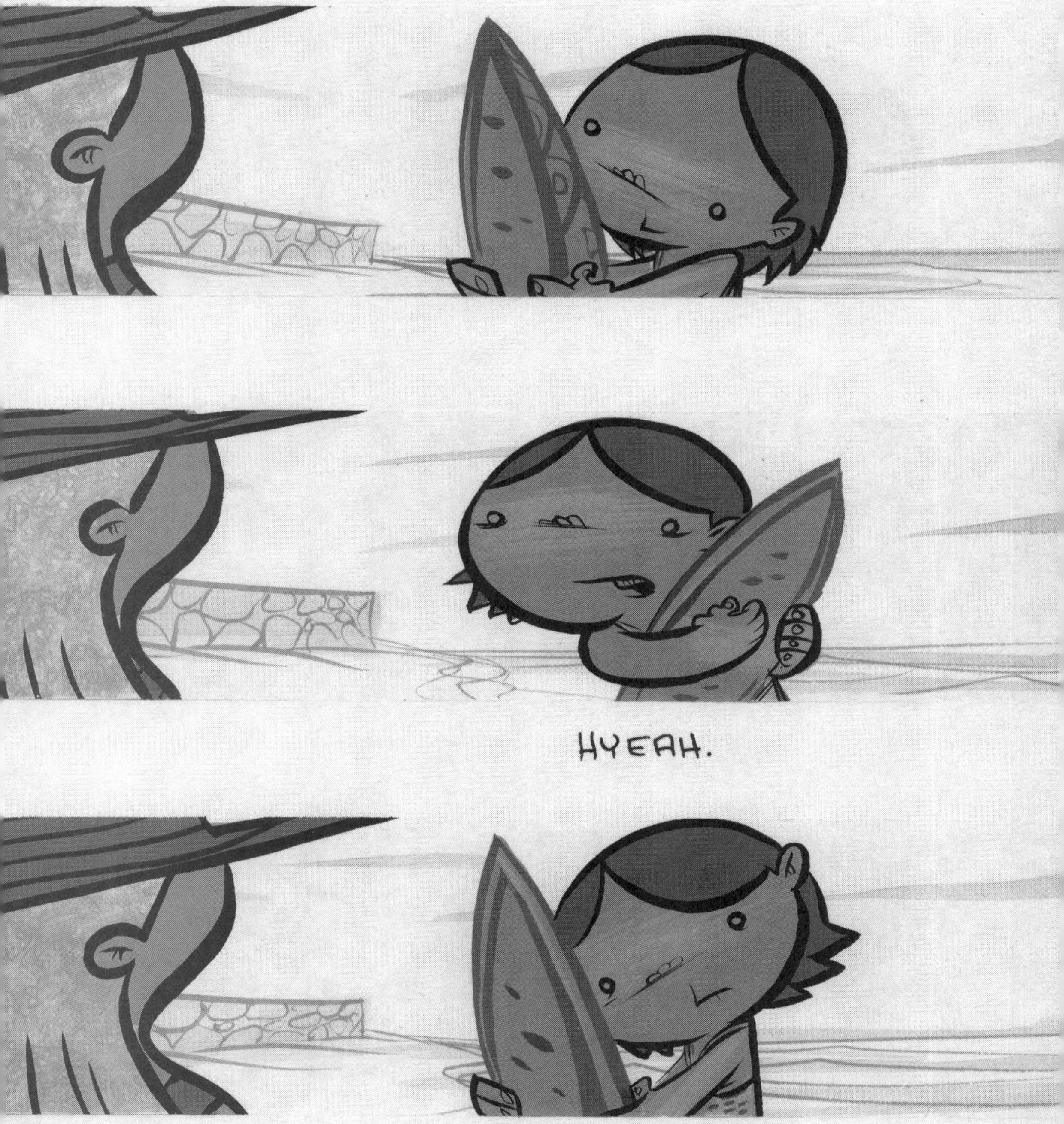
HYEAH.

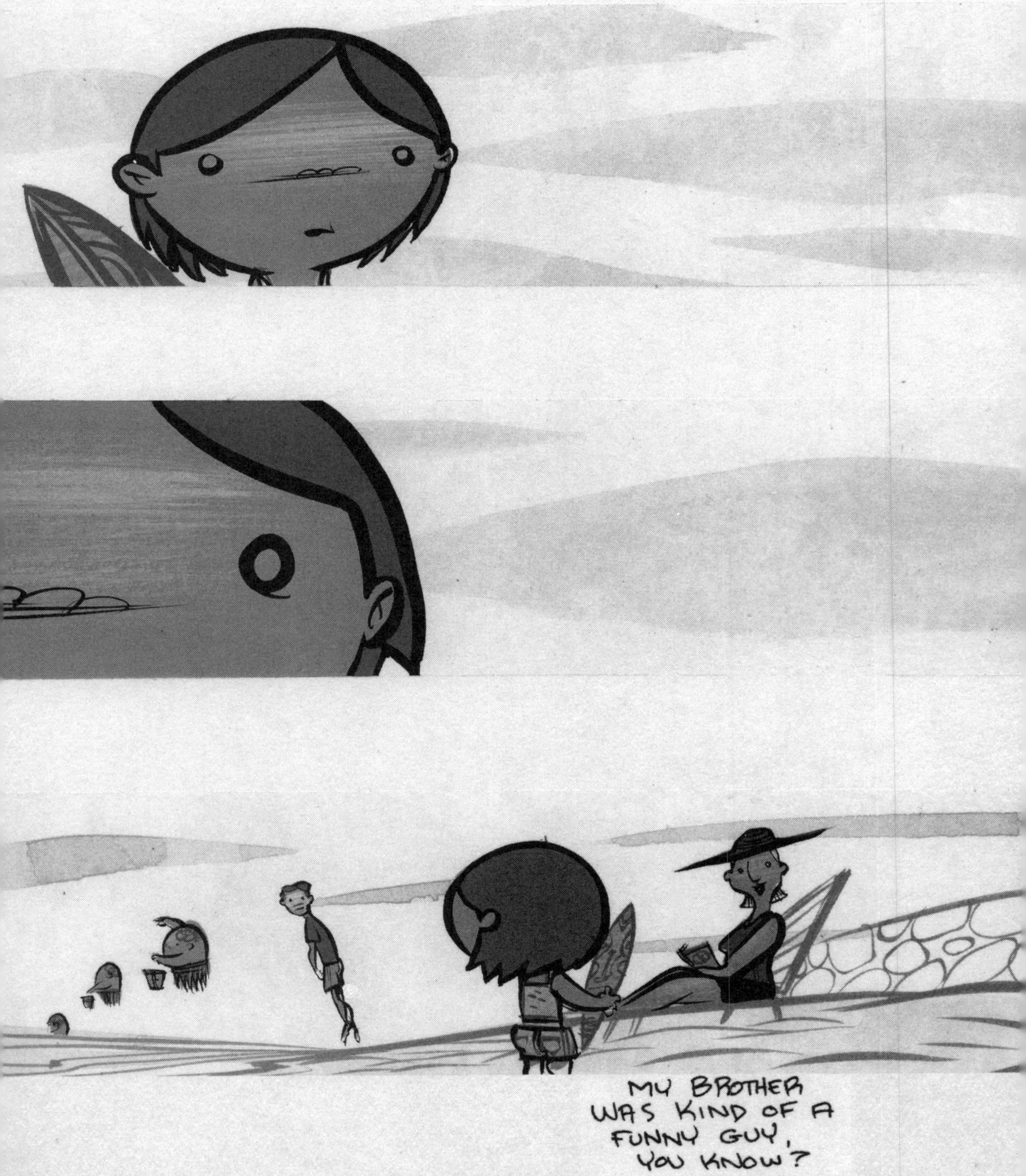
MY BROTHER WAS KIND OF A FUNNY GUY, YOU KNOW?

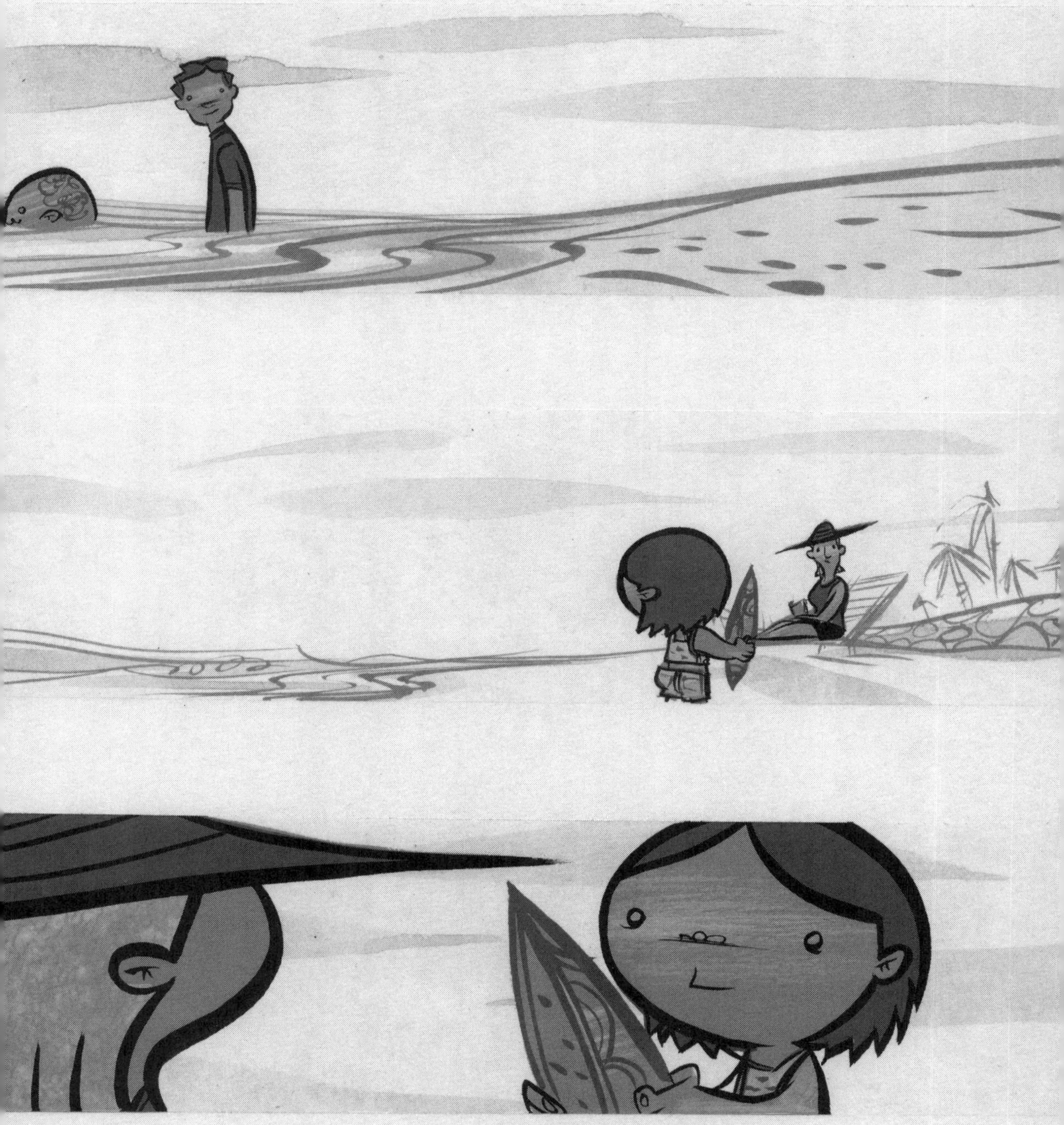

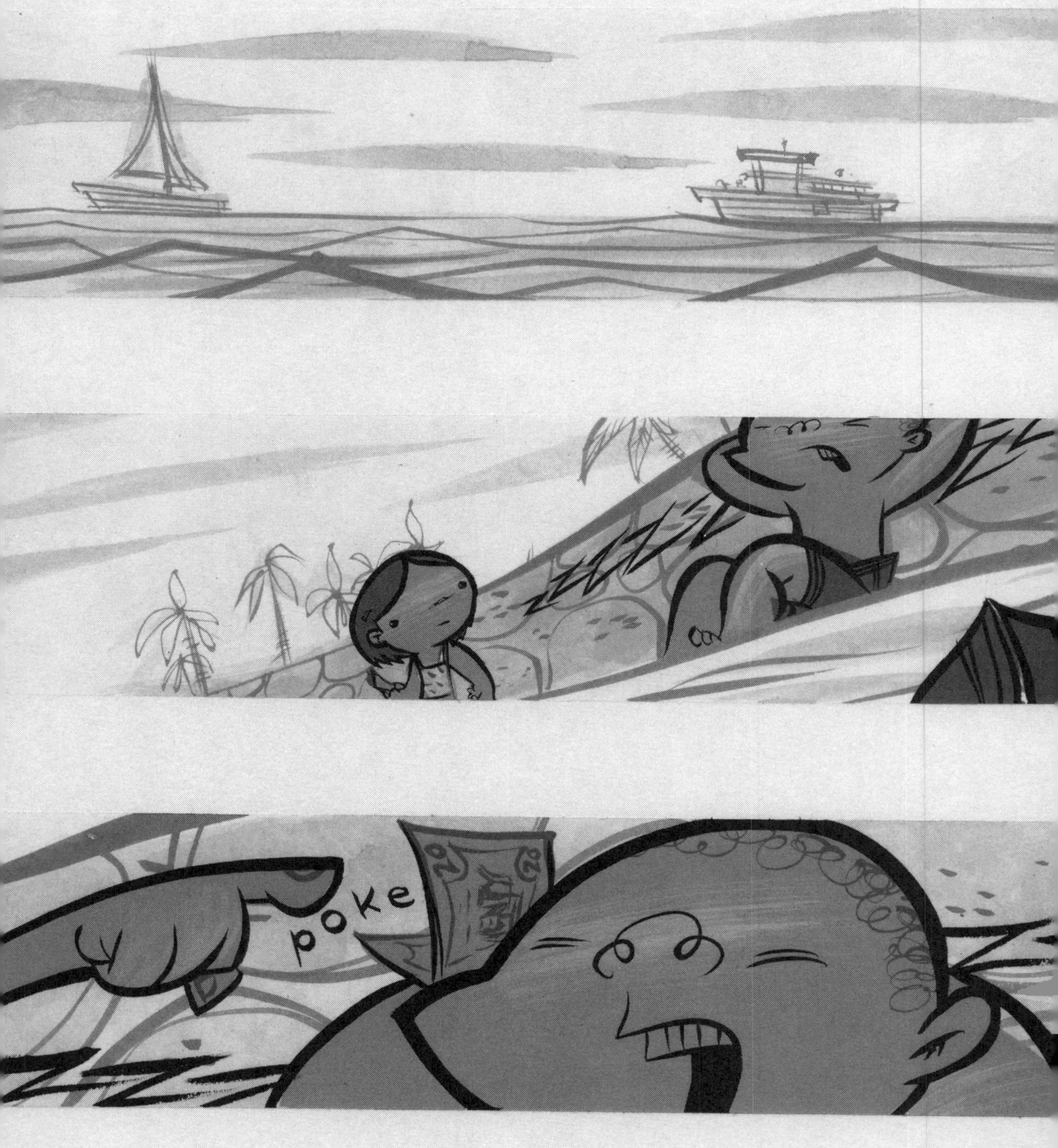
poke

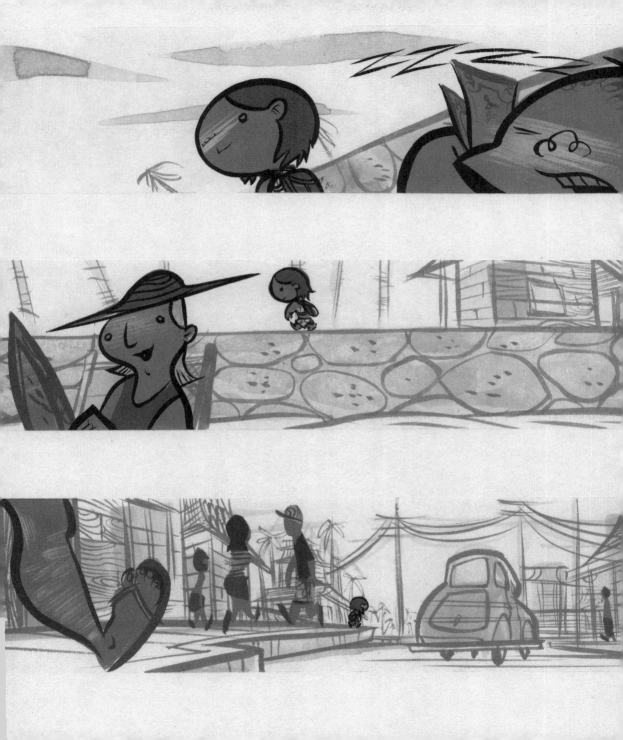

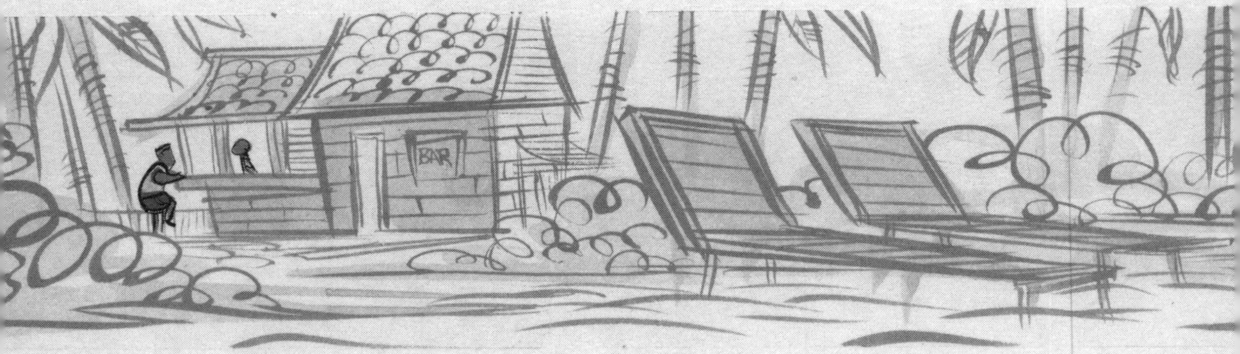
BAR
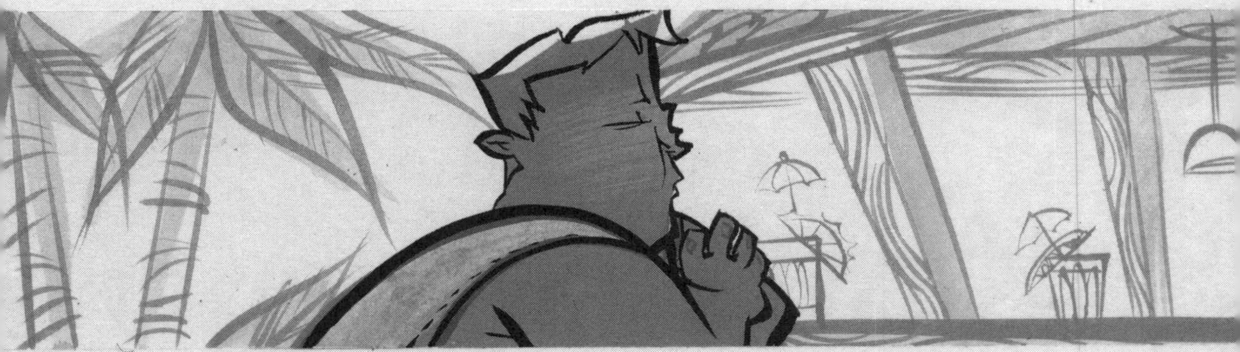
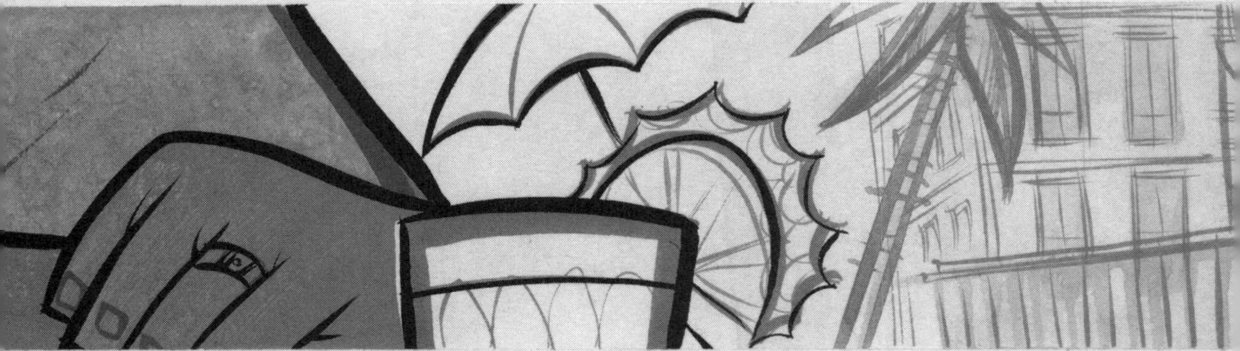

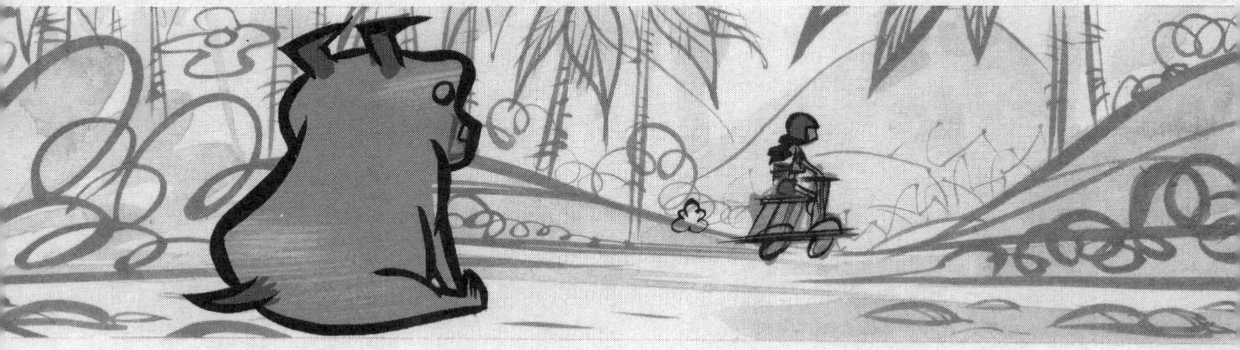
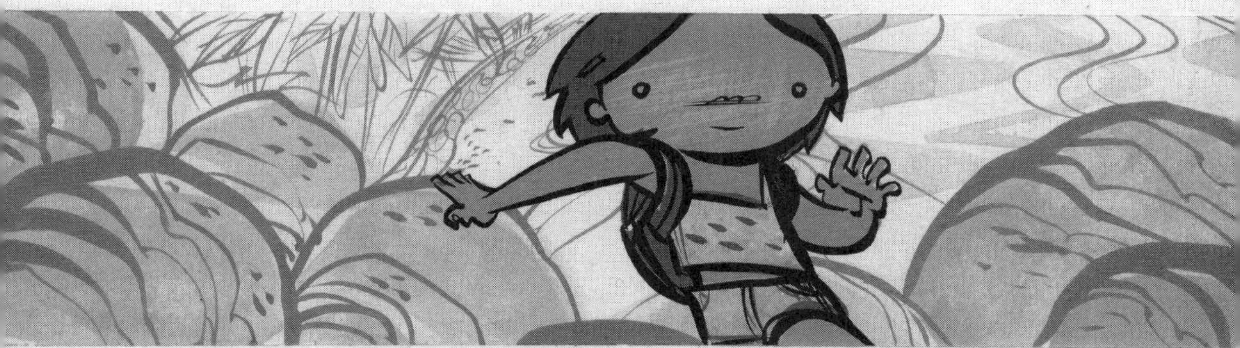
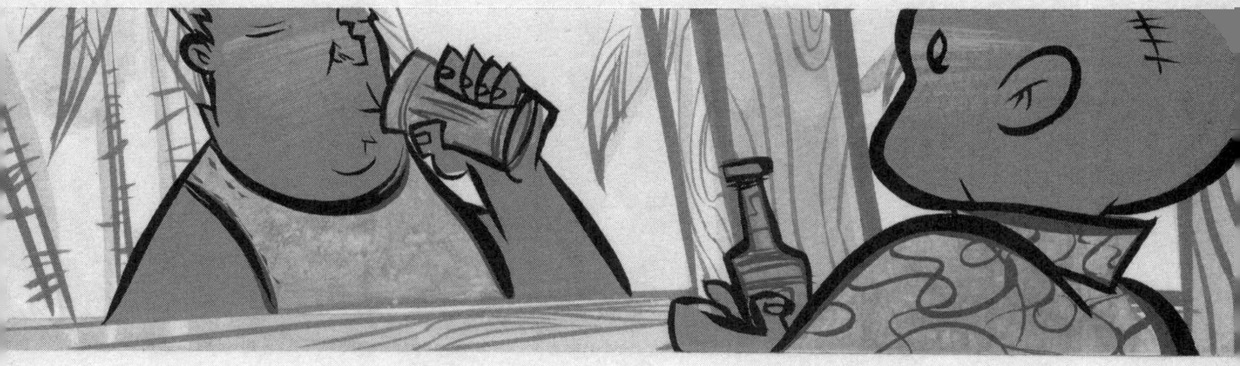

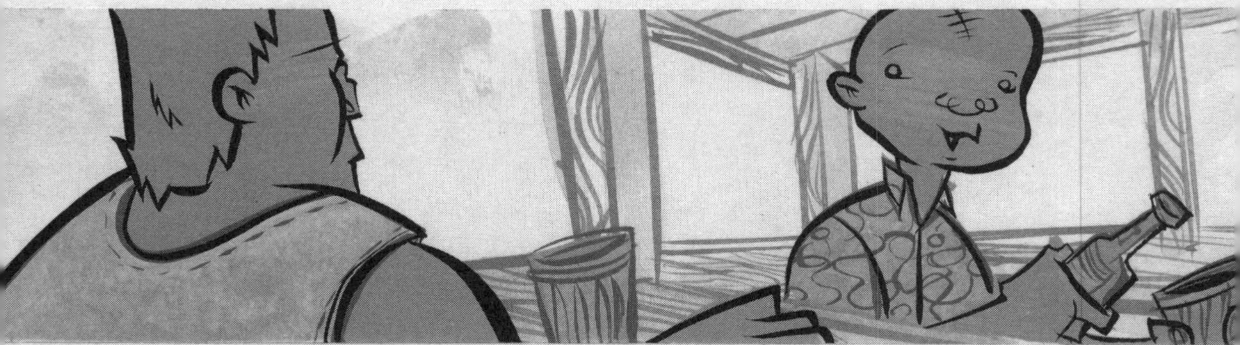

MAI TAI, RIGHT?
WHERE YOU VISITING FROM?

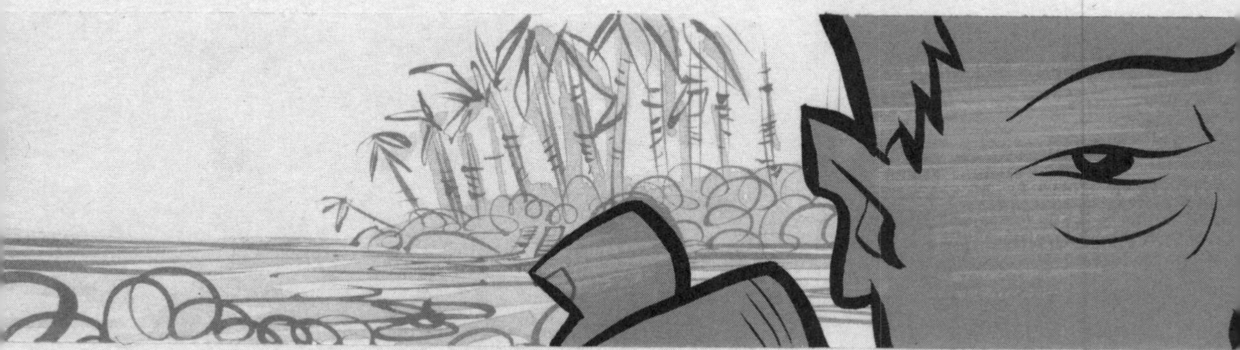

FROM TH' BEACH OVER THERE.

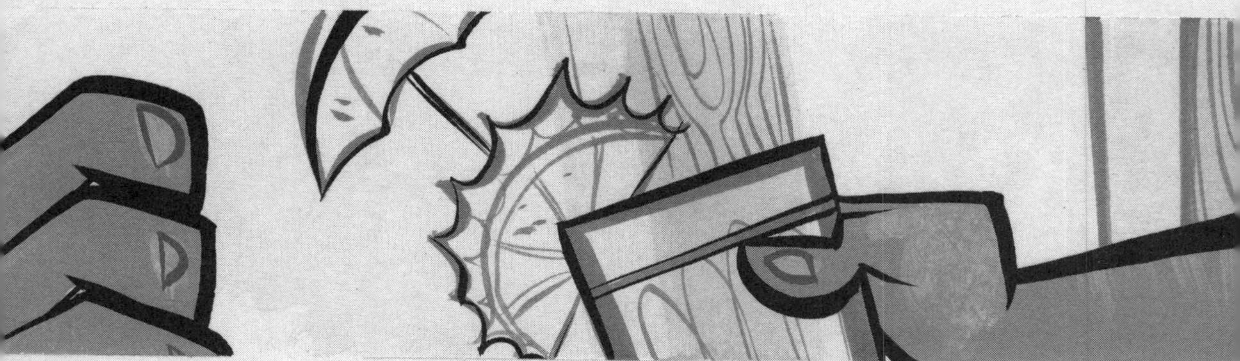

NICE, NICE.
WHAT YOU DO BACK HOME?

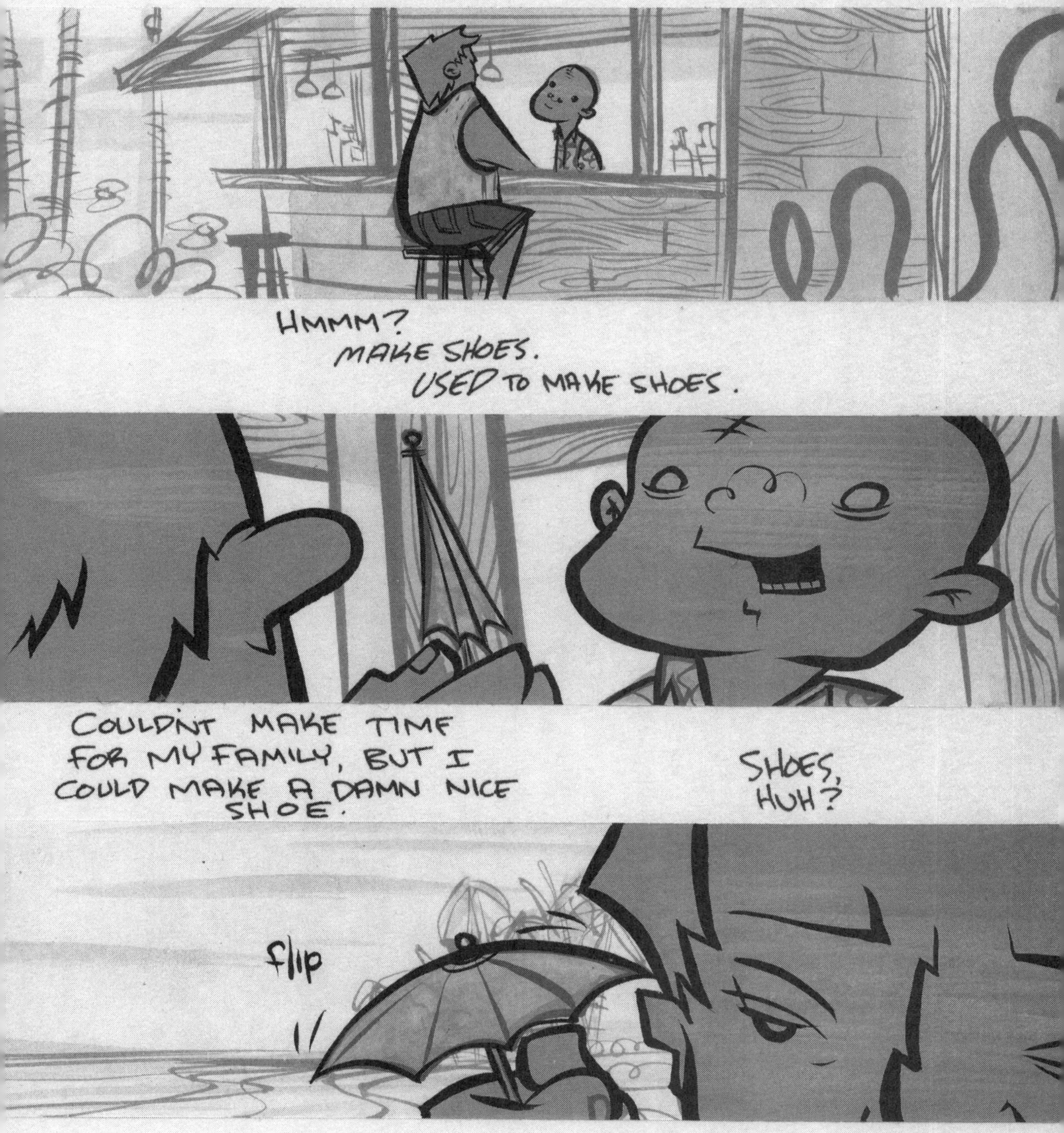
HMMM?
MAKE SHOES.
USED TO MAKE SHOES.
COULDN'T MAKE TIME FOR MY FAMILY, BUT I COULD MAKE A DAMN NICE SHOE.
SHOES, HUH?
flip

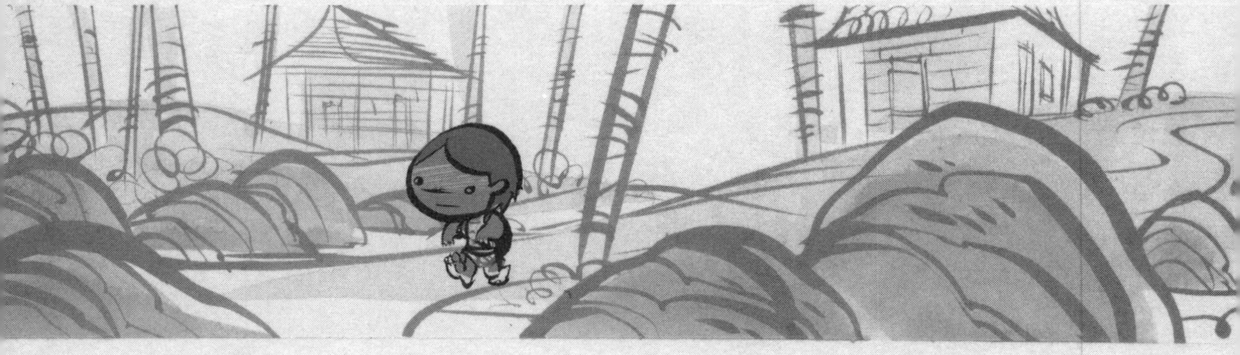

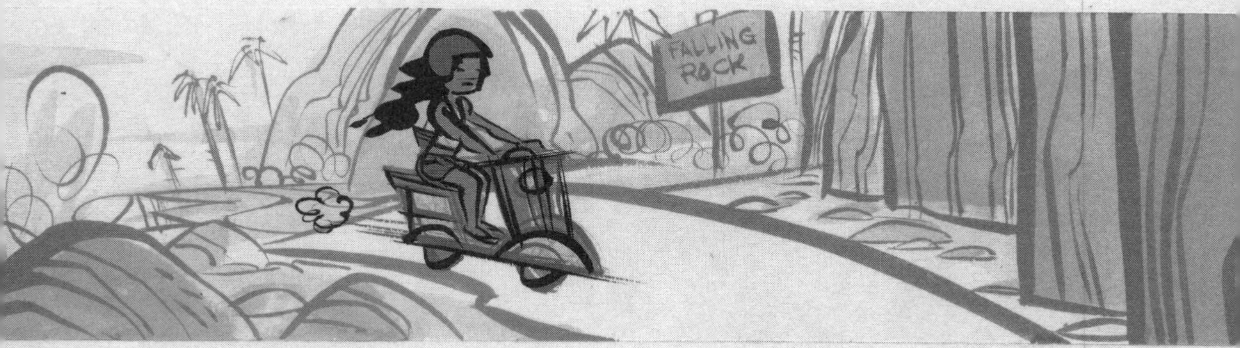
FALLING
ROCK

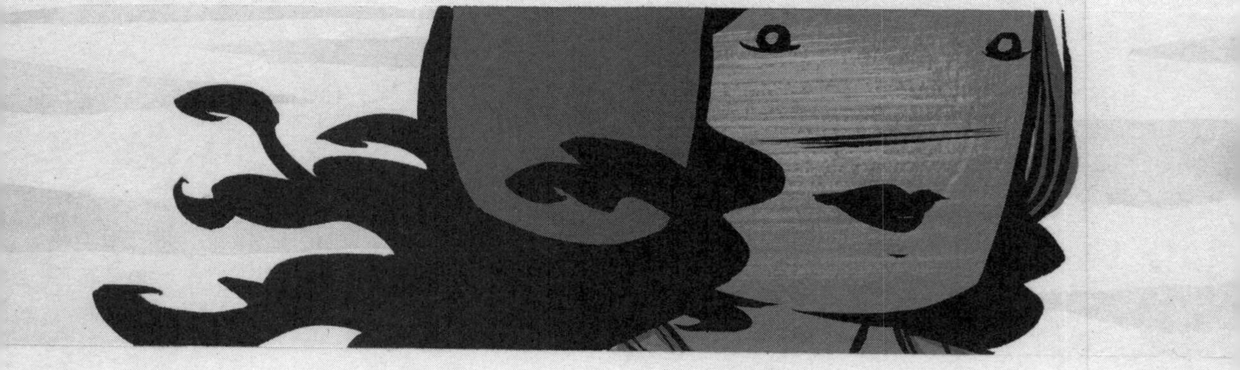

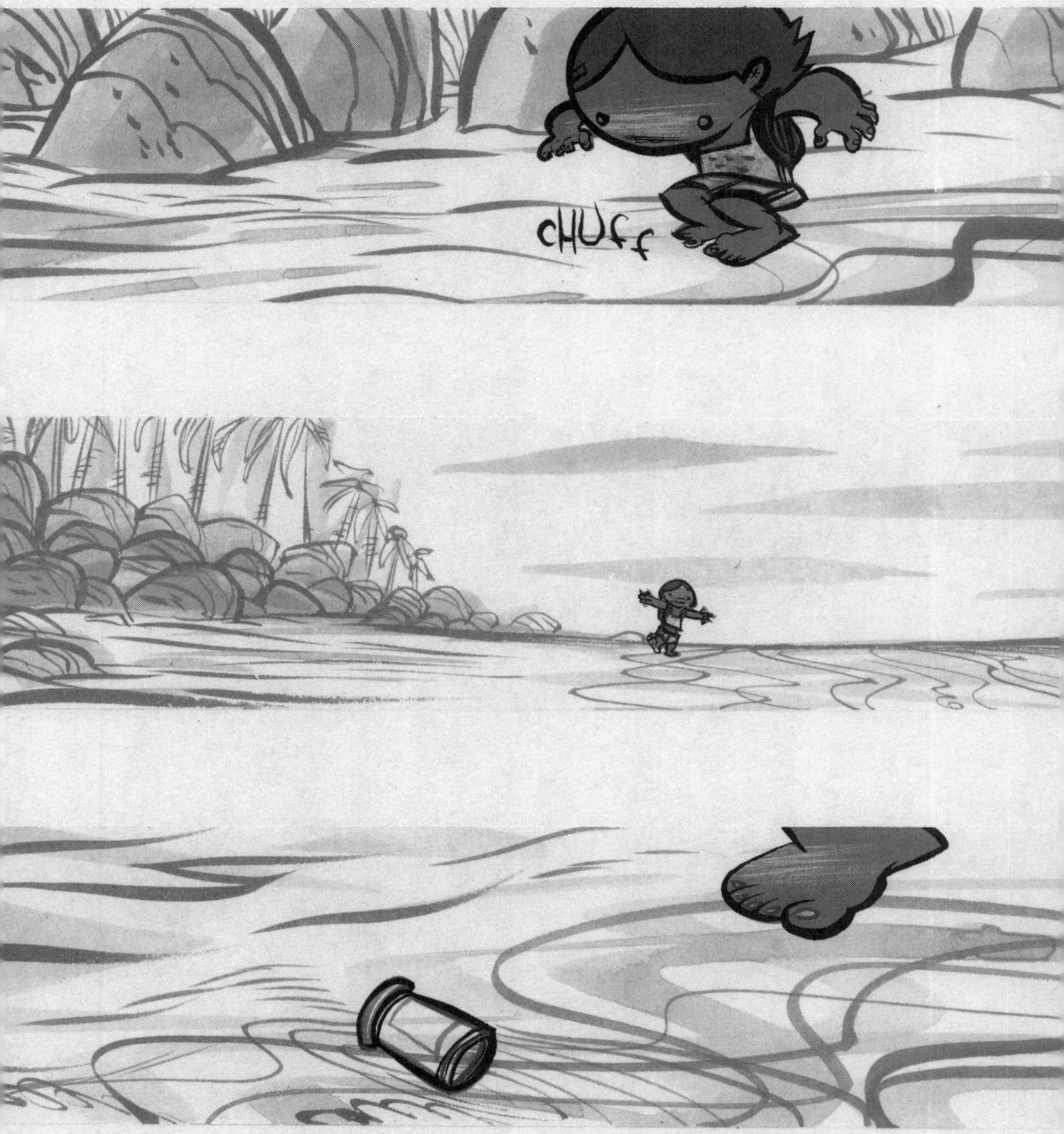
CHUFF

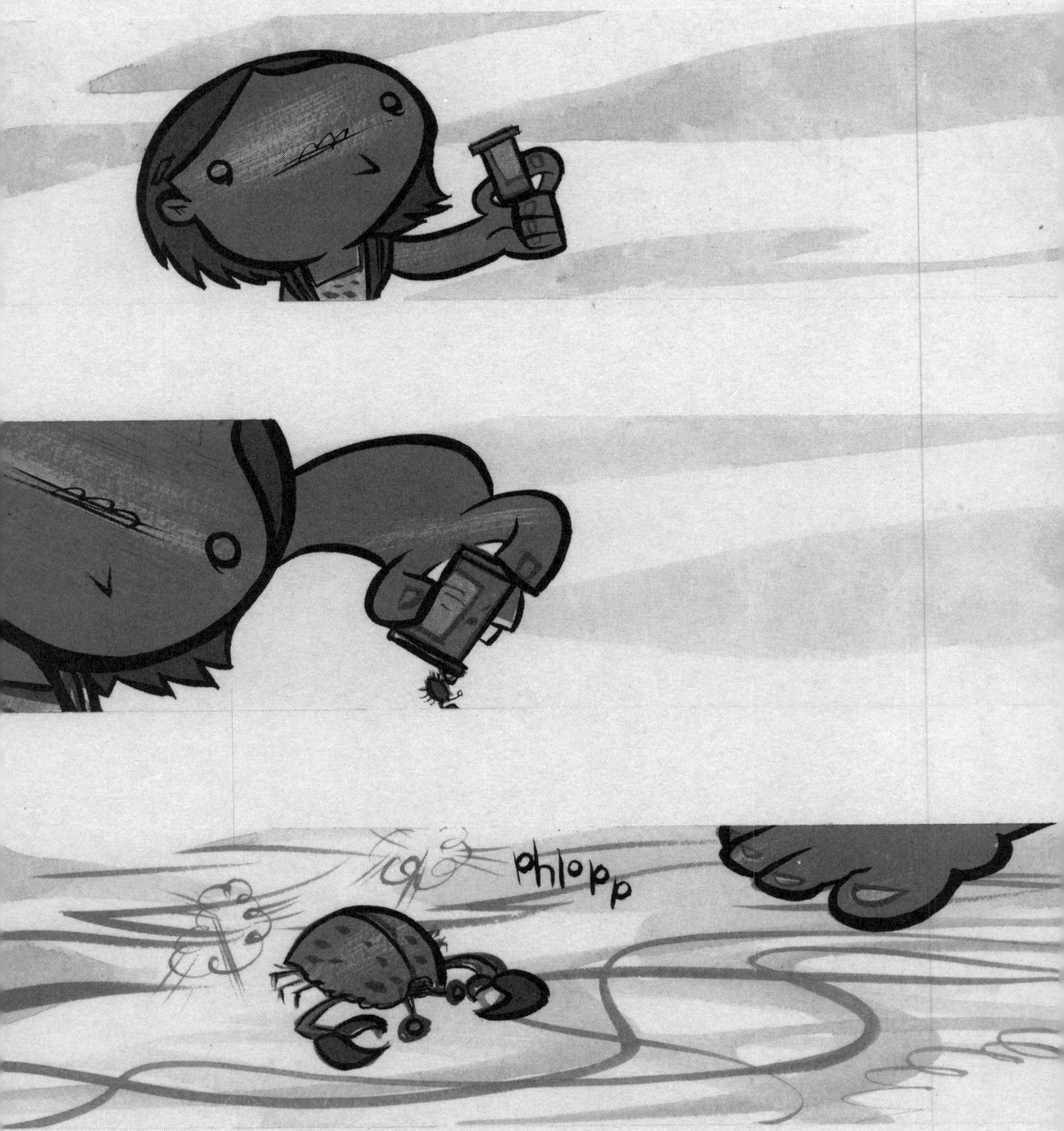
phlopp

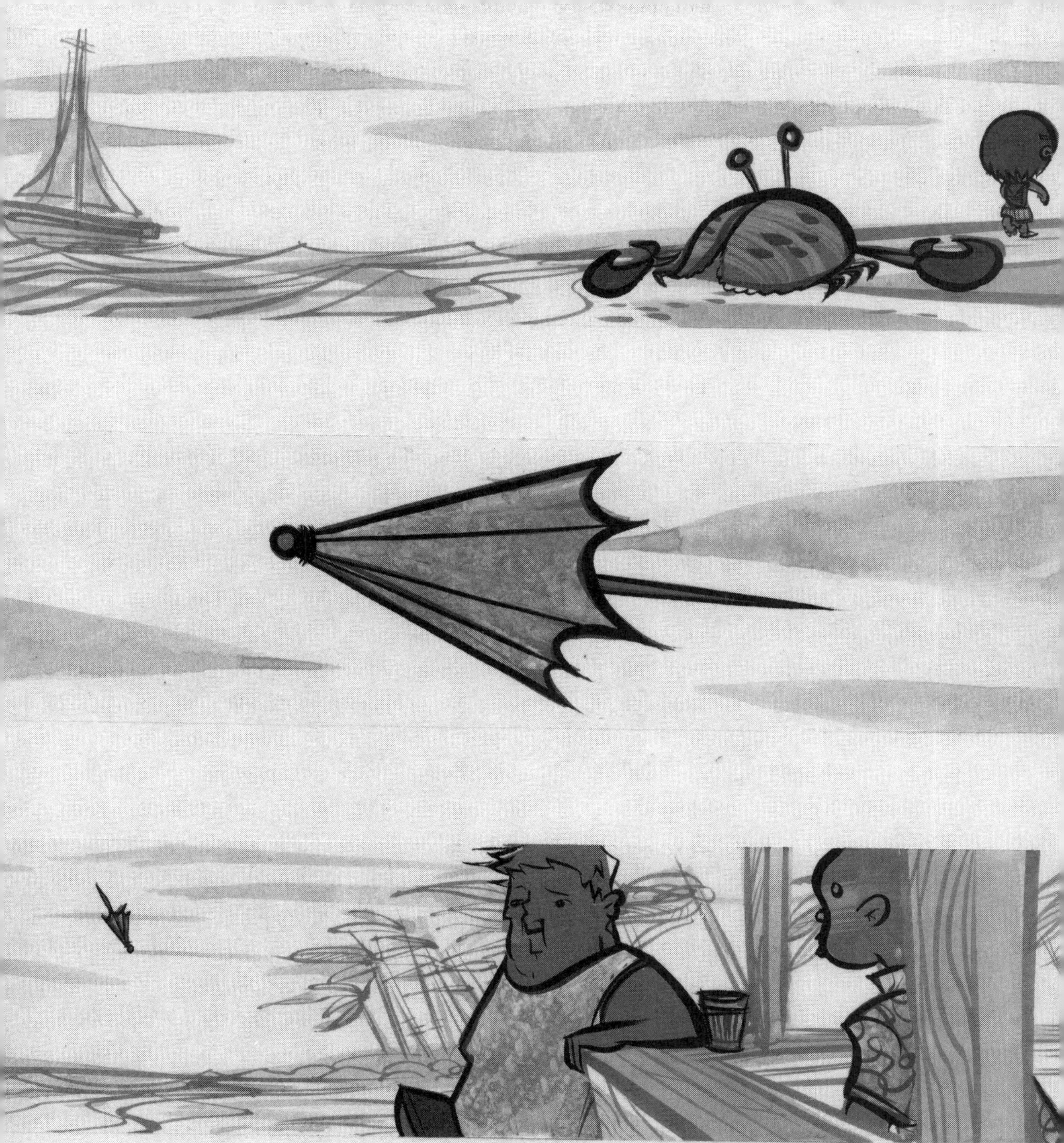

GOTTA WATCH OUT
FOR DEM TRADE
WINDS.

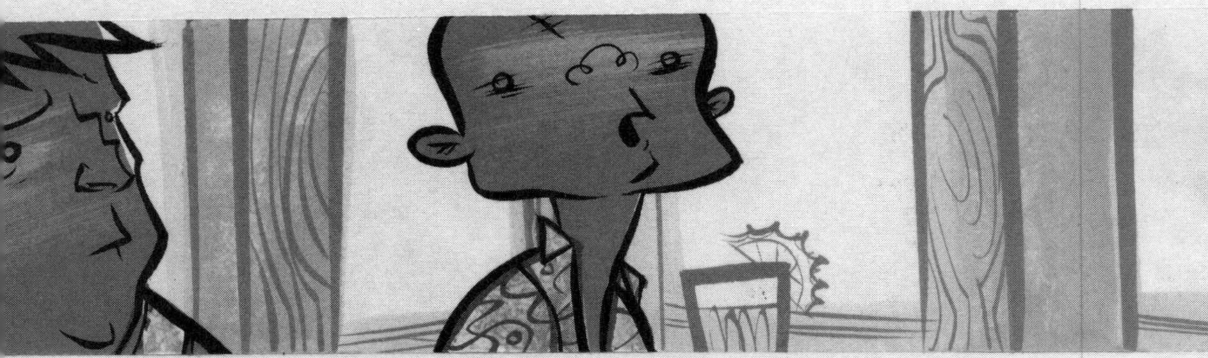

DEY KICK UP
EVERY NOW
AN' DEN.

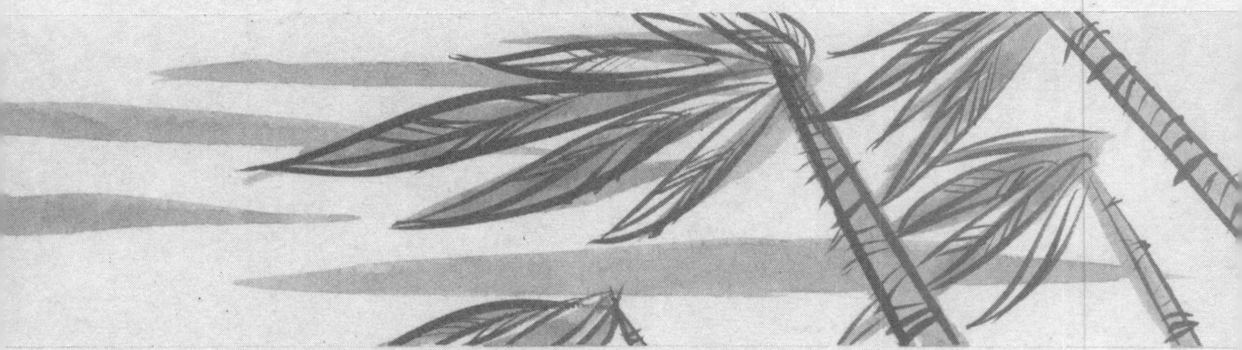

BLOW *SCARY* SOMETIMES.

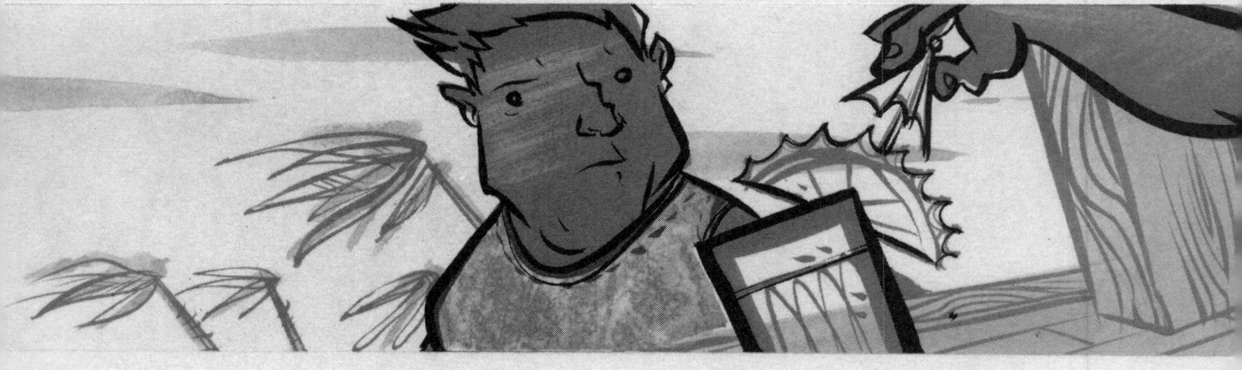

BUT IT AINT
NEVER TOO BAD.

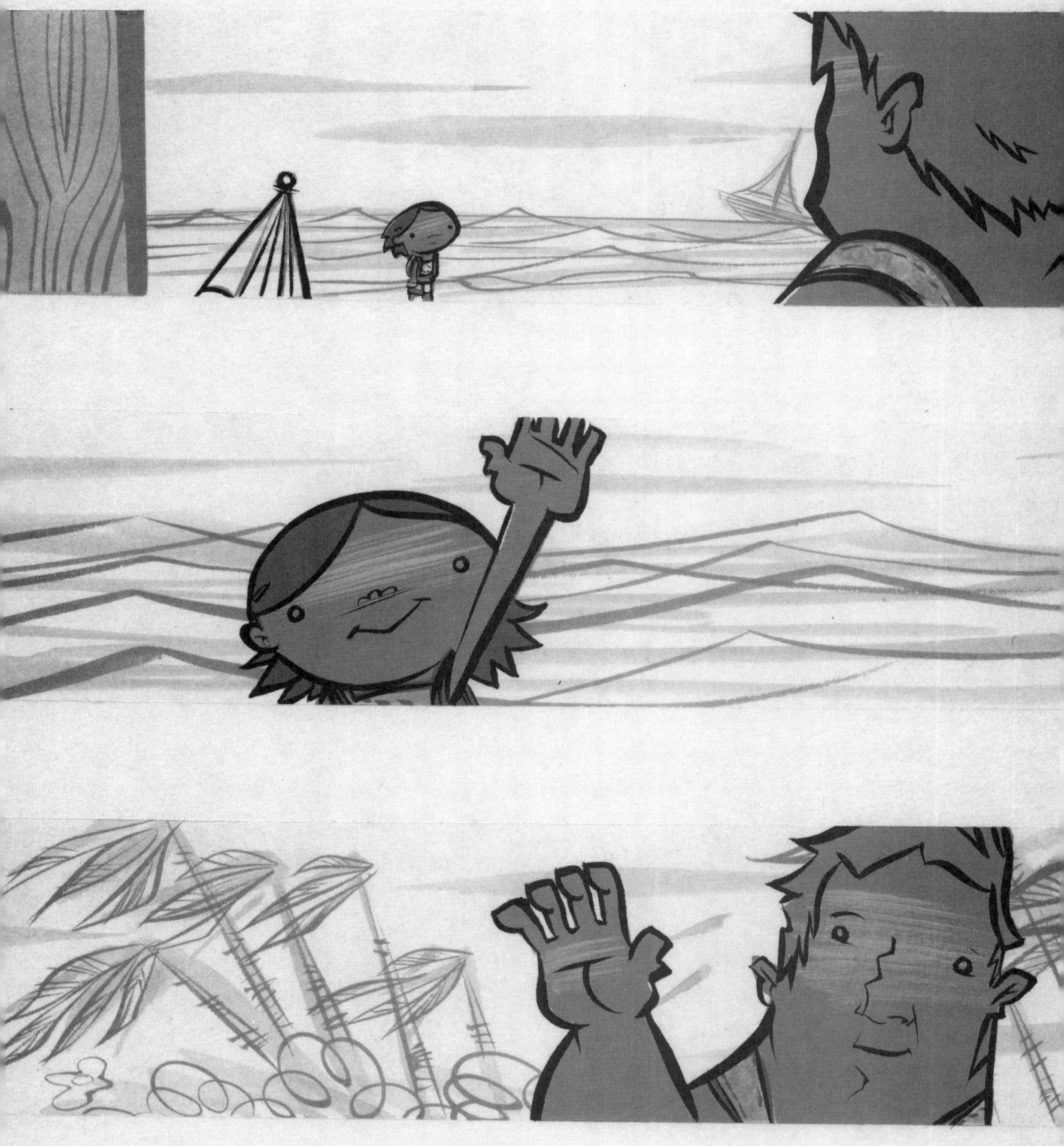

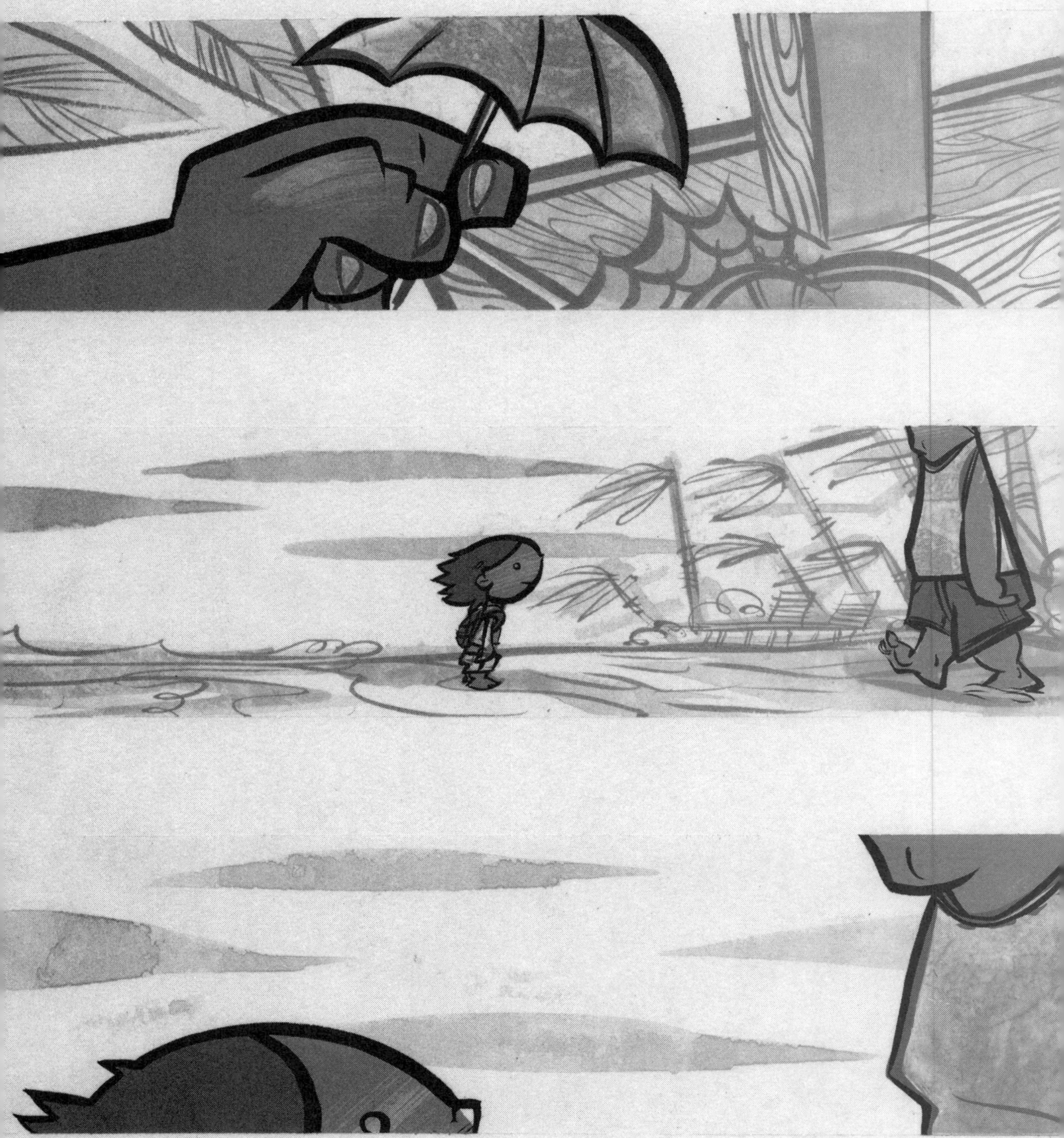

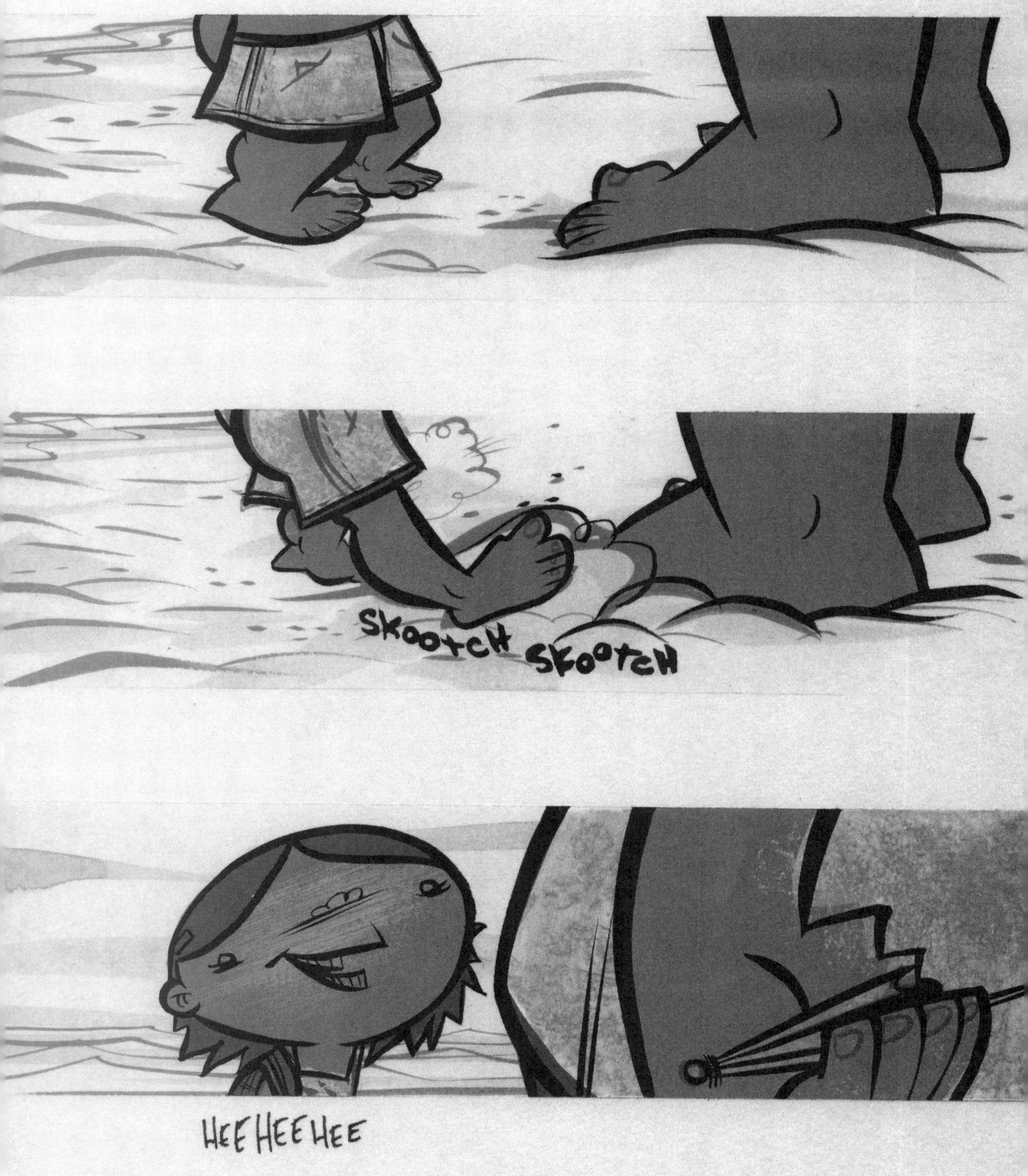
SKOOTCH SKOOTCH
HEE HEE HEE

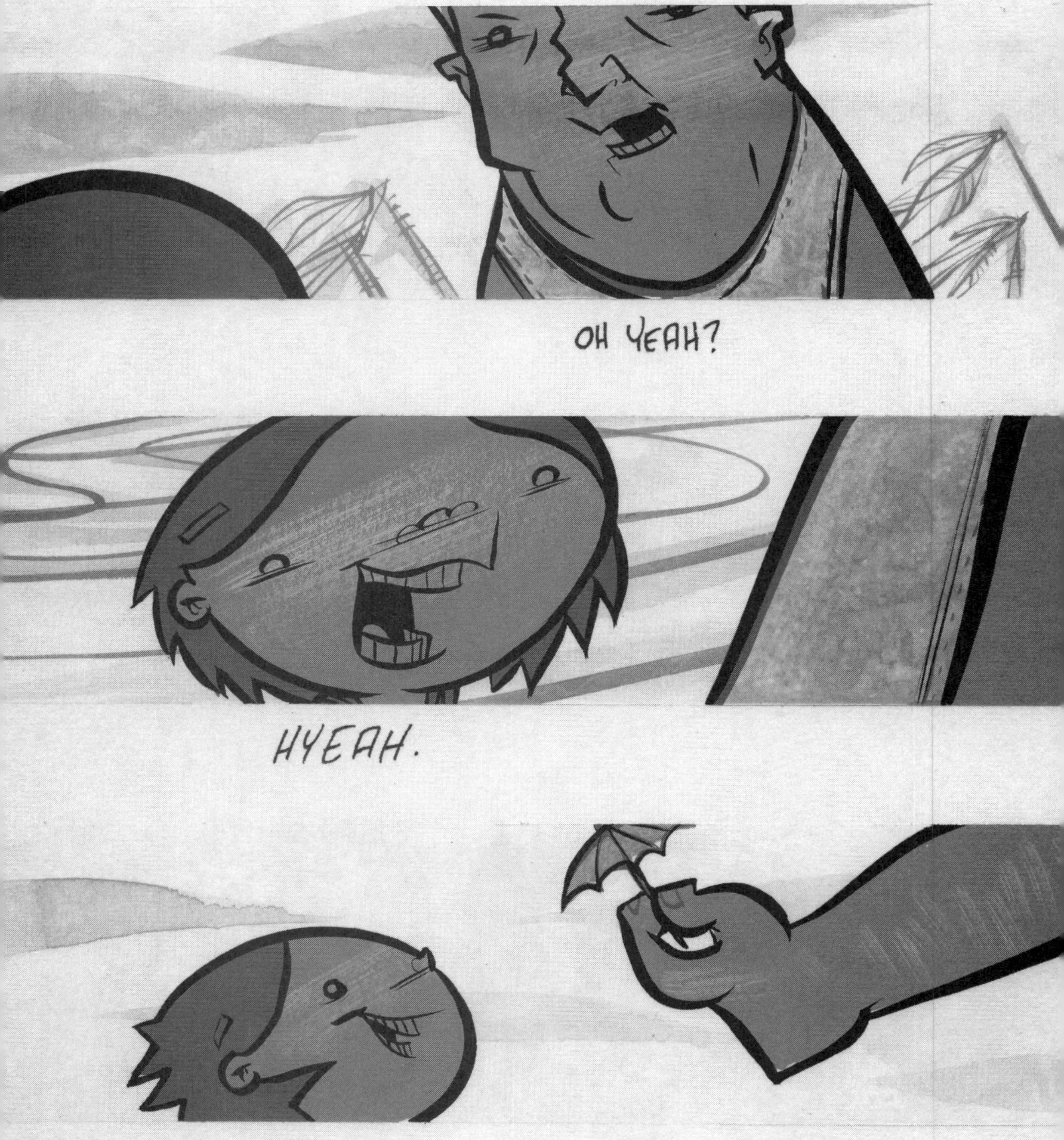
OH YEAH?
HYEAH.

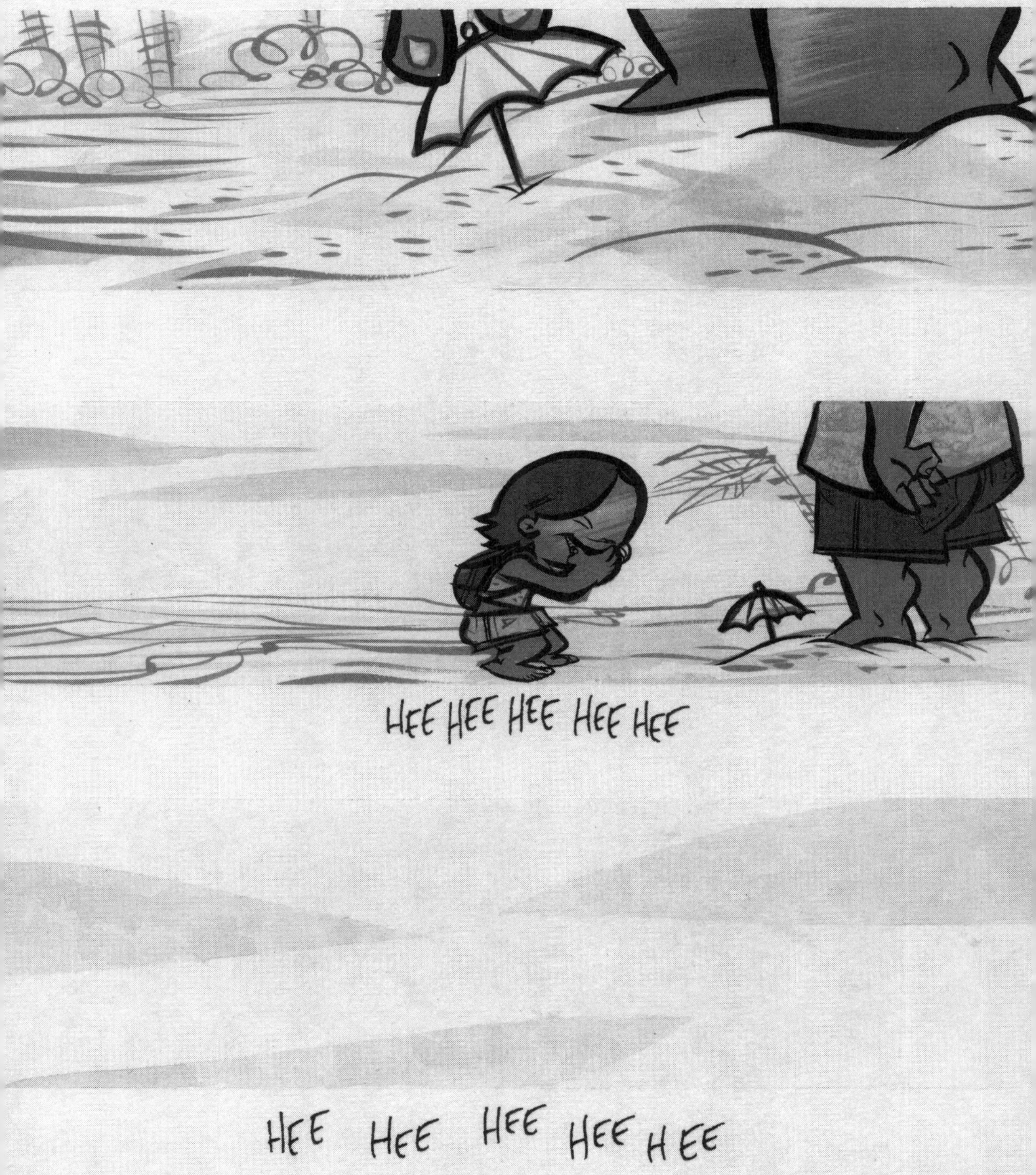
HEE HEE HEE HEE HEE
HEE HEE HEE HEE HEE

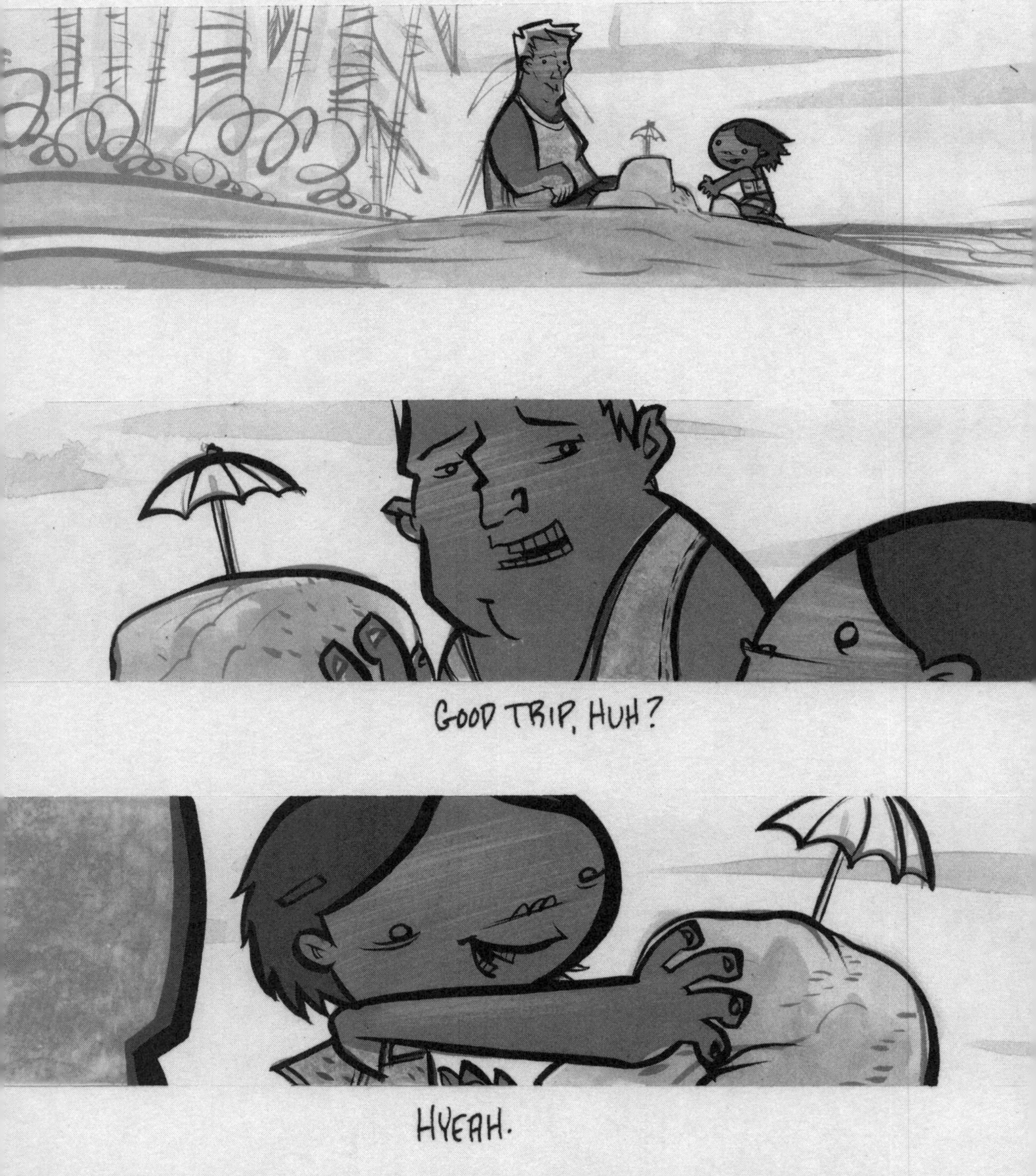
GOOD TRIP, HUH?
HYEAH.

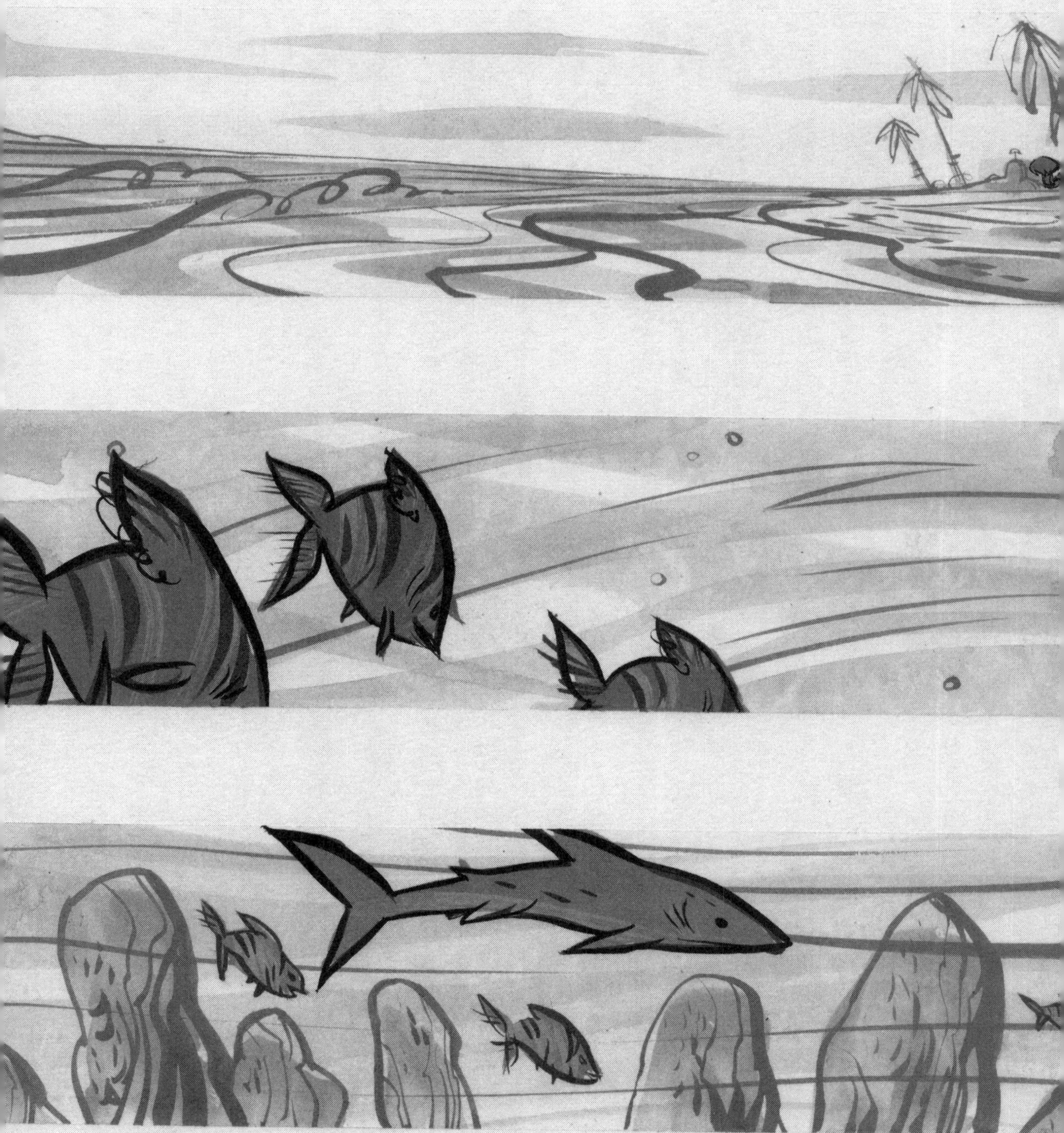

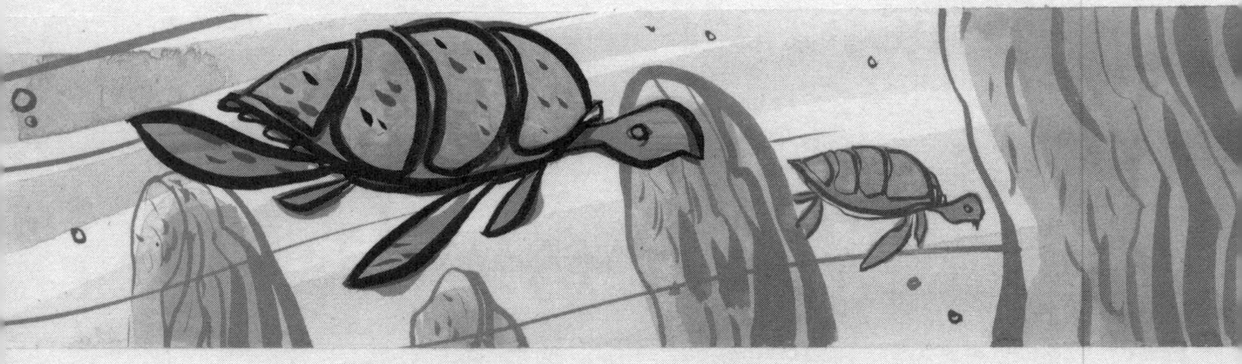
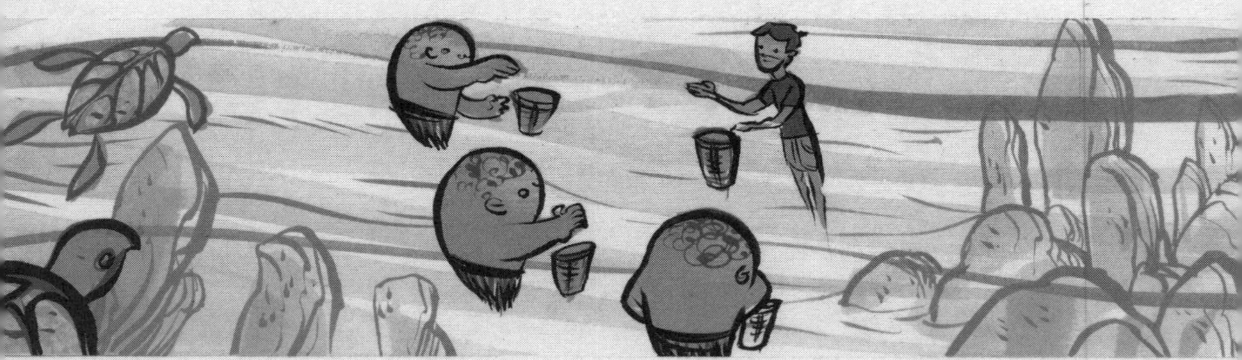
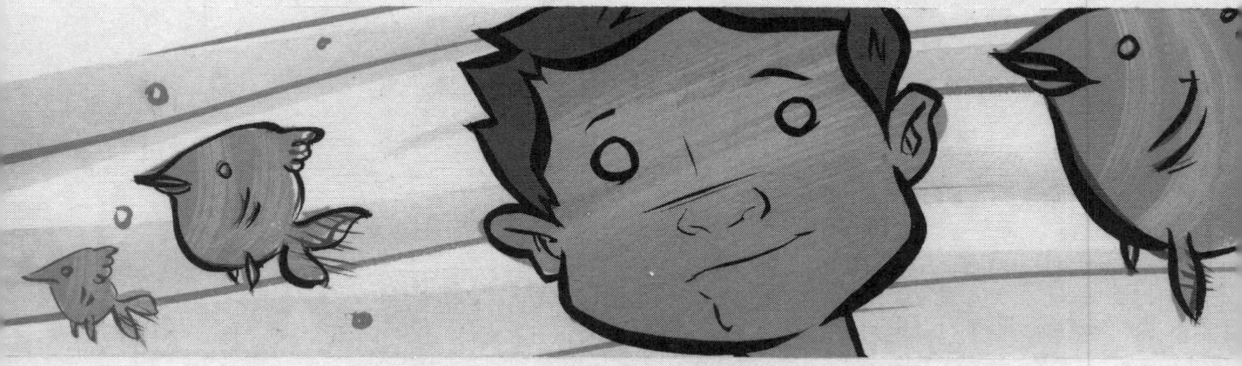

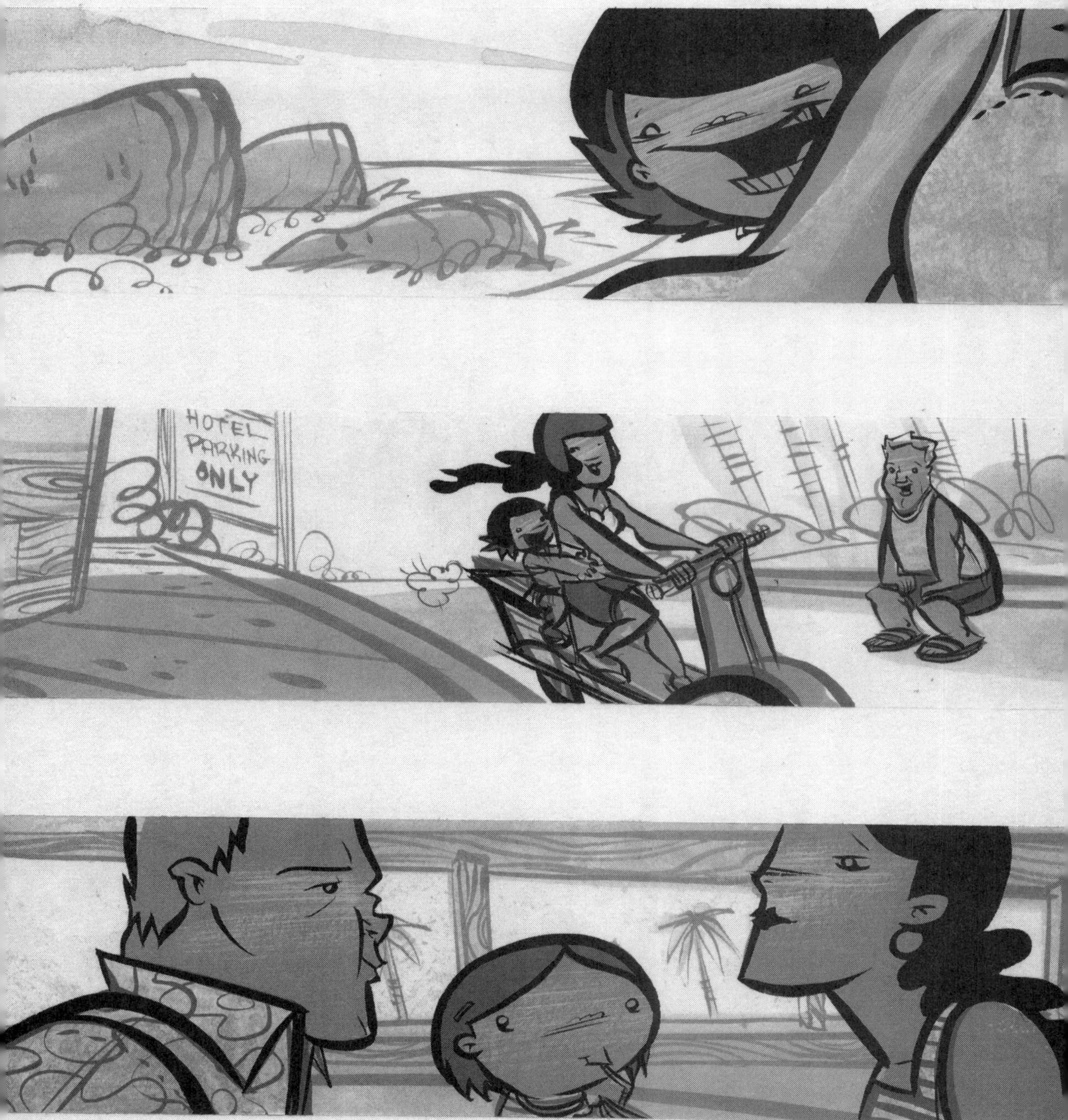
HOTEL
PARKING
ONLY

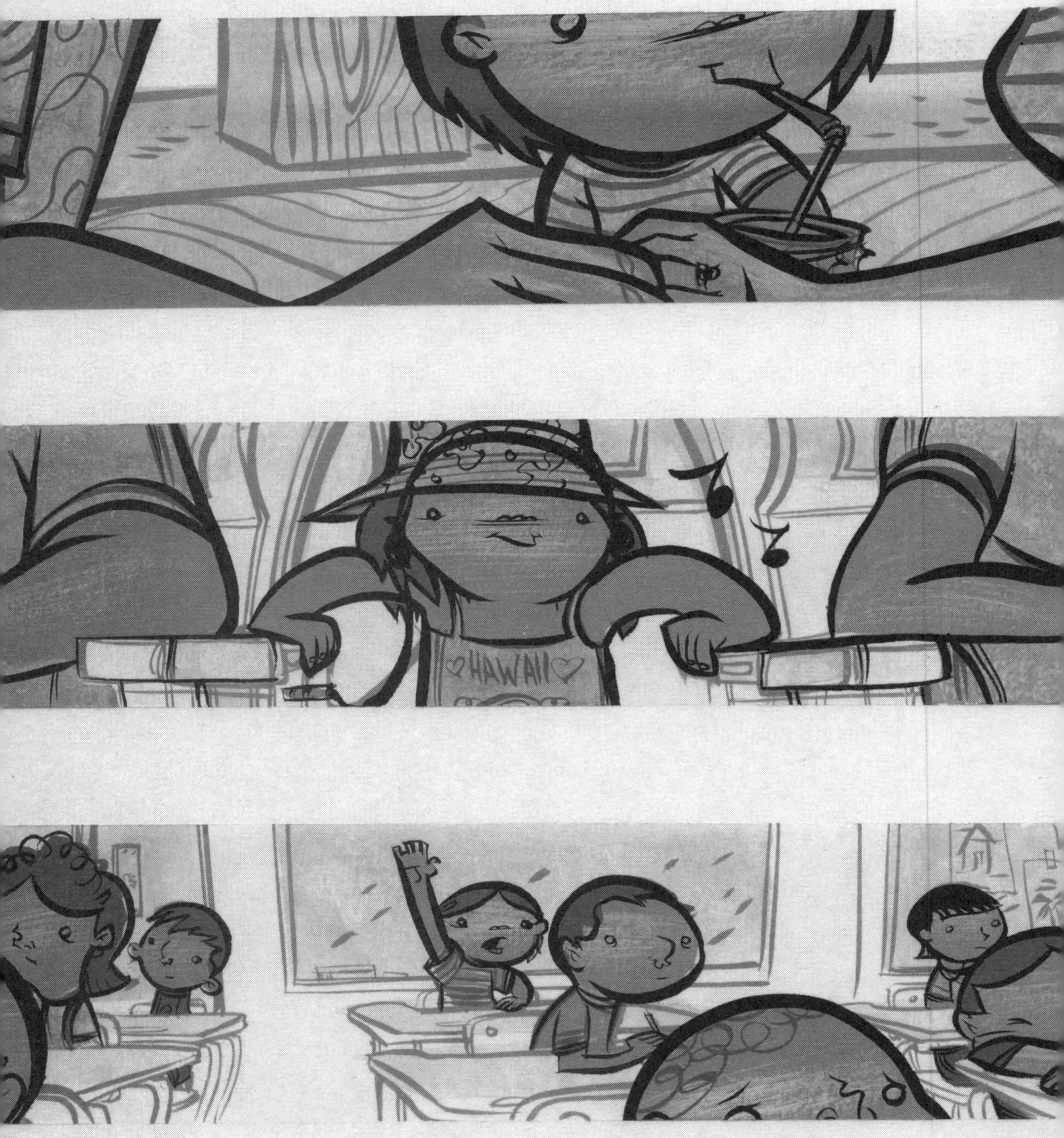
HAWAII

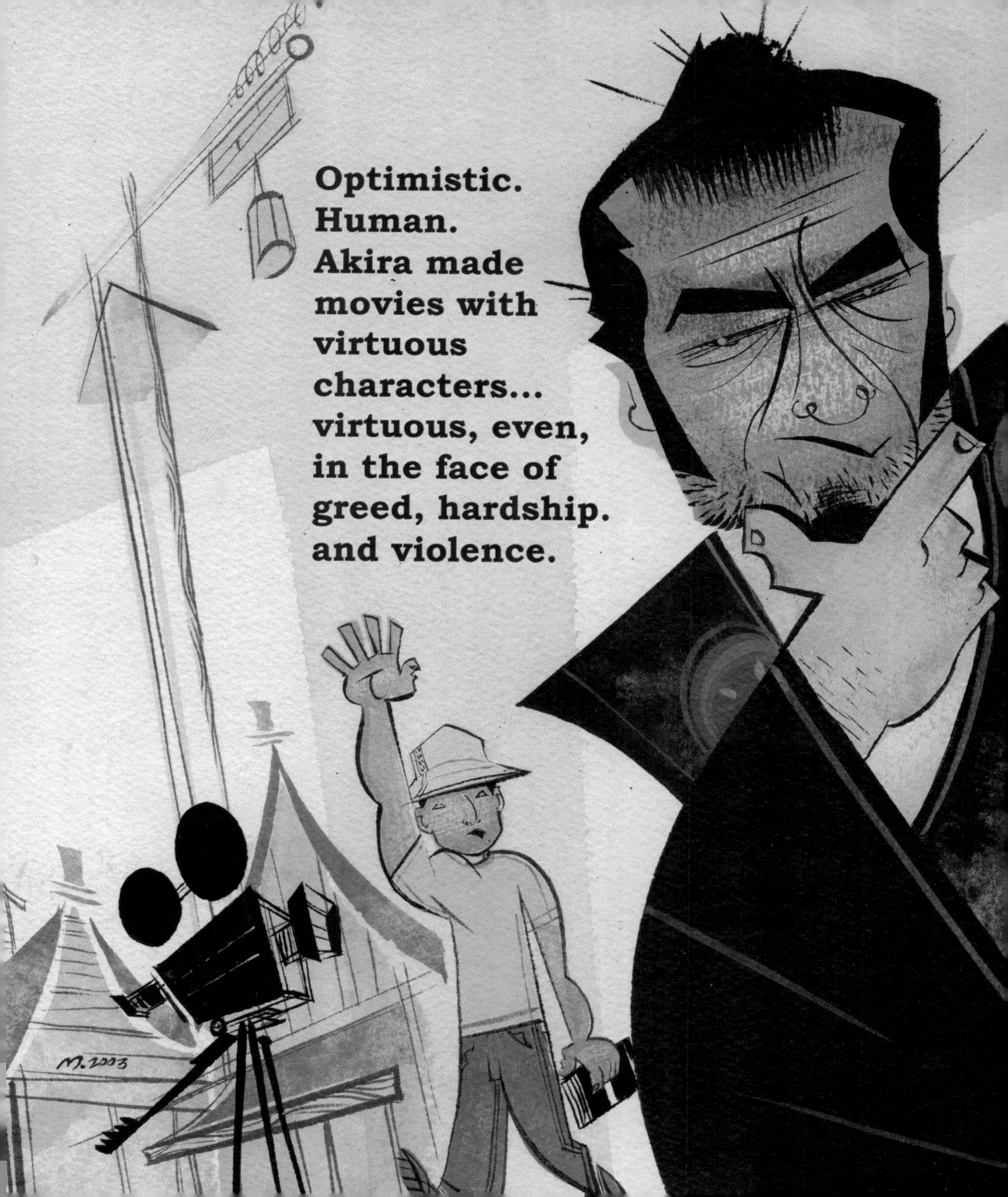
M. 2003

**Optimistic.
Human.
Akira made
movies with
virtuous
characters...
virtuous, even,
in the face of
greed, hardship.
and violence.**

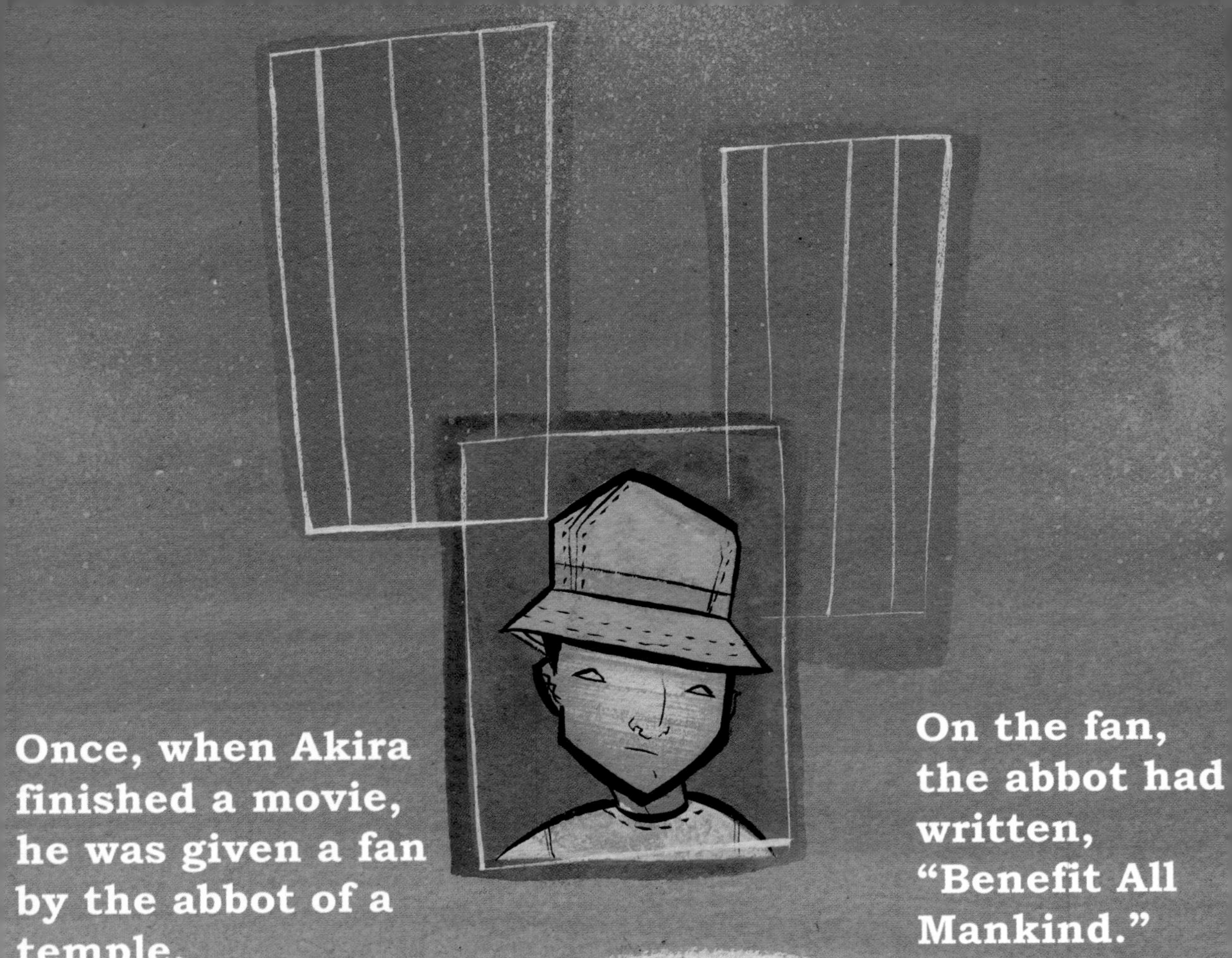

Once, when Akira finished a movie, he was given a fan by the abbot of a temple.

On the fan, the abbot had written, "Benefit All Mankind."

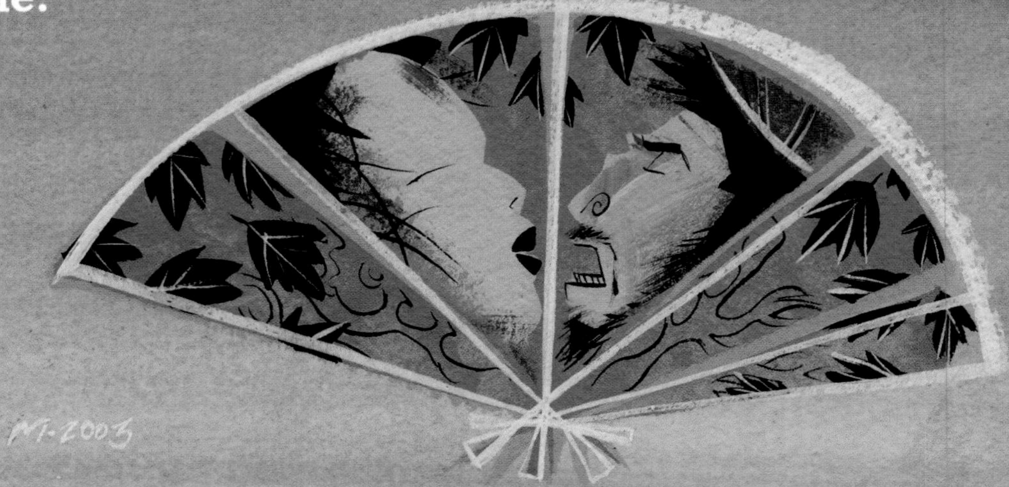

Soon after, the film won a big festival, and the world smiled on Japan.

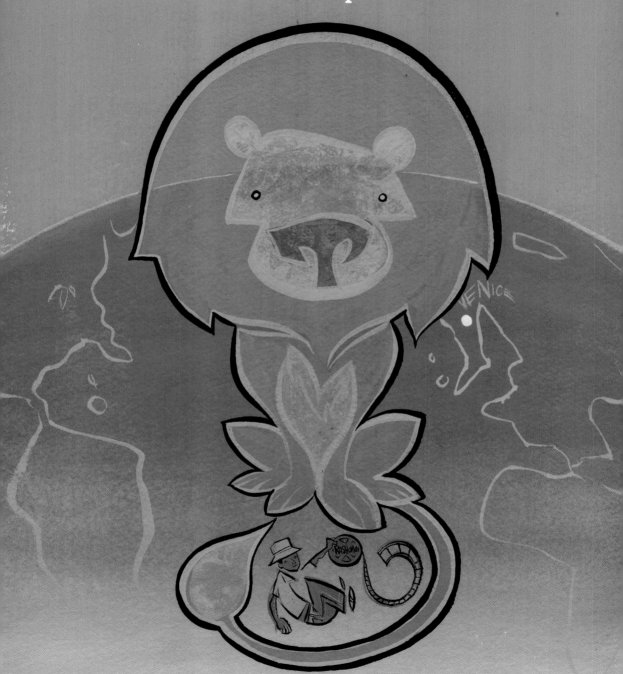

It was the
gentle touches,
the humanity,
that shined
through.

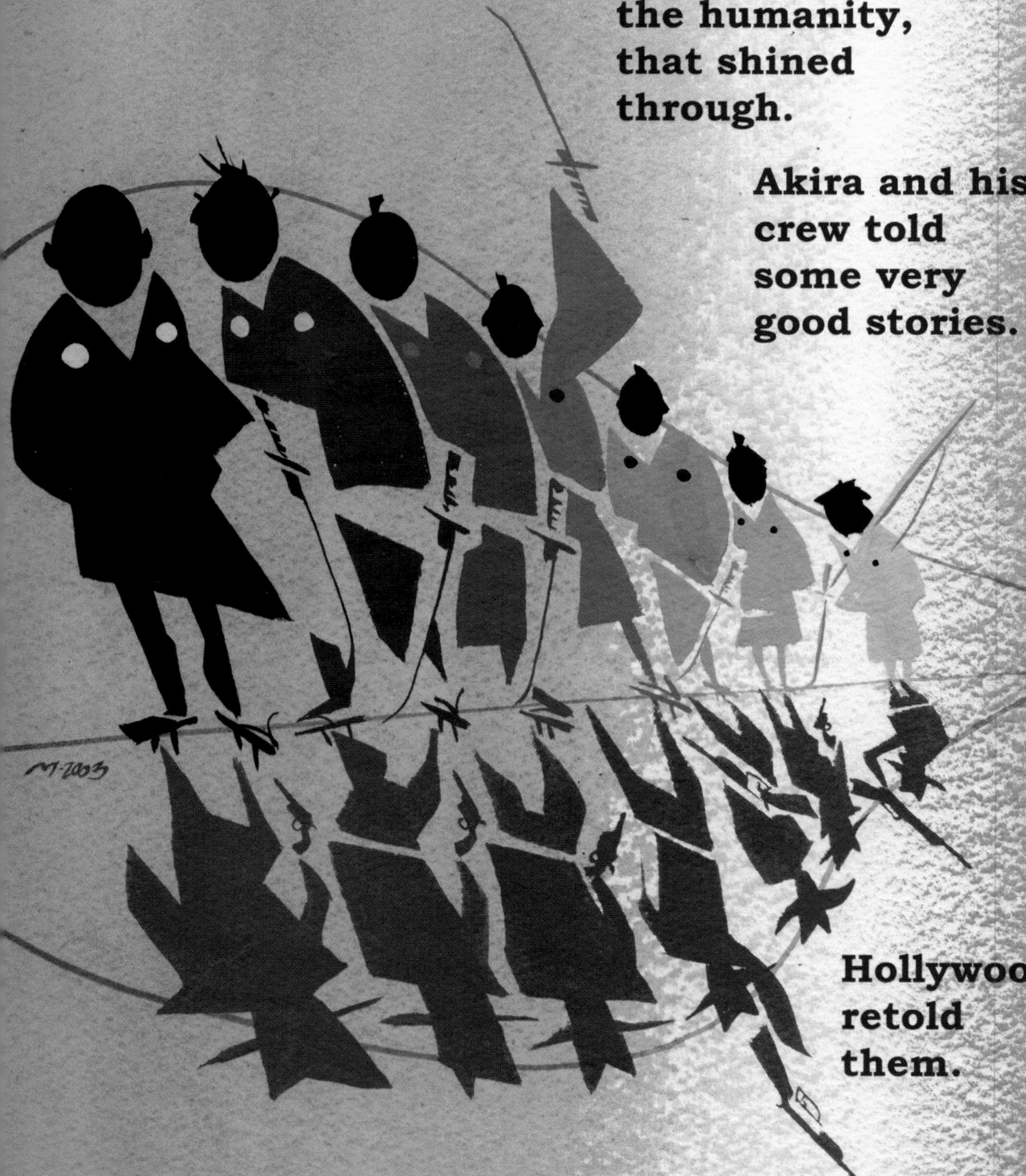

Akira and his
crew told
some very
good stories.

Hollywood
retold
them.

Akira's views as an artist were direct and precise.

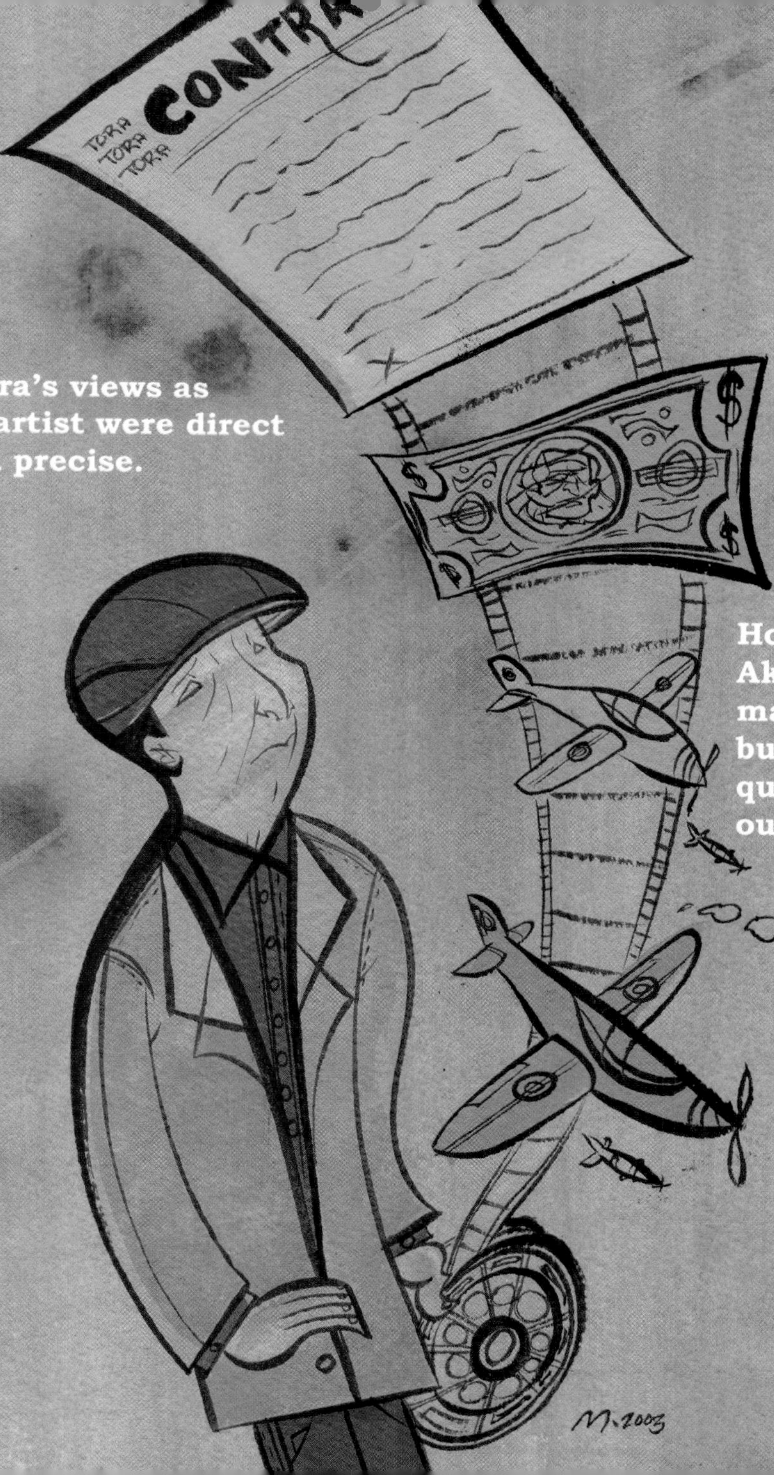
TORA
TORA
TORA
M. 2003

He earned a reputation for being stern.

Hollywood wanted Akira to help them make a movie, but things didn't quite work out.

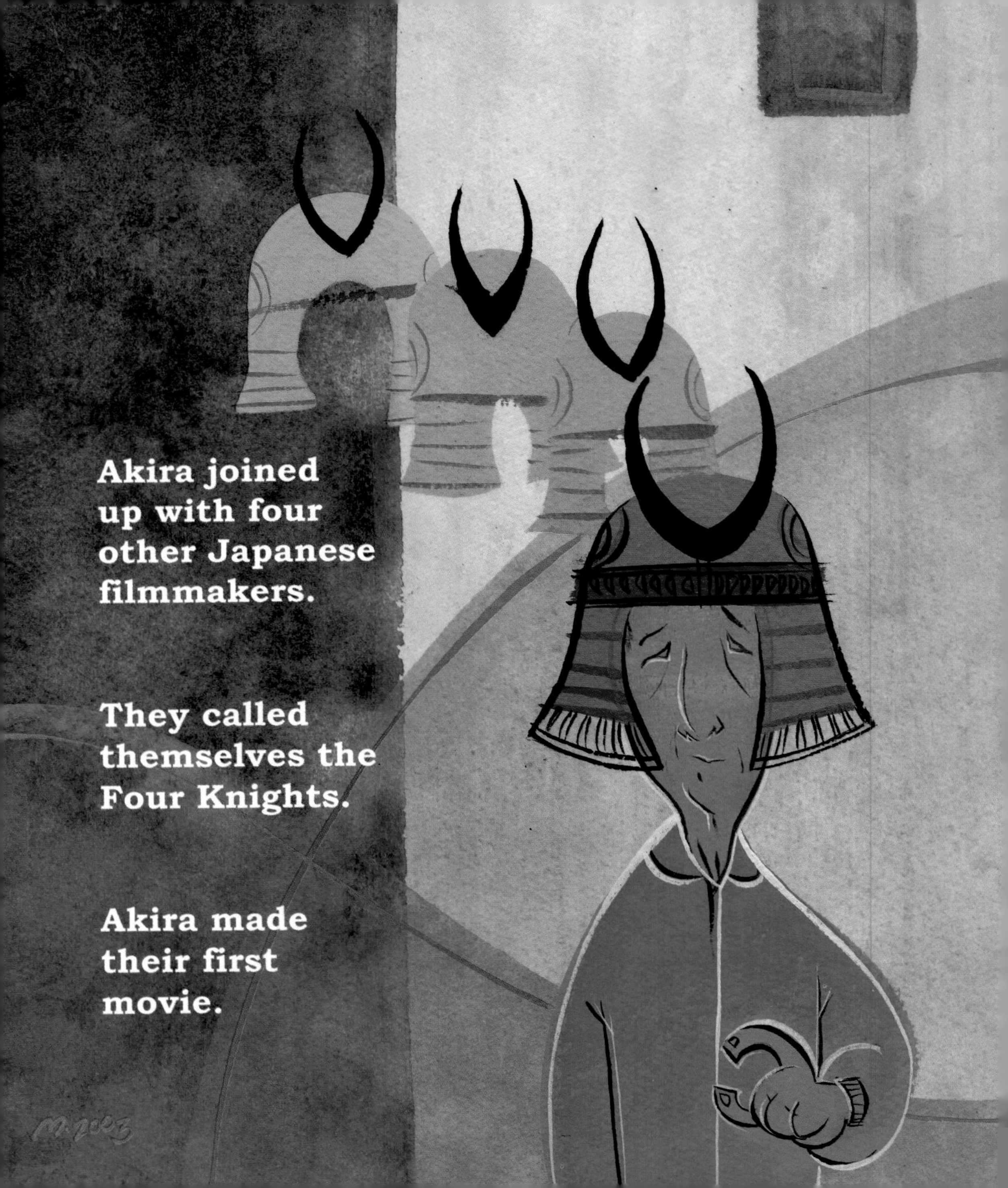

Akira joined up with four other Japanese filmmakers.

They called themselves the Four Knights.

Akira made their first movie.

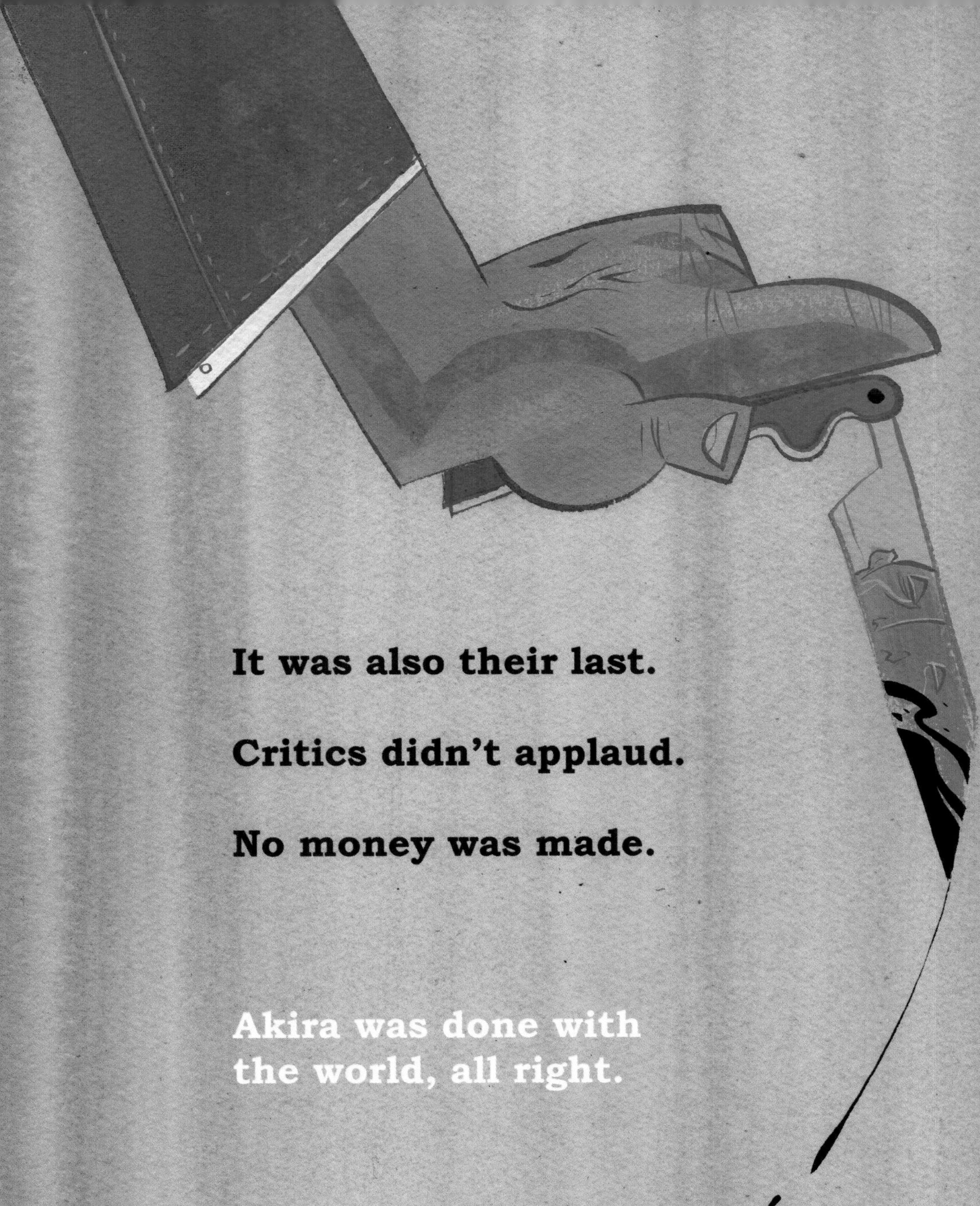

It was also their last.

Critics didn't applaud.

No money was made.

Akira was done with the world, all right.

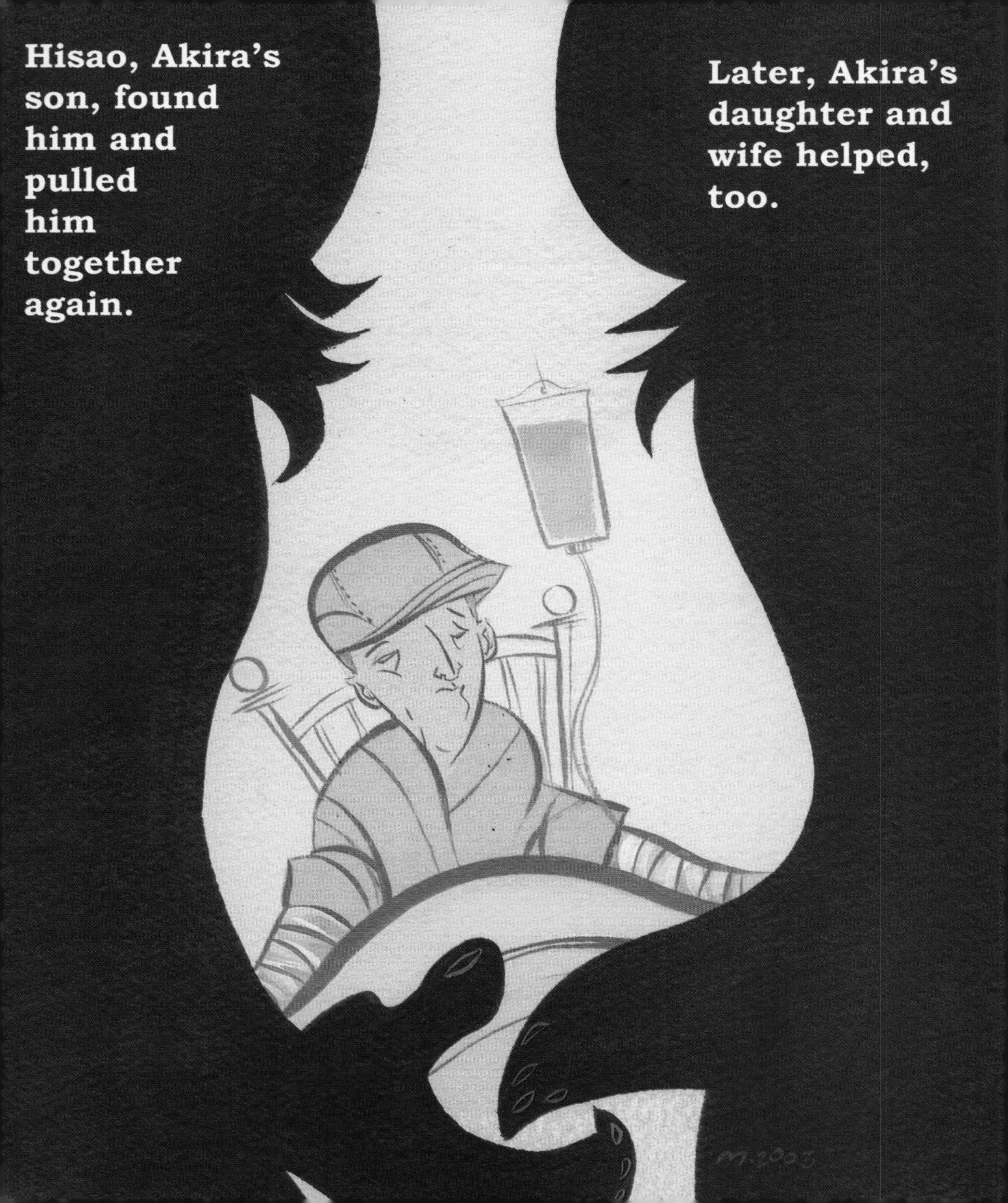
Hisao, Akira's son, found him and pulled him together again.
Later, Akira's daughter and wife helped, too.

Akira knew, inside,
without movies, he
felt empty.

He slowly painted
out new ideas.

And got
money.

And made
more movies.

And won
more
awards.

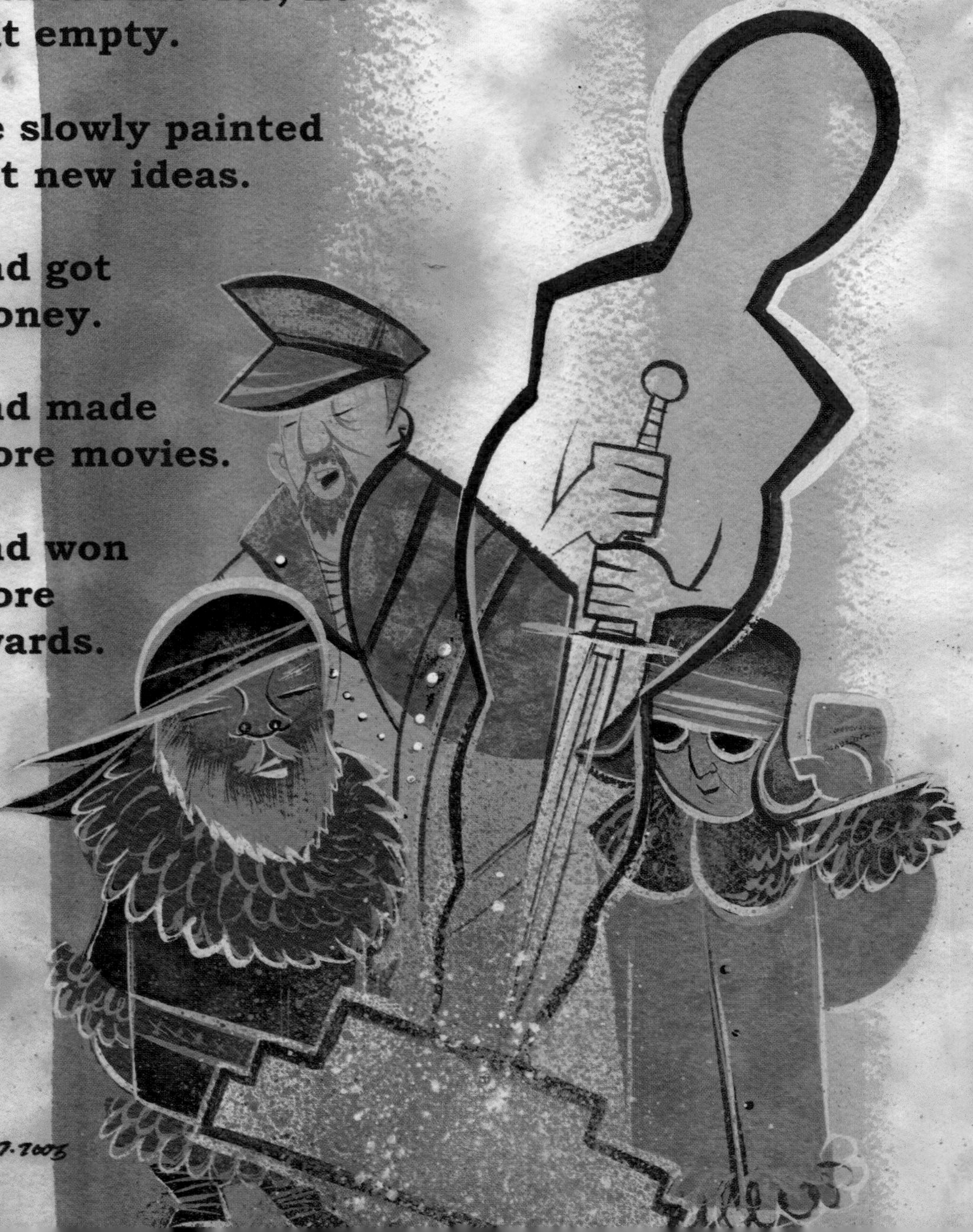

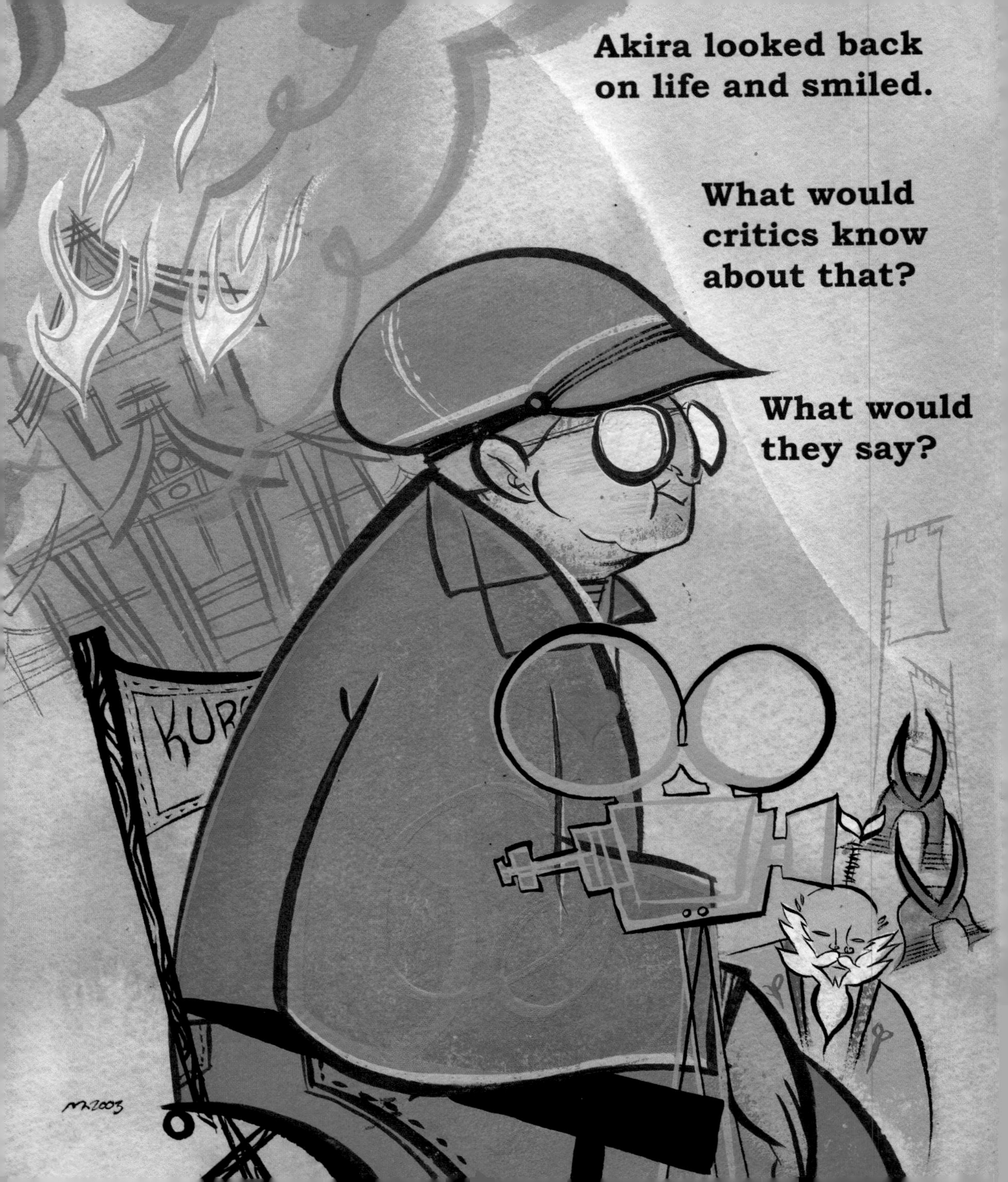
Akira looked back on life and smiled.
What would critics know about that?
What would they say?
KUR

And what would
it matter, anyway?

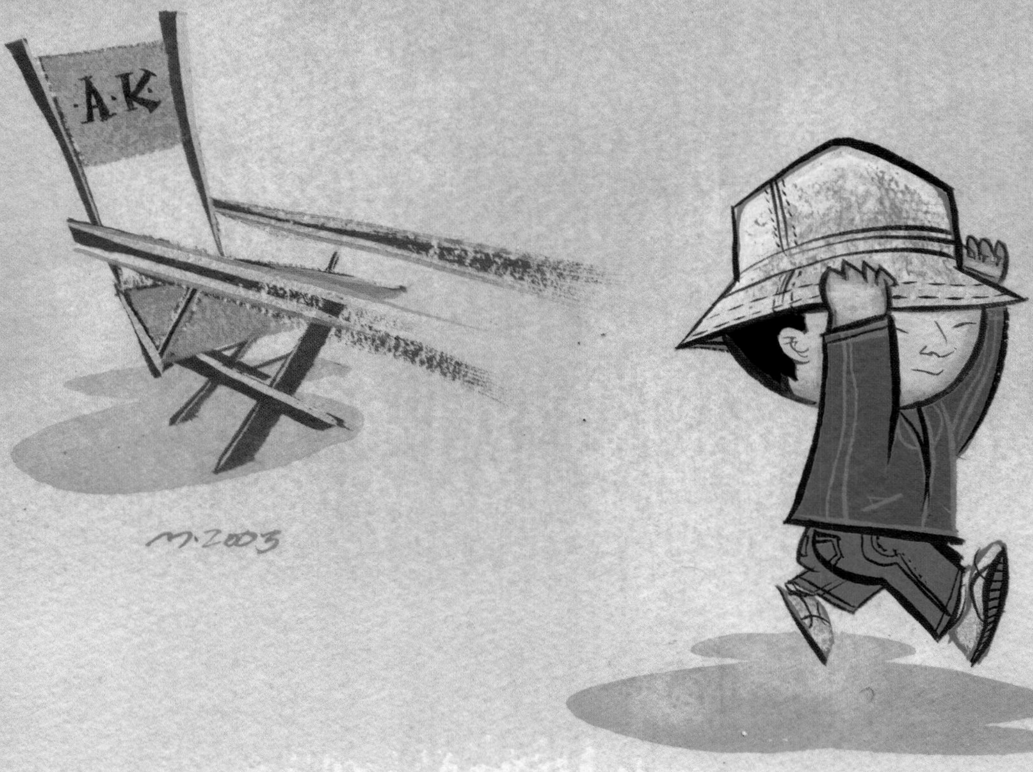
A·K
M·2003

It is a rare instance when a given piece of work from master filmmaker Akira Kurosawa fails to enrapture an audience with multiple layers of meaning and symbolism. With *The Barefoot Serpent*, I attempt to replicate this dynamic, juxtaposing biographical material about Kurosawa himself with a fictional story that echoes many of the themes, symbols, and events associated with the man. The astute reader may notice certain occurrences of familiarity with many of Kurosawa's films. These occurrences were woven into the fabric of the fictional tale to honor and support an over-all theme of Kurosawa's work: hope.

Direct examples of motifs from the films of Akira Kurosawa that played a part in the making of *The Barefoot Serpent* include the appearance of the Night Marchers of Hawaiian legend. These spirits are reminiscent of the fox wedding appearing in the film *Dreams*. The idea of the painter on the beach trying to get his subject right is also inspired by *Dreams*, specifically the sequence featuring Van Gogh. The Hawaiian boy is meant to echo the spirit of the wandering samurai made famous in *Yojimbo*, out for the money, playing two parties against each other, yet ultimately finding glory through helping another. This boy's relationship with the little girl is inspired by the couple in *One Wonderful Sunday*, out for a good time with little to spend, making the most of their day with what's at hand. The pond that won't give up its dead is meant to echo the stagnant pool in *Drunken Angel*, a symbol of society's depression. The girl's father, a shoemaker who turns his life in a new direction, loosely draws upon the themes of *High and Low* and, to some extent, *Ikiru*.

The title 'The Barefoot Serpent' refers in general to the onset of depression, a prevalent element in Kurosawa's life, especially in his later years. Using suicide as a catalyst in the fiction of *The Barefoot Serpent*, the healing process becomes the story, with hope at its heart. Our path ultimately leads to mystery, but fear, anger, and desperation are signposts that do us little good to dwell upon. Kurosawa left us a shining example through his perseverance as a human being that hope is in itself a reward of sorts, a prize worth living for.

Scott Morse, 2003

Akira Kurosawa Filmography

(1993) **Madadayo**... aka **Not Yet**

(1991) **Hachigatsu no rapusodÓ**... aka **Rhapsody in August**

(1990) **Yume**... aka **Dreams**

(1985) **Ran**... aka **Chaos**

(1980) **Kagemusha**... aka **The Shadow Warrior**

(1974) **Dersu Uzala**... aka **Derusu Uzara**

(1970) **Dodesukaden**... aka **Clickety-Clack**... aka **Dodes'ka-den** (alternative transliteration)

(1970) **Tora! Tora! Tora!** (uncredited)

(1964) **Akahige**... aka **Red Beard**

(1963) **Tengoku to jigoku**... aka **High and Low**

(1962) **Tsubaki Sanj°rÙ**... aka **Sanjuro**

(1961) **Yojimbo**... aka **The Bodyguard**

(1960) **Warui yatsu hodo yoku nemuru**... aka **The Bad Sleep Well**

    (1958) **Kakushi toride no san akunin**... aka **The Hidden Fortress**

      (1957) **Donzoko**... aka **The Lower Depths**

      (1957) **Kumonosu jo**... aka **Throne of Blood**

      (1955) **Ikimono no kiroku**... aka **I Live In Fear: Record of a Living Being**

    (1954) **Shichinin no samurai**... aka **The Seven Samurai**

   (1952) **Ikiru**... aka **To Live**

(1951) **Hakuchi**... aka **The Idiot**

(1950) **RashÙmon**

(1950) **Shubun**... aka **Scandal**

(1949) **Nora inu**.... aka **Stray Dog**

(1949) **Shizukanaru ketto**... aka **The Quiet Duel**

(1948) **Yoidore tenshi**... aka **Drunken Angel**

(1947) **Subarashiki nichiyobi**... aka **One Wonderful Sunday**

(1946) **Waga seishun ni kuinashi**... aka **No Regrets for Our Youth**

(1946) **Asu o tsukuru hitobito**... aka **Those Who Make Tomorrow**

(1945) **Tora no o wo fumu otokotachi**... aka **The Men Who Tread On the Tiger's Tail**

(1945) **Zoku Sugata Sanshiro**

(1944) **Ichiban utsukushiku**... aka **The Most Beautiful**

(1943) **Sugata Sanshiro**

(1941) **Uma** (some scenes) (uncredited) ... aka **Horse**

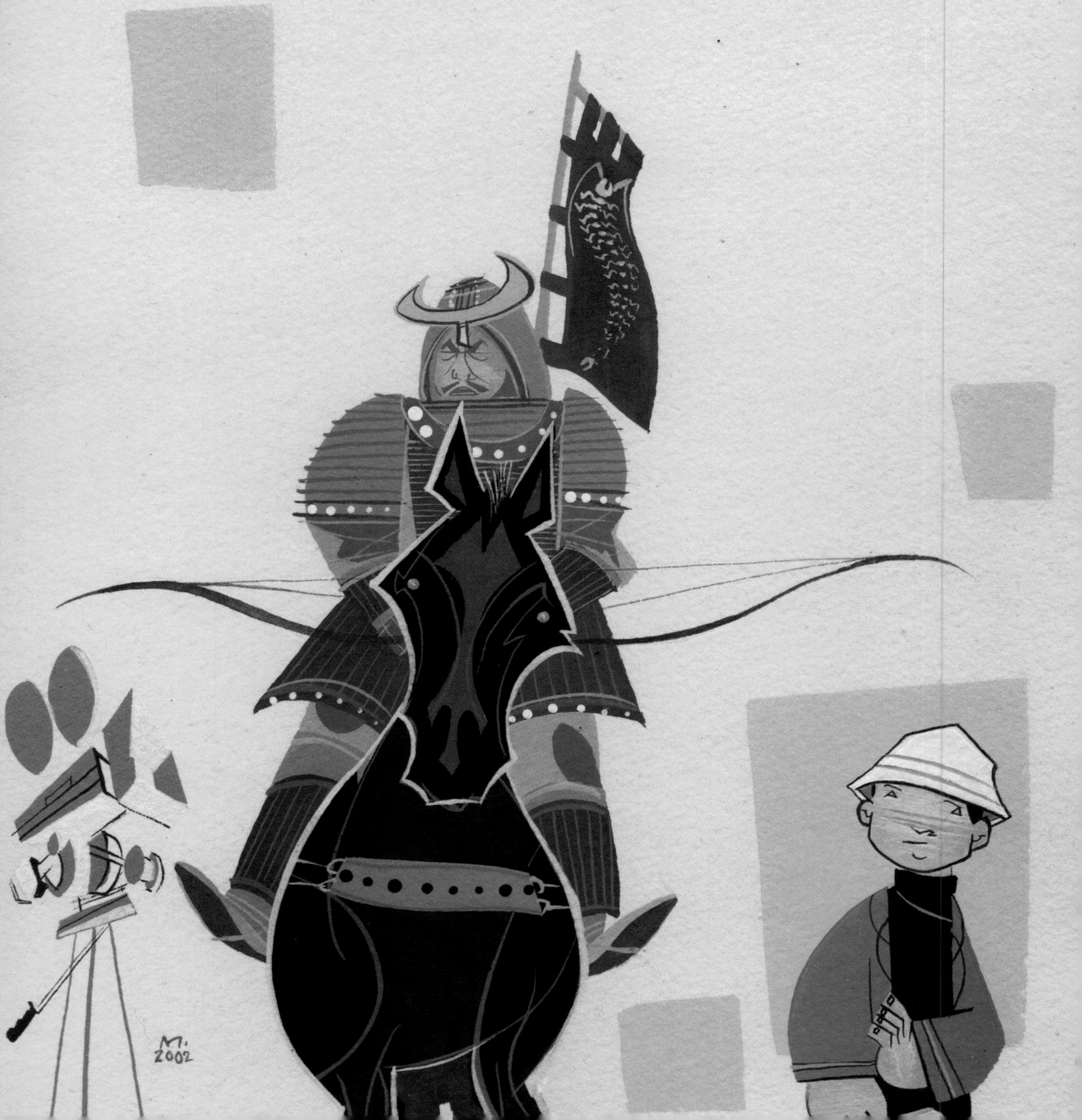
M.
2002

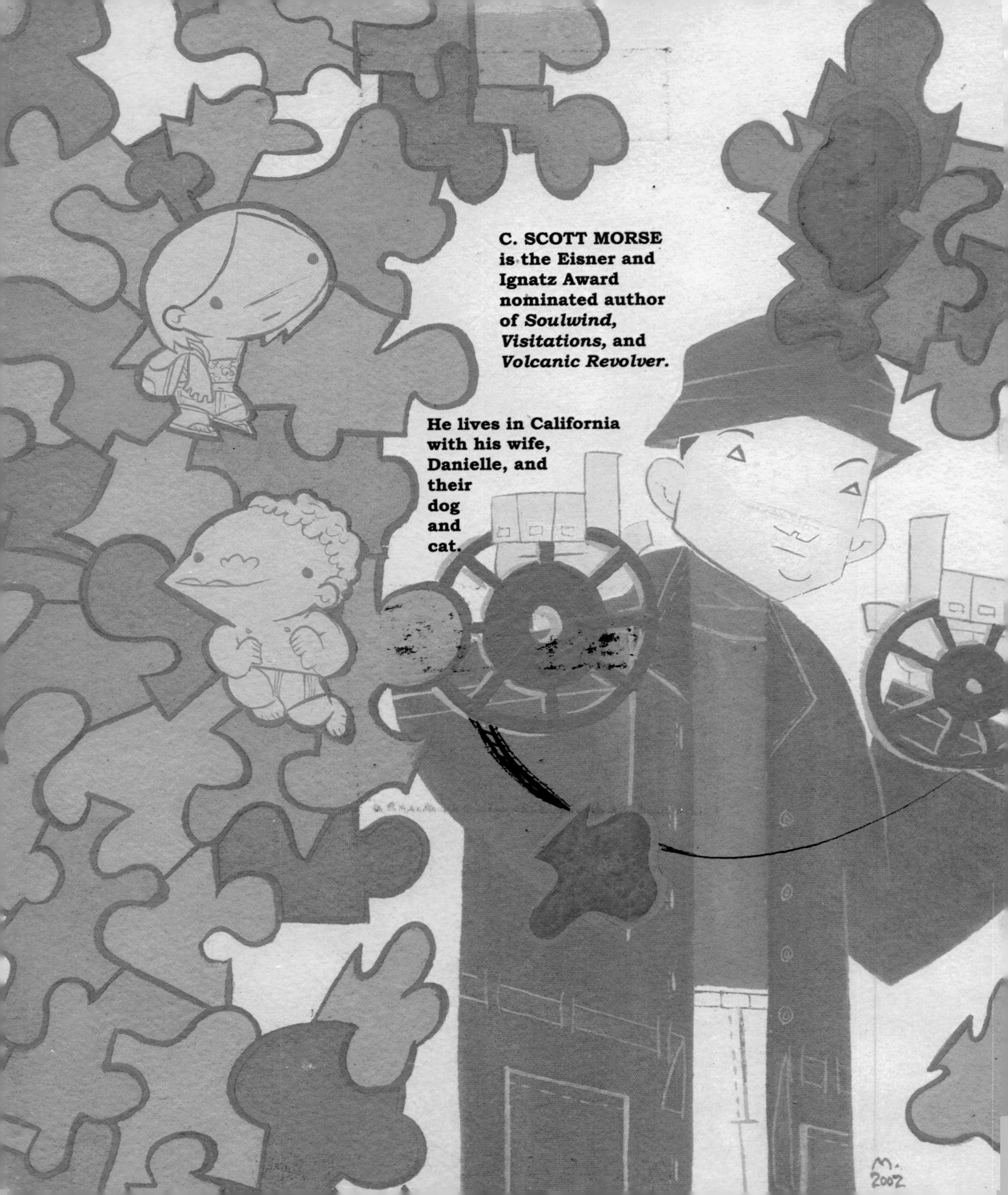
M.
2002

C. SCOTT MORSE is the Eisner and Ignatz Award nominated author of *Soulwind*, *Visitations*, and *Volcanic Revolver*.

He lives in California with his wife, Danielle, and their dog and cat.